Arnulfo L. Oliveira Memorial Library

Landscapes of Hope

Landscapes of Hope

Anti-Colonial Utopianism in America

DOHRA AHMAD

OXFORD
UNIVERSITY PRESS
2009

OXFORD
UNIVERSITY PRESS

Oxford University Press, Inc., publishes works that further
Oxford University's objective of excellence
in research, scholarship, and education.

Oxford New York
Auckland Cape Town Dar es Salaam Hong Kong Karachi
Kuala Lumpur Madrid Melbourne Mexico City Nairobi
New Delhi Shanghai Taipei Toronto

With offices in
Argentina Austria Brazil Chile Czech Republic France Greece
Guatemala Hungary Italy Japan Poland Portugal Singapore
South Korea Switzerland Thailand Turkey Ukraine Vietnam

Copyright © 2009 by Oxford University Press, Inc.

Published by Oxford University Press, Inc.
198 Madison Avenue, New York, New York 10016
www.oup.com

Oxford is a registered trademark of Oxford University Press

Library of Congress Cataloging-in-Publication Data

Ahmad, Dohra.
  Landscapes of hope : anti-colonial utopianism in America / Dohra Ahmad.
    p. cm.
  Includes bibliographical references and index.
  ISBN 978-0-19-533276-6
  1. American literature—History and criticism.   2. Utopias in literature.   3. Anti-imperialist
movements—United States.   4. Authors, American—Political and social views.   5. Race in
literature.   6. Nationalism in literature.
  I. Title.
  PS169.U85A75 2009
  809'.93372—dc22   2008028927

9 8 7 6 5 4 3 2 1

Printed in the United States of America
on acid-free paper

For my father and mother

Acknowledgments

I have dedicated this book in part to Eqbal Ahmad, the first utopian thinker I knew and one of the most intellectually grounded and resolutely optimistic I have yet encountered. It was from him that I came to know that better worlds are possible, and that they can only come into being through the full self-determination of all people—two of the principles upon which I have based this study. Like many of the figures who appear here, he had a long-standing commitment to solidarity among liberation movements. Even at the end of his life, when his country of birth and his final homeland brandished at each other the world's most destructive weapons, he never took refuge in despair.

The idea for this study first came together during the dim and difficult months following his unexpected death in May of 1999. It took shape with the guidance of my wonderful graduate advisors: Ann Douglas, Jean Howard, Robert O'Meally, Bruce Robbins, Gayatri Chakravorty Spivak, and Gauri Viswanathan. I thank all of them for their inestimable contributions to my thinking about the topics here, as well as about literature and culture more generally. I also benefited enormously from the careful reading and consideration of Amanda Bowers, Jolisa Gracewood, Amy King, Michael Malouf, Gary Okahiro, Marisa Parham, Lily Shapiro, Sandhya Shukla, Robin Varghese, and the members of Columbia's Postcolonial and Cultural Studies dissertation group. Orin Herskowitz read and commented on every line, well before I could consider any of them remotely fit for wider consumption.

Tanya Agathocleous, Sarah Cole, and Amy King offered invaluable advice on publication. Shannon McLachlan championed the book from the beginning and provided helpful feedback at every turn. I am grateful as well to the anonymous reviewers for Oxford University Press and the *Journal of Commonwealth Literature* for their thoughtful comments, and to Shannon McLachlan and Jon Thieme, respectively, for facilitating their reviews. In the final stages, Erin Fiero dove valiantly into the world of indexing, and Paul Hobson patiently guided the book through production.

A portion of chapter 2 appeared in an earlier version as "'More than Romance': Genre and Geography in Du Bois' *Dark Princess*" in *English Literary History* 69:3 (2002): 775–803. A portion of chapter 3 appeared as "The Home, the World and the United States: *Young India's* Tagore" in *Journal of Commonwealth Literature* 43:1 (2008): 23–41. I also appreciated the opportunity to present some of the ideas at panels organized by the Society for Utopian Studies, the Rutgers Comparative Literature Department, and the Modern Language Association's Division of Late Nineteenth and Early Twentieth Century Literature. The staff of Butler Library and Mule Café provided congenial places to work. The St. John's English Department has been an ideal institutional home for me: collegial, humane, and intellectually vibrant. Most importantly, during the years of working on *Landscapes of Hope* I have been lucky to have around me an immensely supportive group of family and friends who entertained my daughters, cooked me food, pulled me out of the doldrums of early writing and revision, and generally gave the most material substance to my thoughts on the importance of community. Foremost among them are Orin Herskowitz, Eliya Sage Ahmad, Melina Rose Ahmad, and Julie Diamond; to those four go my deepest gratitude and love.

Contents

Landscapes of Hope

Introduction:
Real Networks and
Imaginary Vistas

> The impossible gives birth to the possible.
> —Karl Mannheim, *Ideology and Utopia*

On September 21, 1917, New York's Intercollegiate Socialist Society sponsored a joint lecture by local luminary W. E. B. Du Bois and exiled Indian nationalist Lala Lajpat Rai. The lecture provided an opportunity for a truly global analysis of economic and cultural oppression, and both men rose to the occasion. Despite his central importance within American sociology and African-American historiography, Du Bois had long been committed to thinking about slavery, colonialism, and their enemies in a transnational frame. Lajpat Rai's focus had previously been more limited—to India and especially the Punjab—but during his exile years in New York his particular brand of nationalism developed a cosmopolitan character as he enlisted the solidarity of Du Bois as well as Irish nationalists and American labor organizers. "The problem of the Hindu and of the negro and cognate problems are not local, but world problems," he stated at that event, anticipating sentiments if not vocabulary that would recur throughout the century.[1] Elaborating on Du Bois's famous formulation regarding "the problem of the color line," Lajpat Rai reflected on the forces that had produced so many hyphenated experiences in the United States and abroad.

My aim in *Landscapes of Hope* is to give substance and context to Du Bois's and Lajpat Rai's brief encounter. The deeper story of their cooperation brings out both the parallels and the divergences between two groups that shared the general goal of emancipation for the colored people of the world. Despite the opening connection between Du Bois's elegantly phrased problem and Lajpat Rai's dysphonic one, in this book I am less interested in problems than solutions. Du Bois's and Lajpat Rai's Socialist-sponsored joint lecture represents one emblematic moment during a period in which anticolonial organizing developed in a holistic, worldwide form. Their cooperation belongs to the same tradition that fostered the Association of Oppressed Peoples, the 1911 Universal Races Congress, and the 1927 Brussels Congress of Oppressed Nationalities; this last event brought together an illustrious group including Jawaharlal Nehru, Lamine Senghor, Ho Chi Minh, Madame Sun Yat Sen, Romain Rolland, and Albert Einstein. Written texts reflected and bolstered the emerging transnationalism: Du Bois's 1927 novel *Dark Princess* envisioned the post-colonial order taking the form of a supranational "world of colored folk," while Lajpat Rai's New York–based periodical *Young India* reported not only on its titular landmass but on promising anticolonial developments in Ireland, Egypt, and China.[2] Throughout this sadly ephemeral period, exile nationalism merged with metropolitan dissent to forge a transformative politics that aimed to transcend race and nation, a forgotten but significant precursor to the "globalization from below" that Michael Hardt and Antonio Negri have called for in our own century.

During this time of intimidating potential, the architects of decolonization carried out the exhilarating work of imagining independent states. Du Bois and Lajpat Rai, along with Pauline Hopkins, Rabindranath Tagore, Sarojini Naidu, and others, did this by marshaling the goals and methods of utopian fiction. How else could one navigate the vast realms of possibility that lay ahead? Like Milton's hapless mortal protagonists at the end of *Paradise Lost*, "the world was all before them." In response, the writers I study here made use of their literary prowess to create better worlds that they and their readers could inhabit together. Through fiction, poetry, and reflective essays, they began the process of constructing a better future. Lajpat Rai cobbled together an eclectic mix of documents—the latest poems of Mohammed Iqbal, Sarojini Naidu, and Rabindranath Tagore; ancient art reproductions; reports on nationalist activities in Amritsar, London, and Minneapolis; and sympathetic patriotic lyrics by dead American abolitionist poets—into the transnational periodical *Young India*. In so doing, he and his multi-national editorial collective circulated every month a vibrant and often contradictory image of an ideal independent India. Pauline Hopkins, in her messianic novel *Of One Blood*, carries her American-born hero to Ethiopia's Hidden City of Telassar, where he fulfills his unknown destiny by bringing the cloistered utopia into the modern world. W. E. B. Du Bois in *Dark Princess* audaciously merges India, Africa, and the American South to produce a global Black Belt on the verge of true emancipation.

Landscapes of Hope traces the shape and character of the anti-colonial utopias that these radical thinkers dared to imagine. Together they inhabited the realm of the conditional. Lajpat Rai's *Young India*, Hopkins's *Of One Blood*, and Du Bois's *Dark Princess* all usher readers into a space that does not yet exist. For these writers, utopian thinking proved an indispensable exercise toward overcoming present-day injustices. This is true both on the level of product—what we might call the blueprint—as well as process. Most concretely, utopian fiction provides an opportunity to invent wholesale every institution through which people experience their lives: biological reproduction; education; relationships of friendship, passion, and community; agriculture; commerce; foreign affairs; art; and perhaps metaphysical belief. But even more important than any of those concrete details is the pure imaginative audacity that underlies the blueprint. As Fredric Jameson explains, there are "two distinct lines of descendency from More's inaugural text: the one intent on the realization of the Utopian program, the other an obscure yet omnipresent Utopian impulse finding its way to the surface in a variety of covert expressions and practices."[3] It should be obvious from even the most cursory historical reflection that anti-colonial politics participates in both categories of utopianism, the practical and the ideological, despite its complete absence from any catalogue of utopian thought.

Even before they set out the details of a new and better order, tapping into utopian discourse allowed anti-colonial theorists to separate themselves from the existing economic, political, and cultural conditions that determined the possibilities for their activism. In a colonial context, we could call this process intellectual decolonization; within the study of utopian fiction, we would call it defamiliarization or cognitive estrangement. Whatever the name, envisioning an entirely new order helps writers and readers alike to rise out of the constraints of present conditions. Utopia thus falls into the category of "romance." The union of an obviously political mode (utopian fiction) with one long seen as apolitical or escapist (romance) may seem unexpected, but upon closer examination the logic is clear. Utopian fiction opposes realism both as a narrative mode and as a political outlook; it utterly refuses to accept existing conditions, even as a determinant of what one can write. Writing that is counterfactual, as well as carefully textured, changes readers' perceptions of what is factual. Once they have been made to inhabit a new world, even an imaginary one, readers will necessarily see their own surroundings anew.

Because of those enabling formal continuities, my starting point in *Landscapes of Hope* will be the canonical utopian fiction that provided a model for how literary language can forge a way out of present-day injustices. The writers I study both employed and revised prevailing conventions of utopian fiction. As I show in my first chapter, classical utopias have been thoroughly imbricated in the ideologies of empire ever since the inception of the genre. Two successive waves of utopian activity each relied upon a central apparatus of colonial activity: exploration in the sixteenth and seventeenth centuries; and developmentalism in the late nineteenth and early twentieth centuries. The early utopian fiction of More, Bacon, and others derived much of its energy from the discovery of new continents and islands, and it flourished as a way to help its readers make sense of the changing world around them. But by the nineteenth century, the blank spaces had been filled in, and the myth of empty land could no longer provide a tenable vehicle for utopia. The myth of progress—the first secular millenarianism—fortuitously took its place. When Edward Bellamy wrote *Looking Backward* in 1888, though America's frontier would shortly close, a new teleological view of history and biology informed by the works of Marx and Darwin began to offer an alternative frontier of the future. That same developmentalist view of history also undergirded the colonial project, relegating what had been the blank spaces to the temporalized category of primitive and backward.

Given that racialist and expansionist legacy, how does one write an anti-colonial utopia? Both because it flattens out cultural difference and because its utilitarian calculus figures racial purification as an aspect of progress, anti-colonial writers could not afford to subscribe to the logic of developmentalism. Instead, they created new utopias that replace bordered nations with loose networks of transnational solidarity, developmentalism with nostalgia, and utilitarianism with romance. Bellamy in *Looking Backward* and Charlotte Perkins Gilman in *Herland* predicated the success of their utopian societies on homogeneity and, more specifically still, "Aryan stock."[4] The strategic response of Du Bois and Hopkins as well as Mohandas K. Gandhi and

J. E. Casely Hayford (major contributors to the literature of Indian nationalism and Pan-Africanism, respectively) was what the anthropologist Richard
Fox has called "affirmative Orientalism": a counter-Orientalism that retains
the associations enumerated by Edward Said (mysticism, antirationality, vol-
atility) but alters their valuation.[5] If Anglo-American racist discourse united
nonwhite people into a single figure of irrational barbarity, these writers
reformulated that imposed unity into a positive continuity.[6] Both the Pan-
African writings that set the stage for the literary achievements of Négritude,
and the Indian nationalist texts that bolstered the Swadeshi movement,
turned received categories on their head to offer essentialized versions of
Asian and African civilization not only for their own people, but as a spiritual
antidote for a moribund West.

Anti-colonial writers were not alone in their use of a utopian mode that
directly opposed the perceived constraints of modernity. The writings of Du
Bois and the others swirled within prevailing currents of anti-modernism,
non-conformism, metropolitan dissent, social reform, and cosmopolitanism. This was, after all, a period marked both by faith in human agency and
also by dissatisfaction with the materialistic outlook of social reform thus far.
If the turn of the century saw the emergence of a reactive, nostalgic opposition to modernity, as T. Jackson Lears demonstrates in his cultural history
No Place of Grace, the devastation of World War I produced further skepticism toward the achievements of mainstream Western culture.[7] My writers
share the anti-modern stance that Lears identifies; they are also, in their anti-
materialism, affiliated with the many spiritualist creeds that had been flourishing since the mid-nineteenth century, like Spiritualism, Mesmerism, and
Theosophy. In the beautifully humane and open-ended *Affective Communities*,
Leela Gandhi outlines the "discursive and ethical continuities" among dissenting positions like vegetarianism, animal rights, homosexuality, and anti-
colonialism.[8] To these we should add the young nationalisms that arose
during and just after the Versailles peace conference. As I will discuss further in my second and third chapters, Irish nationalism, Indian nationalism,
Pan-Africanism (both Du Boisian and Garveyite), and Zionism had close
connections both logistical (as in Du Bois and Lajpat Rai or Marcus Garvey
and Eamon de Valera lecturing together) and conceptual (as in the use of
a romantic motherland rhetoric).[9] Whatever their primary stimuli, all the
associated dissenters and reformers had to perform the same philosophical evaluations, weighing moderation against extremism, elitism against

democracy, modernization against nostalgia, and derivativeness against indigeneity.

Further, Communism figures throughout *Landscapes of Hope* as a powerful complementary force for the reorganization of the perceived world. Every writer who appears here needed to determine where she or he stood in relation to Marx and his followers. After decades of operating alongside Communist organizers, Du Bois finally declared his official allegiance at the age of 93. Lajpat Rai, on the other hand, disavowed the activities of the only other Indian nationalist group in the United States, the West Coast–based Ghadar Party. In both cases, participating in the genre of utopia placed them outside the purview of approved Marxian activities. Utopia is a fundamentally anti-dialectic endeavor. In direct opposition to Marx's understanding of history, utopian texts use literary language to envision and thus create a better order. Counterfactuality, perhaps their key characteristic, is not something in which doctrinaire Communism can be invested. However, we might still describe Communism—especially in the form of the various socialist internationalisms flourishing during this period—as a utopian endeavor in its determination to forge a better and entirely new future.

All of the movements described above—anti-modernism, Spiritualism, Communism, and anti-colonialism—took shape and gained energy through periodical publishing. From the work of Benedict Anderson, we now recognize periodicals as one venue where modern nation-states became consolidated.[10] But so did other forms of imagined community—ones that never reached the same level of institutional solidity as Anderson's nations. International anti-colonial resistance also took shape in serial form. In that way it was able constantly to be re-formed and re-imagined—unlike the manifesto, for example, as another important contemporaneous political form. By presenting his idealized India in the form of a journal, Lajpat Rai creates an entity that is loose, fractured, and collaborative, with change over time intrinsically built in. *Young India* is far from the only place where a periodical creates an imagined world and solidifies a reading community committed to actualizing that world; it is no accident that the hero of J. E. Casely Hayford's *Ethiopia Unbound* is a newspaper editor. As F. Nnabuenyi Ugonna writes in his introduction to that fascinatingly hybrid 1911 novel, "the part played by the press in awakening the political consciousness of the masses of African people has been profound." Ugonna cites a large number of papers that proliferated in the areas that would become

Nigeria and Ghana in the period from 1880 to 1930, the height of the anti-colonial florescence with which I am concerned.[11] As I will discuss later, Indian periodical publishing thrived during this time as well. In a metropolitan setting there was Dusé Mohamed Ali's *African Times and Orient Review*, published intermittently in London between 1912 and 1918, featuring the writing of George Bernard Shaw, H. G. Wells, and Marcus Garvey. Complementing Leela Gandhi's excavations of linked communities of dissent, Ian Christopher Fletcher writes of "the emergence of an imperial public sphere in which various forms of anti-colonial criticism could find expression."[12] Fletcher writes of *The Modern Review*, a well-known Bengal Renaissance journal, and it is evident that *Young India* belongs to that alternative public sphere as well—but so do Du Bois's *Crisis* and Hopkins's *Colored American Magazine*. Periodical publishing, as has recently been observed, is a wide-open field.[13] Room is available especially for scholars interested in breaking the hermetic seal that can so often encase national literatures. This book contains an in-depth study of a single transnational, anti-colonial periodical among several, but it also carries the hope that others may pick up the many strands I have inevitably dropped. I intend *Landscapes of Hope* in part as an opening gesture toward what I hope will be many more investigations of the diverse anti-colonial utopias that flourished in the heady days of possibility.

From a vast global arena I have inevitably had to narrow my focus to a concrete set of analytical objects, and have settled in the New York milieu with which I began this introduction. Focusing on literary utopias produced in the United States, for U.S. readers, will allow for a better understanding of how the anti-colonial utopia took shape in this particular local context. In the case of Du Bois, Hopkins, and Lajpat Rai, the unexpected quarter where we find a vital anti-colonial nationalism is the belly of a younger beast: a neo-imperial United States. Now erased from the study of the counter-cultural nineteen-teens, anti-colonial organizing in the United States formed an important part of that Great War–era radicalism. The United States and especially New York unwittingly furnished a hospitable environment for anti-colonial imaginings by placing these writers in proximity and thus allowing for the emergence of a discourse of solidarity. Removed from both colony and metropolis, Lajpat Rai found a place to negotiate between the perilous extremes of nationalism, reconciling narratives of progress and nostalgia, nationalism and internationalism, romanticism and pragmatism. Rooted in an American literary tradition, Hopkins and Du Bois adapted and appropriated that tradition to suit their own emancipatory aims.

I am aware that such an organizational framework could be seen to reproduce the equation of America and utopia, and even the nationalistic organization of American Studies, both of which I set out to challenge. In addition to mere feasibility—a perennial Area Studies rationale—this scheme has the conceptual advantage of showing exactly how global is the U.S.-produced dream. The United States may provide the origin of these utopian imaginings, but it is far from the destination. Here I have the advantage of coming after years of excellent scholarship that recasts American Studies in an international frame. While informed by valuable recent work like John Carlos Rowe's *Literary Culture and U.S. Imperialism*, Amy Kaplan's *The Anarchy of Empire in the Making of U.S. Culture*, and their important precursor *Cultures of United States Imperialism*, I will take a quite distinct emphasis: not on America's emerging role as an imperial power, but rather on the anti-colonial resistance that paradoxically sprang up within that growing power. Just as Said's exposure of the workings of colonial discourse in *Orientalism* prompted a rush of work to track the voice and agency of colonized people, so the "New American Studies," with its emphasis on neo-imperial complicity, necessitates awareness of the limits of imperial ideology and of the emerging vocabulary and iconography of opposition.[14] Lajpat Rai, Hopkins, and Du Bois produced utopias that were far more global in scope than that of Edward Bellamy; my analysis of them, accordingly, aims to be more global than Lears's limited view of anti-modernism in *No Place of Grace*. However, it will also be grounded in one place and thus in its political contingencies.

Indeed, operating inside the United States had the contradictory effects of forging cross-group alliances, while simultaneously threatening those alliances. For Indian nationalists in New York, we see the pressures generated by the need to appeal to a government that was at once emblematic of world opinion, a rising imperial power in its own right, and a war ally to India's own colonial occupier. For anti-colonial Americans of African descent, there is the problem of theorizing the relationship between racism on a domestic and an international level. Both Du Bois and Lajpat Rai encountered the stifling effects of the Great War, which demanded a choice between dissent and patriotism. If at points in *Landscapes of Hope* America appears as a beacon for freedom, elsewhere it is a neo-colonial threat. *Young India* appeals to the self-image of a growing world power by presenting India and the United States as analogous rebels against English rule, thus anticipating the specious notion that the latter falls under the rubric of postcolonial.[15] Yet both *Looking Backward* and *Dark Princess* make clear that despite its own history as a rebellious colony and despite the lingering rhetoric surrounding that history, even the most cursory attention to existing power relations will show the early-twentieth-century United States in a new imperial relationship to the Philippines and Latin America, not to mention its own "internal colony" of African-Americans. As we will see in the epilogue especially, those imperial adventures would later endanger solidarity in the most significant and long-lasting ways.

The conjunction of anti-colonial rhetoric and neo-imperial reality results in many of the fractures of solidarity that recur throughout this study. Others arise from disparities between each group's relationship to dominant elements like the United States government, canonical utopian fiction, and the discourse of developmentalism. Lajpat Rai had the luxury of seeing the United States as a host and a model, whereas for Du Bois it was the most important and immediate of many adversaries. As in Brent Edwards's *The Practice of Diaspora*, these are "subjects with different historical relations to the nation."[16] One group was made up of exiled colonial subjects, and the other of a recently enslaved internal minority; one group was racially ambiguous, and the other aggressively classified. Thus they necessarily had different relations to Anglo-American literary traditions and associated race ideologies. As I will show in chapter 1, canonical American utopian novels imagine a nation that is racially homogenous, and a world that is unevenly developed. They thoroughly excise black Americans, while allowing Asians and Africans to aspire to a predetermined utopian telos. Development—here, in the form of developmentalist utopian fiction—affects and even envisions each group very differently. Throughout *Landscapes of Hope* we will see that anti-colonial utopian writers stand in different places in relation to the complex legacy of the developmentalist utopia. Each group and individual, too, buys into different dominant myths. Where Pauline Hopkins responds to the white supremacy of canonical utopian fiction by celebrating an Africanist essence, and Du Bois by valorizing racial hybridity as basis of global emancipation, *Young India* expediently attempts to classify Indians as white. Lacking the dubious luxury of defining themselves as Aryan and thus on the winning side of an implicitly eugenic ideology, Hopkins and Du Bois offer clearer rejections of developmentalism. They also offer stronger endorsements of affirmative Orientalism, the non-Western romance that can too easily become romanticization when marketed to an American public hungry for spiritual vitality.

Clearly, as a structural basis for a utopian vision, transnational solidarity has its shortcomings. But if Du Bois's "world of colored folk" and Lajpat Rai's periodical nation are rife with internal inconsistencies, so are the apparently stable utopias of Thomas More, Edward Bellamy, and Charlotte Perkins Gilman. Writing utopia—like writing more generally—necessitates smoothing over an unruly surface. Walter Benjamin's injunction to "read against the grain" may have achieved the status of cliché, but it is still worthwhile to seek out the nubbly knots of meaning that disrupt a deceptively coherent portrayal of an imaginary society. Each of these texts confirms a deconstructionist perspective that anticipates self-contradiction and referential flux. In the case of utopian fiction in particular, we are assisted in deconstructive reading by Karl Mannheim's categories of "utopia" and "ideology." For Mannheim, "utopias" are ideas that challenge the prevailing order, and "ideologies" their exact opposite, ideas that maintain the prevailing order. Both are "situationally transcendent," or incompatible with reality—with the critical difference that the illusions cast by ideologies serve to reinforce existing power dynamics.[17] Despite the purity of these concepts on a theoretical level, upon approaching living texts we find that all utopias are hybrid ones that contain both utopian and ideological elements. From *Looking Backward* to *Dark Princess,* we will see a mélange of progressive and retrogressive, optimistic and pessimistic mind frames. Therein lies the intellectual allure of the utopian text: as a self-contained laboratory for how new worlds are conceived and conveyed.

I begin with a thematic survey of the now-canonical utopian fiction of Edward Bellamy, William Morris, William Dean Howells, and Charlotte Perkins Gilman. Despite their apparent diversity, Bellamy's *Looking Backward,* Morris's *News from Nowhere,* Howells's linked Altrurian novels *A Traveler from Altruria* and *Through the Eye of a Needle,* and Gilman's *Herland* all hold to a teleological model of history that we could anachronistically call developmentalism: a new evolutionary outlook that disparages any form of primitivism and sees little of value in the past. From More to Bellamy and Gilman, classical utopian novels participate in Weber's "disenchantment of the world."[18] Utopian fiction transforms resistance into dominance, and the underground into the state. In one of the genre's many inherent paradoxes, in order to guarantee stability, a utopian society must prevent further resistance. There is no room for the occult in Bellamy's well-regulated Boston: as in More's original capital of diffused surveillance, "you can see how nowhere is there any license to waste time, nor any pretext to evade work—no wine shop, no alehouse, no brothel anywhere, no opportunity for corruption, no lurking hole, no secret meeting place. On the contrary, being under the eyes of all, people are bound either to be performing the usual labor or to be enjoying their leisure in a fashion not without dignity."[19] These are positivist lands devoid of magic, mystery, and subterfuge. My opening chapter, "Developing Nations," considers these five relatively canonical turn-of-the-century utopian novels from an anti-colonial point of view. Such a method entails identifying which of their techniques will be useful for my later writers, and which will run counter to the purposes of colored self-determination. Many techniques prove worth appropriating, mostly obviously and importantly the utopian endeavor itself, the bold premise that one can write one's way out of a present injustice. Equally generative are some of the formal elements of utopian fiction: especially the device of a utopian stranger who can mediate the reader's experience (inherited from More); and the corresponding device of a female character who can at once personify the new order and also provide narrative motion through romance (added by Bellamy and imitated by his followers). The overarching endeavor, the inheritance, and the invention all prove useful for Hopkins and Du Bois in particular. However, the line of influence is not an unbroken one. The chapter also elucidates the elements of turn-of-the-century utopian fiction that opposed colored emancipation. All of the novels of Bellamy and his school, I show, retain as their unit of governance a bordered but expansionist nation, imagine a unidirectional evolution toward Eurocentric civilization, and insist on racial purity and religious unity.

It is only a small step from the turn-of-the-century developmentalist utopias to the anti-utopian parodies of Aldous Huxley, Eugene Zamyatin, and E. M. Forster. *Brave New World*, *We*, and the short story "The Machine Stops" all portray not a dystopia—a terrible place per se—but rather something even more chilling, a place that functions exactly as it should, whose inhabitants are content with the utopian compromise to which they have acceded.[20] In rendering successful utopias as horrific, those authors contest the very premise of utopian thought. Zamyatin especially asserts that a rationalized utopia could never accommodate such threatening intangibles as dreams and love. Developmentalist utopianism, these authors show, opposes romantic individuality. Indeed, the horrors of Nazi Germany would soon justify Huxley's and Zamyatin's apprehensions regarding utopian aims. This point in the history of utopian fiction is a difficult one for those who survey the genre. Krishan Kumar writes that "after the First World War, utopias were everywhere in retreat," while Tom Moylan concurs that after the turn-of-the-century heyday, "utopian writing came upon hard times."[21] The inherent stasis of utopian fiction, a critical consensus holds, leaves the genre too easily prey to totalitarian abuses. Only by inventing new terminologies, it appears, were late twentieth-century thinkers able to resuscitate the idea that it is worthwhile to fight for a better social order. Toward that end have come Tom Moylan's "critical utopias," John Rawls's "realistic utopia," and Immanuel Wallerstein's "utopistics," among others.[22]

The implication of all these worthwhile recuperative projects is that the period between World War I and the 1960s was thoroughly devoid of utopian activity. This approach has overlooked the often utopian goals and methods of the many anti-colonial nationalisms active during that period. By straying from the genre of utopian fiction proper, we can identify the redemptive qualities of the 1960s' critical utopias—dynamism, process, and critique—in that unexpected quarter. Indeed, the texts that make up the topics of my subsequent chapters adapt and appropriate utopian techniques to very different ends. Neither a bordered nation nor a developmentalist historiography that equates progress with racial purification could serve the needs of diasporic writers of color. Accordingly, Lajpat Rai, Hopkins, and Du Bois radically revise evolutionary thinking to embrace both biological and cultural hybridity. Their imaginary worlds are romantic in their nostalgia, belief in a folk spirit, appreciation for mysticism and spirituality as positive forces, overt opposition to Benthemite utilitarianism, and deliberate reversal of a developmentalist trajectory. Whereas Bellamy follows his nearest ideological kin, the English Fabian Socialists, in accepting contemporary bourgeois "civilization" as superior and universal, these writers forge and celebrate a genuinely emancipatory culture of liberation. As such, they anticipate Marge Piercy's powerful and poignant *Woman on the Edge of Time,* a 1976 feminist and anti-racist science fiction novel that transports its beleaguered Chicana protagonist to a utopian twenty-second century. In deliberately engineering a full range of biological characteristics, its inhabitants "broke the bond between genes and culture, broke it forever. . . . But we don't want the melting pot where everybody ends up with thin gruel. We want diversity, for strangeness breeds richness."[23] Decades before Piercy, the twentieth-century anti-colonial utopians, too, envision strange new worlds of mixed-race babies and syncretic faiths. In their loose borders as well as their attention to the needs of minority populations, theirs is a newly cosmopolitan utopianism.

In chapter 2, "A Periodical Nation," we will depart from a classical definition of utopian fiction to investigate the imaginative space produced by a periodical. Benedict Anderson's notion that a periodical may foster an "imagined community" of readers applies to *Young India;* but unlike the reactionary and intolerant nationalisms that Anderson and others have studied, that of *Young India* is a transnational and transcultural one that insists on diversity of race, religion, and opinion as one of its defining characteristics. Far from being limited to the subcontinent of South Asia, it projects a constituency of colonized and other working people in Ireland, Egypt, Turkey, Persia, Japan, China, and the United States. Naidu and Tagore may follow Bellamy in personifying that nation through an emblematic female, but their women are agents of change rather than mere figureheads. If, as the editors of the *Post-Colonial Studies Reader* claim, "the idea of the nation is often based on naturalised myths of racial or cultural origin," *Young India*'s nation is based on a myth of pluralism.[24]

Hopkins and Du Bois, too, grapple with the problem of how to write an extraterritorial utopia. American Afrocentrism in all its incarnations—first Pan-Africanism and later Black Nationalism—has had a uniquely troubled relationship with place. Descended from people hijacked from what would become an increasingly romanticized homeland, and having already forged a new culture in America, where ought Afrocentrist utopians direct their desire for a better social order? The solution, for Pauline Hopkins and W. E. B. Du Bois, is to manufacture idealized and ahistorical versions of colored empires: Ethiopia and India. Hopkins goes fancifully abroad and underground, while DuBois uses the force of imagination to link disparate regions into a cohesive but still multiplicitous whole. Hopkins posits utopia as not a unidirectional process of development but a resurrection of an earlier order, while Du Bois strategically employs romance to overcome the limitations of a pragmatic politics of compromise. Chapter 3, "Worlds of Color," situates their romantic utopianism as a reaction to Booker T. Washington's "uplift" ideology, and also as part of a larger philosophy of internationalism emerging in response to colonial rule. Du Bois's and Hopkins's valuable contribution to utopian discourse, as I show, is to construct a grounded, specific collectivity separate from the nation. Some of the many problems with that collectivity, however, come across clearly in Richard Wright's *The Color Curtain*, with which this chapter ends.

The writings of Lajpat Rai, Naidu, Tagore, Hopkins, and Du Bois present a borderless utopianism that is at once local and global. Perfect worlds can be found, for Du Bois, in a tiny apartment in Chicago and also a worldwide movement; and for the *Young India* writers, in a reading room in New York and also a loose solidarity network. Their borderless quality allows the writings to evade some of the generic shortcomings of utopian fiction. By portraying the new as old, classical utopias provide an imaginative ground for comprehending, assimilating, and ultimately containing social change. As in any piece of writing, execution is double-edged: to carry out is also to destroy, to foreclose possibility. With its punctuated time frame and collective structure, *Young India* harnesses the transformative energy of utopian fiction while evading the perennial problem of closure, both national and narrative. Hopkins's and Du Bois's novels, too, suggest a new order but stop short of fully realizing it on paper. Like the subtitle of Samuel Delany's 1976 sci-fi novel *Triton*, the results are ambiguous heterotopias. *Landscapes of Hope* charts a path from a set of expansionist nations to a loose network, from teleological and predetermined visions to open-ended ones, from racially pure to polycultural populations.[25]

Recognizing the utopian elements of anti-colonial writing allows us to rehabilitate utopian fiction from its associations with authoritarian rule. These texts replace the statism of canonical utopian fiction with diffusion, surveillance with an acceptance of internal contradiction, and stasis with an immanent or punctuated time frame. They present new anti-totalitarian strategies like messianism, incompletion, and collaboration: where time, for a classical utopia, is threatening and potentially destructive to imaginary sustainability, here it is a constitutive force.[26] As worthy as utopian fiction is as an artistic exercise, the problem with utopian novels is that nobody wants to live in the rigid and time-bound worlds they depict. Here, on the other hand, are incomplete utopias that invite and even demand reader participation.

Like Kamau Brathwaite's "nation language," they operate within a continuum of meaning that is unintelligible without an audience.

At the same time, I intend *Landscapes of Hope* to contribute to ongoing debates within postcolonial theory regarding the dynamics of agency and the possibilities for resistant thought and action. Identifying the utopian elements of anti-colonial thought allows us to understand it as not simply reactive but productive. Rather than seeing anti-colonial writing as crudely dependent upon prevailing conditions, we can recognize a substantive body of imaginative work that arose out of the crucible of colonial domination. This is not to say that the issue of derivativeness plays no role. If nationalism is a derivative discourse, so too is utopianism. A central question that occupies this book is whether a colonially informed genre—another of the "master's tools," along with the English language and the nation-state—can aid national liberation. The texts themselves are alive to these issues of imitation and indigeneity. As Du Bois's protagonist Matthew Towns reports early in *Dark Princess*, colored American organizations "chime and accord with the white world" (58). This is certainly true of affirmative Orientalism, which, as noted above, originates from the terms and categories set out by colonial administrators. However, looking at the resulting works through a utopian lens brings out the material value of the new worlds they audaciously create. Further, because the utopias produced are transnational ones, they demand a critical framework that transcends the potentially stifling relationship between colony and metropolis. Thus *Landscapes of Hope* also documents both the linkages between postcolonial and ethnic American writing, and the limits of those connections. As such, part of what this book provides is a prehistory of the later Afro-Asian solidarity so convincingly documented by Vijay Prashad and others.[27]

Largely because of my archival excursions, I may not appear as optimistic as some of the historians and critics whose work I so deeply admire. This is not my intent; for despite the many problems with solidarity that come up in the course of *Landscapes of Hope*, I still believe in the quest for a better order, and I offer this book on that idealistic premise. To proclaim definitively that no effective solidarity movement can ever be forged would fragment opposition in a classic "divide and conquer" maneuver familiar both from colonial India and from the contemporary United States. However, the optimism with which I began my research has been tempered by the texts themselves, which so clearly signal the need for real sensitivity to differences in historical experience. I intend my attentions to the failures of solidarity to be more cautionary than admonitory, for clearly we have not yet arrived where we want to be. It is my own hope that *Landscapes of Hope* will attest to the power of the imagination in helping us to reach that place.

1

Developing Nations

> The country that is more developed industrially
> only shows, to the less developed,
> the image of its own future.
> —Karl Marx, *Capital*

We must begin by identifying the legacies of the utopian tradition in which the prewar anti-colonial writers participated. On the credit side of the balance, to use the crudest metaphor, there are several. Most significant is the ability, indeed the generic *raison d'être*, to step outside present conditions and imagine an improved order. Further, that process has the effect of divorcing readers from their accepted ideological assumptions through the technique of defamiliarization. On the other hand, utopia was from its very inception a colonial genre. For the turn-of-the-century utopias discussed in this chapter, their immersion in a colonial outlook translates into an ethos of developmentalism and an implicit preference for racially homogenous populations. As it stood at the cusp of the twentieth century, utopian fiction conveyed a model of human history that regards the past as hopelessly primitive. This, combined with bordered nations organized on the basis of racial purity, entails an imperialist model that predicts and even predicates a world arrayed in various stages along a preset, hierarchical line of civilizational progress—in other words, what we would now call "uneven development." Utopian novels from Bellamy to Gilman exhibit a perfect faith in developmentalism, the doctrine that Gilbert Rist has identified as an Enlightenment-era linear model of history, merged with the novel pseudo-science of social Darwinism.[1] That new myth of linear progress represents a misapplication of Darwin to human history, one that comes across clearly in the five canonical utopian novels I will examine here.

Within utopian fiction of the turn-of-the-century period, what I call developmentalism entails several easily recognizable elements: linear, teleo-logical models of history; increased regularization of human activity; societal improvement through selective reproduction; and a perception of the "prim-itive" as a benighted and long-vanished condition. Canonical utopia's imbri-cation in the colonial ideology of developmentalism (both on its own and expressed as a belief in the value of eugenic breeding) results in the discred-iting of the genre as inherently totalitarian. Thus this chapter will end with a brief survey of the dystopian and anti-utopian fiction that followed—and directly resulted from—such discrediting.

It is precisely to this developmentalist ethos, I would contend, that Bellamy's novel owes its contemporary success and its endurance. As the conventional wisdom has it, *Looking Backward* single-handedly revived the utopian genre after its disappearance following the early modern period. Frank and Fritzie Manuel, the grand old couple of utopian studies, credit *Looking Backward* (along with *News from Nowhere* and Theodor Hertzka's *Freeland*) with prompting "the rebirth of the utopian novel"; their heir appar-ent Krishan Kumar states that "Bellamy's influence can be traced directly in a spectacular burgeoning of the utopian imagination at the close of the nine-teenth century."[2] I will not depart from the central importance placed on *Looking Backward,* but will offer a new explanation for Bellamy's impact. For the Manuels, Bellamy and his contemporaries managed to render into litera-ture almost a century of utopian political theory. For Kumar, Bellamy's par-ticular contribution is the uniquely sociological approach of the novel.[3] While both of these are indeed critical elements of Bellamy's success, *Looking Backward*'s model of history provides a still more significant innovation. As Rist shows convincingly in his valuable demythologizing study *The History of Development,* the ideology that would go on to define global relations in the twentieth century—namely, developmentalism or modernization theory—gained force during this period as both a dominant philosophy of history and also a justification for colonial rule.[4] My aim in this chapter is to show how *Looking Backward,* as well as the canonical utopian novels that followed it, revitalized the defunct genre of utopian fiction by merging it with the ideology of development.

The turn of the century marked not the first but the second time that utopian fiction relied upon a central apparatus of colonial activity. For the genre's first wave, during the sixteenth and seventeenth centuries, that central apparatus was exploration. The early utopian narratives of More, Bacon, and others derived much of their energy from the discovery of new continents and islands, and flourished as a way to help their readers make sense of a changing world. In the sixteenth and seventeenth centuries, spatial utopias—apparently self-contained islands—reflected England's experimentation with early imperialism and colonialism. Utopian fiction generally feeds off another more popular genre, borrowing its structure and conventions; if by the twenty-first century we have come to think of utopian fiction as a subgenre of science fiction, in this initial phase it closely resembled travel literature. The New World and especially its temperate, fertile islands seemed to offer boundless hospitable locations for an isolated and therefore eternally stable Christian order. Gradually, that perfect locale began to migrate farther and farther from England. In 1516, Thomas More located Utopia in an unnamed sea in the new world. By the time that Francis Bacon composed *New Atlantis* in 1624, he had to move his happy island of Bensalem past the contested Americas, all the way to the South Seas. Even as early as 1621, when Robert Burton inserted a satiric utopia into his *Anatomy of Melancholy*, the idea of uninhabited land had already become somewhat of a cliché. Burton, having resolved egotistically to "make an utopia of mine own, a new Atlantis, a poetical commonwealth of mine own," muses that "it may be in *Terra Australi Incognita*, there is room enough (for to my knowledge neither that hungry Spaniard nor Mercurius Brittanicus have yet discovered half of it), or else one of those floating islands in Mare del Zur . . . or one of the fortunate isles, for who knows yet where, or which they are? there is room enough in the inner parts of America, and northern coasts of Asia."[5] As Burton suggests, the myth of empty land could not indefinitely accommodate utopian yearnings.

Not for another two and a half centuries would a compensation emerge for the loss of that useful myth. Meanwhile, the intervening period saw utopian energies directed elsewhere. In the eighteenth century, the utopian urge took shape less through recognizable utopian fiction than through other means: travel accounts, Orientalist writings, and constitutions of budding republics all used language to create better worlds. By Bellamy's time, utopian fiction could no longer rely upon the myth of empty space as a generic rationale. The United States Census Bureau would declare the American frontier closed in 1890, and in 1899 Conrad would declare through his epic seaman Marlowe that Africa too "had ceased to be a blank space of delightful mystery—a white patch for a boy to dream gloriously over."[6] But if the myth of empty space was no longer tenable, the myth of progress would soon take its place. If no empty lands were available to serve as repository of utopian visions, those visions could find a home in centuries yet to come.

We now have the intellectual means to recognize developmentalism, or modernization theory, as one of the central ideologies of both colonialism and neo-colonial relations. Practically a textbook example of ideology, developmentalist ideas and vocabulary had been almost invisible in their ubiquity and credence until scholars like Walter Rodney, Samir Amin, Arturo Escobar, Gilbert Rist, and Sylvia Wynter put the tools of multiple disciplines to work to demystify those ideas. Rist's *History of Development* is an indispensable source in that it takes the longest possible view of how the discourse of development itself developed over the several thousand years. Developmentalism, writes Rist, is "part of our modern religion."[7] Where many others limit their study to the post–World War II period, Rist takes the concept back to Aristotelian and Augustinian models of history. However, the late-nineteenth- and early-twentieth-century period with which I am concerned marked a decisive break in how the ideology of progress took hold in the popular imagination. Bolstered by the theories of Charles Darwin and to an even greater extent Herbert Spencer, the notion of progressive improvement became linked with doctrines of European superiority. Rist demonstrates a fundamental—i.e., at the very base—connection between developmentalism and race supremacy, one that comes across clearly in the utopian fiction of this period. It is also important to note the conceptual affinity between Marxist historiography and developmentalism, in that both are teleological and universalizing. As Ania Loomba explains, "'progress' was understood in similar ways by capitalists as well as socialists—for both, it included a high level of industrialization, the mastery of 'man' over 'nature,' the modern European view of science and technology."[8] Thus between social evolutionism and dialectical materialism, new philosophies of progress provided utopian fiction with ample material to stage the improvement of humankind over time.

We can see a clear distinction in core values, then, between utopias in space and utopias in time. As opposed to the spatial utopias of the sixteenth and early seventeenth centuries, futurist utopias function as the perfect literary expression of developmentalism. Previous uses of the time-travel plot device demonstrate just how vastly Bellamy's and his contemporaries' novelistic visions of time and history differ from that of their predecessors. Washington Irving in his 1819 short story "Rip Van Winkle" forces his protagonist forward in time, but no further than the Federalist period. Even with the aid of supernatural forces, the hapless rustic cannot reach as far as the author's own era. Such a move—recasting the past as future—would become more common in the mid-century works of Nathaniel Hawthorne, in which only those long dead dare to imagine the future, and the farthest span of time to which any of them could aspire is already past for the author. In the profoundly anti-utopian *Blithedale Romance* in particular, any sense of hope or futurity is as long gone as the embers of a fire that burned years ago.[9] By contrast, Bellamy's novel belies its title by never looking backward at all, except intermittently in horror. The book is antinostalgic to the core, resolutely dwelling only in the future.

Looking Backward spawned a whole dynasty of futurist utopias. In the United States alone, over ninety more utopian novels appeared in the eleven years between its publication and the new century. Despite the prolific imitators, Bellamy's own version of the good place remained supreme within the discourse of utopianism, inspiring two periodicals, hundreds of local discussion clubs, and a short-lived Nationalist Party. His innovative form proved still more irresistible than the content of his utopia, for even those who took exception to the technological or the socialistic components of his vision made use of the time-travel device. Titles like *Looking Beyond* (written by Ludwig Geisser in 1891), *Looking Forward* (Arthur Bird, 1899), and *Looking Ahead* (Henry Pereira Mendes, 1899) attest to Bellamy's indelible mark on the genre. One author, Mrs. C. H. Stone, even brought to life a novelist briefly mentioned in *Looking Backward*, publishing *One of "Berrian's" Novels* in 1890.

The vast majority of these books are long since out of print, with only five titles still commonly read. The remainder of this chapter will turn to those five: *Looking Backward*, as well as four other fairly canonical representatives of this turn-of-the-century utopian renaissance. Across the Atlantic, William Morris made his own contribution—also in direct response to

Bellamy, as we will see—with his 1890 romance *News from Nowhere*. The godfather of American realism, William Dean Howells, soon hopped on the utopian bandwagon with *A Traveler from Altruria* in 1894 and its far richer but comparatively unread sequel *Through the Eye of the Needle* in 1907. In writing his utopian novels, Howells rejected Bellamy's futurist innovation, reverting to the older conventions that presented utopian fiction as travel narrative—as did Charlotte Perkins Gilman in her whimsical but immensely instructive 1915 novel *Herland*. Those five novels now regularly appear in surveys of the utopian fiction of this important period. Given the already established prominence of their authors, *News from Nowhere* and the *Altruria* novels quickly joined *Looking Backward* as influential utopian novels. Though not published in book form until 1979, when Ann Lane repackaged Gilman's 1915 serial as a "lost feminist utopian novel," *Herland* now appears in most courses on utopian fiction.[10] Together, the five now form a standard and pre-dictable sequence of texts within the field of nineteenth- and twentieth-century utopian fiction.

Since all are fairly widely studied, my approach will not be a comprehensive discussion of the elements of their utopian societies. Rather, my object here is to trace aspects of these utopian novels that will be useful elsewhere in this book by way of contrast. Experts on turn-of-the-century utopian fiction generally identify the five as quite different, describing Bellamy's utopia as technophilic, Morris's as nostalgic, Howells's as pastoral, and Gilman's as fantastical. Yet in their organization of time and space they have some important common attributes that have yet to be acknowledged as such. My aim in this chapter is to illuminate those particular attributes, especially since the material in the chapters that follow will come in specific opposition to them. What they have in common—beyond their position in the turn-of-the-century utopian renaissance and their enduring canonical status—is their use of a developmentalist model of history: namely, the belief that social conditions will change for the better with the passage of years, whether on their own or through human intervention. As my five representative texts indicate, the vast majority of the utopian novels in this period—not only those set in the future—share the developmentalism inaugurated by Bellamy. The range of styles and political agendas demonstrates just how pervasive his progress-oriented model of history would quickly become. Out of the five, only two are set in the future, for reasons I will explain later. But all five convey Bellamy's unwavering faith in a natural course of societal improvement over time. Though it emerges contemporaneously with futurist utopian fiction, developmentalism permeates even those utopias still set in far-off "undiscovered" lands. As proof of the dominance of developmentalist thinking during this period, we will find it within utopian novels often held to be utterly different.

My focus is on what these "classic" utopias have in common, and what they do not share with the documents of the more inchoate, dynamic utopianism that will provide the focus for the remainder of *Landscapes of Hope*. Where these five, to varying degrees, present utopia as evolving through an often impersonal machinery of progress, romantic utopianism looks nostalgically to the past and hopefully to the future for its ideal order. For this chapter in particular, the terms "form" and "content," always indispensable for the study of narrative, take on slightly different and more specific meanings. I will use the term "form" to refer to the novel and how it lays out its plot, and "content" to refer to the utopian society that it introduces. Those two components of narrative are even more closely linked than in most genres: since "the utopia" may refer either to the work of fiction or to the world it portrays, form and content constantly bleed into each other. Developmentalism dictates both how the imaginary world is written, and also what kind of world it is. Since the utopian society—content—is the triumphant result of an impersonal mechanism of progress, the story that presents that society—form—must move forward in an equally smooth and assertive motion. However, in all these utopian novels the benefits of progress stop somewhere. Even as their model of history pushes relentlessly forward, all these authors hold tightly to the idea that the governing unit for utopia would be a single nation-state, cleanly bordered on the same contours as the author's own. Like the developmentalist model of time, this too comes in direct contrast to the globe-spanning imaginations of the other authors that I will later examine.

I. Evolution: Edward Bellamy, William Morris, and William Dean Howells

With *Looking Backward*, Edward Bellamy formulated the governing vision for turn-of-the-century utopianism. His account of year-2000 Boston presents a centralized, technology-enabled universe of plenty. Narrator Julian

West, a bourgeois neurasthenic who must employ a mesmerist in order to overcome chronic insomnia, awakens from hypnotic sleep into a twenty-first century purged of both Mesmerism and insomnia, along with all other forms of mystery and malaise as well as any social inequality. The novel's invented historiography attributes the complete change in social organization not to any human intervention, but simply to a natural progression from monopoly capitalism to state socialism. This naturalized social-Darwinist evolution transforms a world of injustice and subterfuge into a rational and explicable order. The change came about through the least possible effort: merely that of not standing in its way. As West's patient and apparently omniscient host Dr. Leete explains, "The solution came as the result of a process of industrial evolution which could not have terminated otherwise. All that society had to do was to recognize and cooperate with that evolution, when its tendency had become unmistakable."[11] The result of this natural and peaceful process is a logical extension of Taylorism: mass production standardized to the utmost degree, until it is controlled entirely by the state.

For his readers, Bellamy's fantasy presented an unthreatening vision of social and economic equality, one in which advances in communication and distribution enable a heavily centralized state to distribute all the benefits of civilization—including literature, music, art, fine cuisine, and genteel after-dinner conversation—to the masses. *Looking Backward* renders the utopian urge into a rationalized, bureaucratized, utterly static state. The peaceful evolution brought about perfect equality but no accompanying cultural transformation; rather, the entire population now conforms to nineteenth-century bourgeois standards. With the exception of more comfortable (though still distinct and recognizable) dresses for women, no aspect of culture has changed since 1887. Leete immediately recognizes West as a "man of culture," suggesting that the definition for that nebulous term has remained stable (50). Relaxation, for West and Leete, consists of late-night conversation over a glass of wine and a cigar. Speech patterns have been regularized, with the language of the "cultured ancestors of the nineteenth" century as the standard (59). With "what you used to call the education of a gentleman" universally available, all now love "music really worth hearing," while popular literature now coincides with that of "real merit" (161, 99, 129). Accordingly, working-class culture has disappeared entirely. As Leete explains, "manual labor meant association with a rude, coarse, and ignorant class of people. There is no such class now. . . . Brutishness is eliminated" (162–3). With such a monolith of gentility as his ideal society, Bellamy conforms perfectly to Marx's description of the bourgeois socialists, who "want all the advantages of modern social conditions without the struggles and dangers necessarily resulting therefrom. They desire the existing state of society minus the revolutionary and disintegrating elements. They wish for a bourgeoisie without a proletariat."[12] Marx found such socialists reprehensibly unimaginative and damagingly moderate—but in fact, Bellamy himself would have objected to even that moderate designation as overly radical. He stopped short of identifying himself as any kind of socialist at all, writing to William Dean Howells in 1888 that "the word socialist is one I never could well stomach . . . it is a foreign word in itself and equally foreign in all its suggestions. It smells to the average American of petroleum, suggests the red flag, with all manner of sexual novelties, and an abusive tone about God and religion."[13] In *Looking Backward*, he seizes the socialist goals of equality and nationalization and renders them familiar, unthreatening, and palatably American.

In a parallel process to his cure of the bourgeoisie through the surgical removal of the proletariat, Bellamy also cures the ills of Reconstruction by neatly excising the novel's only character of color. That would be West's "faithful colored man Sawyer," who almost never appears without some indication of his loyalty (46). Upon awakening in 2000, West retroactively kills off his own faithful servant for the sake of narrative logic. As he ponders, "It only remains to assume that Sawyer lost his life in the fire or by some accident connected with it, and the rest follows naturally enough" (61). Bellamy rids his utopia of the race question merely by erasing the presence of the one black man.[14] Bellamy later claimed, in response to a reader's criticism, that "For anything to the contrary that appears in the book, the people referred to in its pages, so far as we remember, might have been black, brown, or yellow as well as white."[15] The fact that West identifies Sawyer as a "colored man" belies that disingenuous statement—as do Edith Leete's "deep-blue eyes" and "delicately tinted complexion." In fact, Bellamy quite deliberately creates a whites-only twenty-first century; his vision of Reconstruction has the United States centralized, supreme, and racially pure.

The unit of governance for Bellamy's utopia would have been as recognizable to his readers as the habit of an after-dinner cigar. It is a cleanly bordered United States, so taken for granted that Leete and others generally refer to it as "the nation." That nation mediates all relationships. When explaining how service positions have lost their demeaning quality (the problem of service being a favorite theme of both Bellamy and Howells), Leete tells West that "the individual is never regarded, nor regards himself, as the servant of those he serves, nor is he in any way dependent upon them. It is always the nation he is serving" (126). It makes perfect sense that the movement inspired by *Looking Backward* would be called Nationalism, indicating exclusivity as well as state control of industry, for his blueprint retains and even strengthens the model of the nation.

At the same time that it is a nationalist one, Bellamy's is also a thoroughly imperialist vision. Our familiar United States now serves as a model for the rest of the world, particularly the civilized but less evolutionarily advanced nations. As Dr. Leete tells it, "the great nations of Europe as well as Australia, Mexico, and parts of South America, are now organized industrially like the United States, which was the pioneer of the evolution" (115). Given Bellamy's racialized universe, we can presume that Europeanized Argentina and color-stratified Brazil fall into the opportune category of "parts of South America"; the implication is that the darker world has resisted rationalization. Together, those satisfactorily developed nations have joined into "a loose form of federal union of world-wide extent." One critic cites this passage as evidence for the "inherently globalizing tendencies" of Bellamy's thought.[16] Yet for Bellamy the nation is still a viable unit for governance—in fact, the only viable one. It is important that Leete describes the world's other 'great and civilized' nations as being organized "*like* the United States," not with it: they duplicate that original utopia rather than bleeding into it. Though the exotic flavor of the "Turkish Reveille" is available over a proto-radio, this utopia has no diasporas. Meanwhile Bellamy attests to and endorses the new late-nineteenth-century model of uneven development, which I will discuss more fully in the section on William Dean Howells. "The more backward races," Leete continues, "are gradually being educated up to civilized institutions." Now we learn what has become of the other "parts": under the tutelage of the "great nations," they too will experience evolution in time. With the "more backward" still organized into "races" and only the civilized identified as "nations," Bellamy frames nationalism as a necessary stage in societal evolution. By continuing the ongoing developmentalist push toward perfection, he allows his utopia to be at once nationalist and universalist. Once fully evolved, utopia may export its philosophy and structure around the world; until that time, perfection remains within national borders.

Despite his disavowal of socialism, Bellamy essentially translates the contemporaneous English movement of Fabian Socialism to an American context.[17] *Looking Backward* accepts the English Fabian dream of a peaceful evolution into equality, while adding as a native element the prediction that monopoly would assist in that transition. The Fabians, like Bellamy, lacked a transformative theory of culture, placed full faith in evolution, evinced absolutely no nostalgia for any past order, and favored conciliation over dialectical conflict. When Beatrice Webb defined the Fabian aim as collectivizing "the kitchen of life" so that "all may have freedom for the drawing room of life," she could well have been describing Bellamy's Boston.[18] Like Bellamy, the Fabians departed from the various internationalist socialisms in their endorsement of both nationalism and imperialism. In his history of radical dissent to British colonial ventures in Africa, Bernard Porter singles out the Fabians as the socialist group most fully in support of Britain's Africa policy, especially in regard to the Boer War. As George Bernard Shaw put it in a 1900 lecture, "a Fabian is necessarily an Imperialist."[19] As Porter tells it, the war changed the Fabians from parochial social reformers to equally parochial imperial apologists still unable to conceive of a constituency beyond England. Indeed, until that war most of the Fabian Society's ever-proliferating pamphlets present the world outside England as not a real place but a useful source for metaphors and analogies that illustrate the position of the worker in England. Annie Besant's 1886 essay "Why I Am a Socialist" repeats T. H. Huxley's declaration that it would be better to be "a savage in one of the Fiji islands" than a London slum-dweller, while Sidney Webb in a lecture of the same year makes an analogy whereby "the king's house . . . in the African sand" is to "the blood of the slave girls" as a mill-owner's saloon-carriage is to "the task of his serfs."[20] Given that Fiji and Africa represent nothing more than sources of metaphor, it is easy for the Fabians, like Bellamy, to imagine that a benevolent imperialism will uncomplicatedly foster developmentalist improvement everywhere.

Even more central to their shared vision is the unquestioning faith that both Bellamy and the Fabians place in the benefits of evolution. In this, they exhibit—along with a good part of the transatlantic agnostic intelligentsia—the influence of Herbert Spencer. It is Spencer who initiated the misapplication of Darwin to the study of human societies (and who coined the term "survival of the fittest," which is so frequently misattributed to Darwin). If society is a living "organism" that functions analogously to animals, as Spencer often claimed, then it must benefit from the same natural adaptation that Darwin observed in animal species. His optimism deeply influenced Bellamy, who in 1877 summarized Spencer as predicting that humankind would achieve "completer perfection" through "gradual development."[21]

That faith in evolution underlies every aspect of *Looking Backward*. In Bellamy's imagined future, mysticism (in the guise of West's Mesmeric hypnotist) has been banished; social and economic relations regularized; and transparency imposed in all venues. This is Weber's "disenchantment of the world" carried to its farthest extent. As in More's happy island, there are no secrets and no underground. When shopping, for example, West expects to see a familiar crowded market filled with pecuniarily motivated clerks forcing wares on reluctant customers. Instead he finds "a vast hall full of light" in which "legends on the walls all about the hall indicated to what classes of commodities the counters below were devoted" (80). Wondering how customers will learn about the products, "I saw then that there was fastened to each sample a card containing in succinct form a complete statement of the make and materials of the goods and all its qualities, leaving absolutely no point to hang a question on" (81). Commercial relations are defined by objective information, depersonalized and emanating from a centralized state.

A similar transparency applies to class relations, as we learn from Edith. She asks West incredulously whether "in old times people often kept up establishments and did other things which they could not afford for ostentation, to make people think them richer than they were. . . . it could not be so nowadays; for everybody's income is known" (96–7). Nor do subterfuge and secrecy any longer characterize sexual relations. Dr. Leete responds to West's question regarding "the social relations of the sexes" by asserting "the entire frankness and unconstraint which now characterize those relations." According to Dr. Leete, "Coquetry would be as much despised in a girl as in a man. Affected coldness, which in your day rarely deceived a lover, would deceive him now, for no one thinks of practicing it" (178). Dovetailing nicely with Bellamy's general emphasis on efficiency, sexual relations now are never circuitous but instead straightforward.

Bellamy, through the mouthpiece of Dr. Leete, attributes the new transparency in all these arenas to one simple change: the elimination of money as an obscuring and obfuscatory medium. As Dr. Leete explains to an astonished West, money is not the necessary substance that West and his nineteenth century had held it to be, but rather a dispensable medium of exchange, now made superfluous by the nationalization of all industry and commerce. Back when private corporations dominated production, "money was essential as their medium. But as soon as the nation became the sole producer of all sorts of commodities, there was no need of exchanges between individuals that they might get what they required" (71). Money pretended to be determining relations that it was in fact only mediating, and in the process obscuring. Chapters later, West, an apt pupil, demonstrates how well he has internalized this information: "I have a tolerably clear idea of your system of distribution, and how it enables you to dispense with a circulating medium" (127). If money is now seen to have been unreal and misleading, credit takes on an even more occult character. In the eyes of the enlightened twentieth century, it was "but the sign of a sign," and as such caused "prodigious illusions" (161). Those illusory qualities vanish once money and credit are no longer used. The single change away from currency carries with it a host of reformatory implications: the new transparency in sales and class relations are an obvious result, while (hetero)sexual relations have also been reformed because women no longer depend upon men to support them, and thus can initiate courtship on their own accord. A world of secrets and illusions, Bellamy shows, has evolved into a rational and explicable order.

Bellamy integrates that faith in evolution, so evident in the content of *Looking Backward*'s utopian society, into the form of his story as well. In terms of how the story is told, his futurism manifests itself as a concern with narrative motion. As Bellamy and his generation reinvented the utopian genre, retaining many of its timeworn conventions but altering those conventions to suit their new model of historical change, they brought to it for the first time a dissatisfaction with stasis. The problem of stasis, though it greatly occupies contemporary readers of utopian fiction, rarely troubled the early utopian authors. As Frank and Fritzie Manuel point out, eternal stasis was to Thomas More and his seventeenth- and eighteenth-century followers not a liability but a boon: "How often in the eighteenth-century moralists and moral historians does one read praise for the society without a history! History meant wars, devastations, religious persecutions . . . Repetitiveness as a self-destructive, stultifying rut is a new conception that represents a sharp disjuncture in Western thought."[22] If by now "stasis is the perpetual whipping boy of critics of utopia," as Kenneth Roemer claims, it was not until Bellamy's time that it even became a quality to avoid.[23] And having deemed motion to be a desirable quality, Bellamy, Morris, Howells, and

Gilman find ways to generate motion on the level of both form and content, or utopian fiction and utopian society. Since the writing makes the world, stasis is a problem on both of those levels. With utopia as a consummation of desire for a better world, any utopian author must grapple with the question of how to reconcile consummation and desire, or how to write desire into a narrative of achieved consummation.

To ensure the narrative motion that would mirror his evolved society, Bellamy applies and adapts one of the many enduring generic conventions first established by More. Utopian fiction still retains several of More's original conventions: a legitimizing frame; explicit, ongoing comparisons with the author's inferior system; and a narrator who is foreign to the utopian world but familiar to the reader. In combating stasis, writers in this second wave of utopian fiction put the last of those, the "stranger" convention, to uses unanticipated by More. Though Raphael Hythlodae came to Utopia as an outsider, he describes the island to his eager listeners not as he experienced it, but in logically organized, discrete topic areas. More even interrupts Hythlodae's exposition with topic headings like "Of Their Towns" or "Of Their Magistrates," so that the effect is of an organized treatise rather than a protagonist's time-bound experience. In Bacon's *New Atlantis,* the narrator conveys his disorienting experience chronologically, so that the utopian fiction benefits at least from the drama of discovery. The second wave, taking advantage of four centuries of novelistic experimentation, more pointedly employs the stranger in service of narrative by using him to incorporate two genres that had emerged by then: romance and conversion tale. In *Looking Backward*—as in *News from Nowhere,* Howells's Altruria series, and *Herland*—the stranger helps to remedy the problem of narrative stasis by providing the drama of whether he or she (all except Howells's strangers are male) will be converted to the unfamiliar and initially uncomfortable system.

Bellamy creates further narrative tension by involving his hapless stranger in a romance plot, another device that Morris, Howells, and Gilman would all imitate. Ostensibly, *Looking Backward*'s insipid even though quasi-incestuous love story serves only as an antidote to the problem of stasis. As the story's mock preface from December 2000 acknowledges, "the author has sought to alleviate the instructive quality of the book by casting it in the form of a romantic narrative, which he would be glad to fancy not devoid of interest in its own right" (35). Bellamy's vision of the future so lacks in narrative tension that he must overlay a romance story in order to motor the plot. Accordingly, Julian West must be a bachelor when he falls asleep in 1887—though his unmarried state has further symbolism that I will explain shortly. Having lost his fiancée, servant, and mesmerist, he miraculously finds the qualities of marriageability, loyalty, and magnetic attraction in his host family's daughter Edith Leete. Edith clearly returns his sentiments, and after she is eventually revealed to be the great-granddaughter of his long-dead fiancée Edith Bartlett, the two are instantly engaged. That revelation, however, does not come until the novel's penultimate chapter, after two hundred pages of meaningful glances. Within a perfect world, Bellamy had to manufacture some unfulfilled desire in order to keep the reader turning the page—which the lovely Edith graciously provides.

However, that is not Edith's only purpose. In addition to encoding desire into the narrative, she also bestows upon the stranger, who is the [male] reader's double within the text, the productive role that he had initially been denied. The novel opens with the frustration of desire on many counts. For one, the frame is pre-utopian, so that the socially aware reader enters the text in his own world of violent inequality. Thus *Looking Backward* opens with the deferral of the desire to see utopia; at the same time, through West we must experience the more personal deferral of sexual consummation. In the novel's opening chapter, West describes his life as a callow, naïve young man of the benighted era. Just before his long sleep, labor politics and his own romantic life have collided:

> I was engaged to wed Edith Bartlett. . . . Our marriage only
> waited on the completion of the house which I was building
> for our occupancy in one of the most desirable parts of the city. . . .
> When the house had been begun, its completion by the winter of
> 1886 had been expected. The spring of the following year found it,
> however, yet incomplete, and my marriage still a thing of the
> future. The cause of the delay calculated to be particularly
> exasperating to an ardent lover was a series of strikes, that is to say
> concerted refusals to work on the part of the bricklayers, masons,
> carpenters, painters, plumbers, and other trades concerned in
> house-building. (41–2)

Bellamy cleverly links marriage, sex, and fair labor practices: all, of a piece, are "a thing of the future," and indeed the twenty-first century sees all of them realized. With Edith Leete replacing her dead great-grandmother, the romantic plot engine also allows West to enter utopia permanently, thus consummating all readers' desires—again, that collective experience presumes a readership of heterosexual males. Bellamy inserts a further motivation for realizing utopia, here depicted in contrast to the present day as a place where the will of "an ardent lover" would never be frustrated. The future allows the simultaneous consummation of sexual desire, political desire, and consumer desire.

Further, Edith serves to render the twenty-first century comfortable, desirable, and productive for West and for the reader. Throughout the novel, West feels like a stranger in the new well-regulated world; Bellamy reinforces that feeling by repeating "strange" or "stranger" in almost every chapter. The thoroughly disoriented traveler initially perceives his surroundings as strange, describing Dr. Leete as "an utter stranger" and his home as "this strange house" (49, 51). Gradually West locates the quality of strangeness not in his environment but in his own self, fearing "the horror of strangeness that was waiting to be faced when I could no longer command diversion" (60). On his first trip outside the house, "the idea that I was two persons, that my identity was double, began to fascinate me," until finally "I covered my burning eyeballs with my hand to shut out the horror of strangeness" (78, 80). West gradually identifies himself as the stranger, and realizes that he has generated the quality of strangeness rather than merely experiencing it. The continual strangeness culminates in the "double mystery" of Edith's unpredictable behavior, which is resolved when he finds out her identity and embarks in a quasi-necrophiliac, incestuous love—at which point strangeness collapses into itself, and Julian and Edith emerge as stunningly normal lovers, with Julian fully incorporated into the new order (181). Edith's body provides a means for pulling West into utopia, despite his sense that the new century cannot accommodate him. The consummation of West's romance folds the [male] reader into utopia, following the frustration of consummation—of home and marriage as well as utopia—in the 1887 portion. After West's betrothal to Edith, Bellamy toys with the idea of denying happiness to his hero, sending him instead into a frightening dream sequence through a now-defamiliarized nineteenth century. But ultimately he allows West to wake up back in utopia—and to get the girl.

Edith's role marks a complete change in the narrative value of women in utopia. For More and Bacon, utopian women served to ensure continuity in the utopian society through their reproductive capacity. Bizarre and seemingly incongruous details in both *Utopia* and *New Atlantis* attest to that function. In the communal dining halls of Utopia, writes More, the tables are organized with "the women on the outside, so that if they have any sudden pain or sickness, such as sometimes happens to women with child, they may rise without disturbing the arrangements and go to the nurses."[24] Despite allowing them to be soldiers or priests, More imagines the women of Utopia as perpetually pregnant. Bacon, too, indirectly emphasizes the social value of reproduction through his "tirsan" ceremony, which salutes male generativity while only cursorily paying tribute to the women who actually bear children. In an almost comically perfect rendition of women's essential-yet-invisible role in utopia (as outside it, for that matter), the ritual dictates that "any man that shall live to see thirty persons descended of his body, alive together" is treated by the state to an elaborate and highly choreographed feast, at which the "mother, from whose body the whole lineage is descended . . . sitteth, but is not seen."[25] Here Bacon acknowledges indirectly how his island of experimentation relies upon the unheralded productivity of women. Edith's function in *Looking Backward* marks a diametric shift from those earlier texts that use women as vehicles for social continuity. Women exist in *Utopia* and *New Atlantis* to banish change by reproducing; in *Looking Backward*, as well as *News from Nowhere* and others, they provide plot movement and also incorporate the atavistic male narrator into an evolved society—or, as we will see in *News from Nowhere*, deny that incorporation. In the case of *Looking Backward*, Edith allows West to experience an accelerated version of Herlund's eugenic improvement over generations. Rather than assuring stasis, women now function in service to evolution.

Looking Backward set the terms anew for a genre, especially in its setting—the future—and its accompanying ethos of progress and development. Of the seventy-one more utopian novels that appeared between its publication and the turn of the century, the vast majority locate their perfect society in the future. Whereas utopian fiction in its first incarnation had fed off the more prevalent genre of travel narrative, by 1900 science fiction had largely taken over as utopian fiction's host genre. Throughout the twentieth century, the terms "utopia" and "future" have bled together in the minds of general readers and scholars alike. In a bibliographic survey of early-twentieth-century utopian novels, for example, Howard Segal writes that their "outstanding characteristic . . . is their diversity, both of general orientation toward the future and of the specific kind of future envisioned."[26] In pronouncing such "diversity," Segal takes for granted a crucial commonality: that very "orientation toward the future," which for most of the previous century had been alien to utopian fiction. It was not until after *Looking Backward* that spatial utopias gave way to temporal ones, set in the new frontier of the future. But with Bellamy launching the new wave of utopian fiction, even those utopian novels *not* set in the future rely on the closely related rhetoric of evolutionary development—as both William Dean Howells's Altruria series and Charlotte Perkins Gilman's *Herland* will show.

Before moving on to the anachronistic spatial utopias of Howells and Gilman, we can look for proof of Bellamy's success to an unexpected source, namely one of his most vocal critics and a foe of industrial development in its every manifestation: William Morris. Here I depart from the American terrain of this book, but only to demonstrate how fully the utopia most closely associated with nostalgia or antidevelopmentalism in fact adheres to Bellamy's evolutionary values in terms of both form and content. After composing a book review that panned Bellamy as incapable of dreaming up anything better than "a machine-life," Morris promptly set out to right the wrongs perpetrated by *Looking Backward*.[27] He began to submit serialized portions of *News from Nowhere* to his Socialist League organ *Commonweal* within a month of reading *Looking Backward*. Fascinatingly, the far more gifted writer allows Bellamy's earlier utopia to set his own terms entirely. The resulting novel, published in 1890, mirrors *Looking Backward* on all but the most internal levels. Though the aesthetic texture of both the utopian novel and the utopian society differ markedly from those of Bellamy's utopia, leaving an impression in readers' minds of a meaningful shift, in fact Morris imitates Bellamy's plot structure as well as the broadest outline of his state. For Morris as for Bellamy, therefore, a single nation has evolved into a more advanced version of itself while retaining its national borders. Ultimately, the lack of variation demonstrates both the influence of Bellamy's model, and also the power of nationalism as an ideology.

Morris's review, also published in *Commonweal,* is unambiguous in its criticism of both Bellamy's style and his content. "To anyone not deeply interested in the social question," Morris writes, *Looking Backward* "could not be at all an attractive book."[28] He assails Bellamy's lack of imagination ("Mr Bellamy's ideas of life are curiously limited; he has no idea beyond existence in a great city; his dwelling of man in the future is Boston beautified"), his failure to accept the necessity of violent resistance, and his acceptance of the basic conditions of modernity. Within Morrisian vocabulary, this last is the most severe accusation one could level: Morris writes caustically that Bellamy is "perfectly satisfied with modern civilization, if only the injustice, misery, and waste of class society could be got rid of; which half-change seems possible to him."[29] *News from Nowhere* is his response to such an unsatisfactory "half-change," and for generations of English socialists, that novel represents the pinnacle of utopian imaginings. The Marxist historian A. L. Morton in his *English Utopia*, for example, dismisses *Looking Backward* as "flat" and "mechanical," while holding out Morris's utopia as the single work that "forms the final synthesis" of England's divergent utopian traditions and thus embodies "the deep, undying, hopes and desires not of an individual only but of a nation."[30] Morris's acolytes follow the author himself in viewing his and Bellamy's products as opposed in every way. In fact, though, despite their apparent position on opposite ends of a utopian spectrum, the structural underpinnings of both Morris's utopian romance and his utopian state closely resemble those of Bellamy. While Morris presumably intended the deliberate revision to highlight the internal differences in their respective utopian projects, it still has the effect of endorsing Bellamy's future-oriented historiography.

As Bellamy does in *Looking Backward*, Morris infuses his protagonist's travels with a continual sense of doubleness, in which Guest recognizes landmarks even in their unfamiliarity. The effect is a narrative layering of new London and old London, so that the traveler as well as the reader must live both times at once. As Guest passes through Trafalgar Square, "a strange sensation came over me; I shut my eyes to keep out the sight of the sun glittering on this fair abode of gardens, and for a moment there passed before them a phantasmagoria of another day" (77). In *Looking Backward* too, the narrator's present always lingers. In one of West's rare trips outside the Leete home, he finds that "The mental image of the old city was so fresh and strong that it did not yield to the impression of the actual city, but contended with it, so that it was first one and then the other which seemed the more unreal. There was nothing I saw which was not blurred in this way, like the faces of a composite photograph" (79). Typically, Bellamy and Morris use different vocabulary—Bellamy's culled from the arena of technology, and Morris's from spiritualism—to describe essentially equivalent phenomena.

Guest, like West, is ill at ease among the new people, whose youth and vigor make him feel ridiculous, unattractive, and old. To help his narrator,

Morris imitates Bellamy's love story, along with every other major plot element. Just as Edith does for West, the lovely young Ellen rejuvenates Guest when he meets her toward the end of his journey. Once she comes on the scene, Guest declares hopefully that "I felt young again, and strange hopes of my youth were mingling with the pleasure of the present" (207). As in *Looking Backward,* the consummation of utopia, or the transformation of hoped-for future into realized present, is an unquestionably sexual process. Ellen embodies the new world: if it is novel, unfamiliar, and strange, she is the most novel, most unfamiliar, and strangest element of all. Yet she serves the purpose of making the stranger feel normal within that world. Like Edith, she functions—at least initially—as a vehicle for incorporation.

However, as mentioned, Morris does not imitate Bellamy's form in entirety, but introduces a significant twist into the recognizable plot. Unlike West, Guest is expelled from utopia, in accordance with Morris's belief that we can only reach the good society by passing through a crucible of violence. Through Ellen, the new world offers provisional sexual renewal, but it ultimately denies that renewal, along with incorporation: Guest will never become more than the transitory visitor implied by his name. Morris temporarily adapts Bellamy's technique of assimilation before choosing to reject it, and determining thereby to withhold from both narrator and reader any peaceful, easy entry into utopia. So while Bellamy's narrator permanently enters the new society through the conduit of a hospitable female body, Morris's wakes up "in my bed in my house at dingy Hammersmith" (228). We have not yet earned utopia, Morris tells his readers; we will end up just where we began unless we take action. Whereas Bellamy feints pulling West out of utopia and then ultimately allows him to stay, Morris does just the opposite. If the trite sleep device used by Bellamy and Morris—as well as Mercier, Washington Irving, and Mary Griffith before them—indicates a lack of consciousness on the part of the traveler, then Morris certainly cannot allow his traveler to enter the good place in that unwitting manner. For Bellamy, on the other hand, slumbering peacefully is precisely how we will all get there.

The second significant difference in the novel itself is its visual quality. That change is due in part to Morris's commitment to a writing style with the texture and heft of a lovingly handcrafted object; but it also stems from his goal of compensating for all of *Looking Backward*'s deficiencies, specifically Bellamy's failure to provide visual information. From the outset of *News from*

Nowhere, Morris makes clear that revisionist intention. One of *Looking Backward's* simultaneous strengths and defects is a stunning lack of visuality, a technique that would ideally allow readers to insert their own pictures of loveliness. The bulk of the novel consists of conversation and internal reflection, with West's intermittent excursions out of the Leete drawing room coming only every twenty pages or so. Those excursions themselves often contain very little visualizable substance. On his first walk through the new Boston, for example, Bellamy gives us a strong sense of West's visceral discomfort, as quoted above, but no inkling of the city's material and aesthetic presence. A few chapters later, Edith takes West to see the new consumer distribution center that has replaced the sordid nineteenth-century market. This is only his second trip out of the fortunately very comfortable Leete residence, yet once again he has few material details to report. The rare moments of visual information come in the form of negative description, in which West tells us what he sees only by conveying what it is not. As he approaches the distribution center,

> we turned in at the great portal of one of the magnificent
> public buildings I had observed in my morning walk. There was
> *nothing* in the exterior aspect of the edifice to suggest a store to a
> representative of the nineteenth century. There was *no display of*
> *goods* in the great windows, *or any* device to advertise wares, or
> attract custom. *Nor was there* any sort of sign or legend on the
> front of the building to indicate the character of the business
> carried on there. (92; emphasis added)

The following three chapters consist solely of conversation, at which point Bellamy, apparently under pressure to provide another visualizable scene, allows West and the Leetes to walk to the neighborhood dining hall. So uncomfortable is he with this task that he obscures the building's façade and relies on extrapolation instead of direct description. West narrates: "We now entered a large building into which a stream of people was pouring. I could not see the front, owing to the awning, but, if in correspondence with the interior, which was even finer than the store I visited the day before, it would have been magnificent" (123). That interior provides little basis for generalization, since Bellamy never describes it either.

For Morris, that glaring lack of visual materiality represents not an invitation to the reader's imagination, but a failure of the author's. Accordingly,

Morris's skill at providing visual information becomes in *News from Nowhere* a useful aspect of his rejoinder to Bellamy. The novel's opening frame finds the protagonist leaving a particularly contentious meeting of the Socialist League. As the short-lived omniscient narrator tells us, a discussion of "the future of the fully-developed new society" degenerates into a shouting match in which "there were six persons present, and consequently six different sections of the party were represented" (43). Returning home via a "that vapour-bath of hurried and discontented humanity," the Underground, the soon-to-be time-traveler sits "musing on the subject-matter of discussion, but still discontentedly and unhappily. 'If I could but see a day of it,' he said to himself. 'If I could but see it!' . . . He went out of the station, still discontented and unhappy, muttering 'If I could but see it! if I could but see it!'" (43–4). Directly against *Looking Backward,* Morris asserts the importance of visual materiality. And as a deliberate retort to *Looking Backward,* his utopia is most interesting for my purposes in its failure to depart from its predecessor. Guest traipses for miles with his host, stays the night in new cottages and refurbished old castles, sails up the Thames, and helps to harvest hay— but each episode forms a mere diversion within a borrowed plot outline.

Morris, then, applies the basic contour of Bellamy's plot, and alters it with the significant twist that the hopeful protagonist must return to his own time. In terms of utopian society as well as utopian novel, there is also a borrowing and an alteration. Here, the alteration is so palpable, encompassing the aesthetic appearance of the new society—from clothes to homes to all ornamentation—that it tends to obscure the borrowing. The two utopias *look* quite different, with Bellamy holding on to Victorian aesthetics and Morris reviving the best of the medieval age. That difference is far from superficial, pointing to their ideal modes of production as well as to Bellamy's lack of a transformative imagination. However, the underlying similarity is equally critical if far less obvious. Both Bellamy's industrial United States and Morris's agrarian England are cleanly bordered nations that retain the same contours as those of the author's day. The "Nowhere" of Morris's title serves to salute More's utopian pun, but certainly not to indicate remove: this is a far closer place than More's imaginary island. As Guest roams the villages that have replaced London and sails up the now-pristine Thames, his travel diary tells not of a stand-in for England, let alone of a genuinely cosmopolitan utopia, but of England itself. Though Morris claims this to be a postnational society, he cannot sustain that claim throughout the novel. Dick Hammond's

learned great-grandfather, apprising Guest of all matters political and economic, tells the stranger that "the whole system of rival and contending
nations which played so great a part in the 'government' of the world of civilization has disappeared." The enlightened future-dweller looks upon nations
as "artificial and mechanical groups" roped together through coercion and
manipulation (117). Yet at the same time the utopians' "we" invariably refers
only to the English. Similarly, the title "National Gallery" produces confusion
as to the meaning of "gallery" (indicating how fully art has been integrated
into life) but not the meaning of "national." Unlike *Green Mansions* author
W. H. Hudson—who, in his predictably primitivist 1887 fantasy *A Crystal
Age*, makes a concerted point of his future-denizens' incomprehension of
"England"—Morris allows his utopians to use the word readily and comfortably several times, thereby demonstrating the persistence of the nation.

As in *Looking Backward*, that nation stands at the forefront of a global
trajectory of social improvement. Given Morris's vocal anti-imperial stance
(which I will discuss further in the following chapter), it makes sense that
his future-dwellers "have long ago dropped the pretension to be the market
of the world" (101). Yet remnants of England's imperial ideology linger in the
form of the same developmentalist language that Bellamy employs in his
juxtaposition of "backward races" and "advanced nations." Here, too, England
as well as "parts of Europe" are "more advanced than the rest of the world,"
while Morris takes aim at Bellamy and his countryfolk by designating
America and other ex-Commonwealth countries as "very backward" (128).
Luckily for that backward remainder, the English utopians "have helped to
populate other countries—where we were wanted and were called for" (106).
If internally the utopian mode of production and aesthetic sensibility depart
completely from those of *Looking Backward*, on an external level Morris holds
to Bellamy's vanguardist global model and his benevolent expansionism.
Once again we see that, even coming from a writer deeply skeptical of both
industrialism and imperialism, the utopian world consists of a hierarchical
array of uneven development.

Morris may consider "civilized" a pejorative term, but his utopia still
rests on a form of developmentalism. If Marx's description of the "bourgeois
socialist" perfectly captures Bellamy, Morris is far from the "feudal socialist"
that precedes it. The feudal socialist, Marx writes, is "half lamentation, half
lampoon, half echo of the past, half menace of the future . . . always ludicrous in its effect, through total incapacity to comprehend the march of

modern history."[31] His forebear Ruskin would count among them, but Morris added to Ruskin's Gothic aesthetic and his doctrine of labor value a thorough grounding in the dialectical process. No uncritical nostalgist, he shows in *News from Nowhere* just how well he understands "the march of modern history."

Like that of *News from Nowhere,* the pastoral setting of Howells's Altruria series often deceives readers, who tend to overlook the underlying developmentalism of all three novels. *News from Nowhere* may be anti-industrial, but it is by no means anti-progress. Morris's good society embraces newness, endorses progress, and never claims to be participating in any kind of renaissance. Regardless of its inhabitants' clothing, in terms of historiography it looks forward as resolutely as Bellamy's. Similarly, though many readers classify the Altrurian romances as pastoral or nostalgic, Howells's engine of history in fact relies as heavily on the concept of evolution as Bellamy's, if not more so. To cite only one example amid a general consensus, Jean Pfaelzer in Kenneth Roemer's useful reference work *America as Utopia* classifies Altruria as a "retrogressive" utopia. Noting its pastoral setting, she places Howells with those "retrogressive utopists" who "sought a return to a lost age of a simple agrarian arcadia, which they claimed existed in preindustrial America."[32] As we will see, such a description fails to recognize Howells's own account of Altrurian history. In fact, Howells presents Altruria not as America's past but as America's future. With one simple human intervention, Howells insists, America will almost automatically unfold or evolve to resemble Altruria's more advanced society. Pfaelzer opposes her category of retrogressive utopias with "progressive utopias," in which the latter locate their good society in the future, and the former find it through a present-day journey. But Howells collapses those categories, for Altruria represents the future of America even though it exists in the present. Providing further proof of the dominance of evolutionary thinking, Howells asserts developmentalism even without traveling in time.

Though regularly included in surveys of American utopian fiction, Howells's first utopian installment, *A Traveler from Altruria,* contains no view of utopia until its penultimate chapter. Serialized in *Cosmopolitan* from 1891 to 1892 and published in 1894, the novel takes place not in Altruria but in a tony resort in upstate New York. Aristide Homos, the titular traveler, spends the summer there meeting caricatures of familiar high-society types (the pulp novelist, who narrates the novel; the neurasthenic female; "the lawyer";

"the manufacturer"; "the professor"; and a banker, Mr. Bullion) and asking them naïve questions that expose the workings of class in America. His informants consistently allege that the United States has abandoned Europe's rigid social hierarchy at the same time that they all devotedly guard the line between leisure and service classes, with the result that Homos grows more and more confused by the contradiction between rhetoric and reality. Until his long lecture on Altruria, to which Howells dedicates the novel's last two chapters, Homos largely serves as a simple foil to expose the falseness of America's rhetoric of equality.

Those last two chapters of *Traveler* provide our only glimpse of utopia, affixed to the end of a novel that belongs far more centrally to the genre of social satire. Howells's real utopian novel is the far less well-known *Through the Eye of the Needle*, an epistolary expansion of *Traveler*'s conclusion. Part 1 of *Needle*, originally serialized as "Letters of an Altrurian Traveler," continues in the vein that Howells began in his earlier installment. Now in New York, Homos turns his naïve and therefore penetrating eye to the homes, clubs, holiday celebrations, and general parasitism of that degenerate city's ruling class. With *Traveler*'s narrator Mr. Twelvemough freed from the humiliation of recounting Homos's pointed questions and disappointed reactions, Homos himself tells the story through letters to his friend Cyril Chrysostom, Altrurian emissary to England. During his New York visit Homos falls in love with the wealthy widow Eveleth Strange, who in part 2 of the novel travels to Altruria as Homos's wife, thus becoming the first woman to explore and narrate utopia. Her maiden name satirizes Bellamy's heavy-handed use of the "stranger" convention; yet the former Eveleth Strange never feels nearly as strange in Altruria as Julian West and William Guest had in their respective sojourns through the future—for as Homos predicts, women by their nature adapt more easily to Altrurian life. From Altruria, Eveleth writes to her friend Dorothea Makely (*Traveler*'s comic neurasthenic) the letters that provide the series' most thorough exposition of utopia.

Howells's descriptions of Altruria—namely, the last chapters of *Traveler* along with part 2 of *Needle*—demonstrate that even the allegedly "retrogressive" author holds a developmentalist notion of history. Similarly to Morris's England of the future, Altruria incorporates elements of pre-modern social organization, but it also makes use of technological innovations to take best advantage of those elements. More significantly, Howells has Altruria's perfect equilibrium coming about as a result of a smooth, linear historical progression.

He first presents Altruria's history in the last two chapters of *Traveler*, which contain only a vague account of utopia itself but a quite detailed explanation of how it came about. Like Bellamy's United States, Altruria rests on a principle of evolution, here capitalized as "Evolution" and repeated almost ritualistically. And as Bellamy does, Howells naturalizes many of the changes that comprised that Evolution. In both utopias, all else organically falls into place after one simple alteration: for Bellamy, the abolition of money; for Howells, a single genuinely democratic election. Before the Evolution, during the period known as "the Accumulation," Altruria resembled nothing so much as the robber-baron-dominated, monopoly-ridden United States. Within five years of the electoral revolution, "the Accumulation had passed away forever."[33] As in *Looking Backward*, the change comes without violence: "Our Evolution was accomplished without a drop of bloodshed, and the first great political brotherhood, the commonwealth of Altruria, was founded" (181). In response, the very character of the land altered itself effortlessly: "Almost from the moment of the Evolution the competitive and monopolistic centers of population began to decline. In the clear light of the new order it was seen that they were not fit dwelling-places for men" (187). Howells gives so many causes for the great change—at one point all improvements can be traced to the cessation of shoddy manufacturing, at another point to "the disuse of money"—that the ultimate cause becomes simply the application of time (185, 202). With "Evolution day" celebrated as a national holiday, Howells's novel clings even more tenaciously than Bellamy's to a pure faith in beneficial human development.

As opposed to that projected by Bellamy, Altruria's peaceful evolution came about through the application of human will, even named here as "resistance" (181). As a result, the formerly "competitive and monopolistic people" now "have the kingdom of heaven upon earth" (202). In narrating Altruria's history, Howells does something remarkable and yet generally unremarked: he collapses the model of ongoing development into a single time frame—just as the pioneers of anthropology were beginning to do— and puts the United States in the position of a primitive society. This is a quite unprecedented technique, one that recent historians of developmentalism can help us to appreciate. As discussed above, developmentalism owes its genesis to the misapplication of Darwin's doctrine to human history, an unfortunate grafting generative of a mind-set that in turn buttressed the practice of colonial expansion. As Johannes Fabian, Gilbert Rist, and others have shown, a mainstay of this developmentalist thinking is the designation of one region's present as another region's past, a model that the leading nineteenth-century American anthropologist Lewis Morgan perfectly encapsulates when he characterizes the American Indian as "our contemporary ancestor."[34] Such a model of cultural difference interpreted as temporal difference, as Anne McClintock demonstrates in *Imperial Leather: Race, Gender, and Sexuality in the Colonial Contest*, was not limited to intellectual and political spheres, but bleeds out into what McClintock calls "commodity racism."[35] Between Fabian and McClintock, we have a full picture of a racist discourse that encompasses museum exhibits, university courses, exposition displays, and advertisements for Pear's soap—all of which depict the primitive as existing in an anterior time.

Fascinatingly, Howells in the Altrurian novels applies that burgeoning discourse but departs radically from it by placing America in the position of the primitive. In what is probably *Traveler*'s most frequently quoted formulation, Homos pronounces that "America prophesies another Altruria" (193). To most commentators, accustomed to viewing the United States as the singular locus of utopian imaginings, this implies only that America will eventually achieve utopia. Certainly, one item on Howells's agenda is to assert optimistically that things will get better. However, the formulation "America prophesies another Altruria" also contains a value judgment that comes across more clearly in dialogue. When Homos describes the grim conditions in Altruria under the Accumulation, "'Look here!' a sharp nasal voice snarled across the rich, full pipe of the Altrurian, and we all instantly looked there. The voice came from an old farmer, holding himself stiffly up, with his hands in his pockets and his lean frame bent toward the speaker. 'When are you goin' to get to Altrury? We know all about Ameriky'" (176). The emphasis here is not on America's rosy potential, but on its unpleasant current reality. Howells carefully opposes the American farmer's "sharp nasal voice" with "the rich, full pipe of the Altrurian." He consciously relegates America's present to Altruria's past, with all the censure that such a schema implies.

McClintock singles out one aspect of the developmentalism studied by Fabian and Rist, and renames it "panoptical time": namely, the historiographical understanding that allows the imperial eye to view all the world's realms and thus all stages of development, "so that imperial progress is consumed at a glance . . . in a single spectacle from a point of privileged invisibility."[36] In examining Africa's and Asia's present as windows onto Europe's past, late-nineteenth-century historians like Henry Maine exhibit such a viewpoint.[37] Howells turns on its head that image of the producer of knowledge at the forefront of a strictly linear march of progress. The unexpected effect is of an anti-ethnocentric version of McClintock's model. The Altruria novels portray a global system of uneven development, but with the United States as the underdeveloped region. "America prophesies another Altruria" just as Asia's present resembles Europe's past. The advanced Altrurians now view their past—which is also American's present—with disgust. "We . . . who have realized the Utopian dream of brotherly equality, look back with the same abhorrence upon a state where some were rich and some poor, some taught and some untaught, some high and some low," Homos tells his incredulous audience (194). Here, Howells turns imperial "panoptical time" against the United States, placing the Altrurian in the privileged position of seeing all its failings. This is the opposite of Bellamy's model, with the United States at the vanguard and "the more backward races . . . gradually being educated up to civilized institutions." There is some overlap with Bellamy's picture of twenty-first-century horror at the cruelty and selfishness of the past—but writing the advanced civilization into the same chronological year is quite a different maneuver, one that turns the imperial mind-set against itself.

Having introduced his developmentalist model of history in *Traveler*, Howells geographically expands it—along with all other aspects of utopia—in *Through the Eye of a Needle*. As opposed to the characterization of Pfaelzer and others, Howells exhibits no nostalgia; rather, the benighted past lingers on as a dangerous and infested ruin full of "malarial influences." Wandering the countryside with Eveleth, Homos reports to her that "We are not far from the ruins of one of the old capitalistic cities, which have been left for a sort of warning against the former conditions, and [a passerby] wanted to caution us against the malarial influences in it. . . . they ought to abolish that old pest-hole. I doubt if it serves any good purpose, now."[38] As in the novella *Daisy Miller* by Howells's friend Henry James, the values of the past cause the "bad air" that was then believed to spread malaria. But while James has European snobbery generate the "villainous miasma" that kills Daisy, Howells rests the blame on the capitalist era, whose abandoned monuments can still breed disease. Howells consigns America's present to the wrecks of history. Further, he comically and caustically shows the Altrurians doing so themselves, when they decide that Eveleth's impractical and uncomfortable high-fashion dresses belong "in the ethnological department of the Museum, along with the Esquimau kyaks and the Thlinkeet totems" (152). Howells's use of ethnological display as a marker of primitive backwardness is perfectly in line with Fabian's indictment of anthropology's racism; but he departs from the discourse by placing the United States in an unexpected position on the developmentalist scale.[39] After being immersed in Altruria's system of pure gender equality, the enlightened Eveleth, too, declares that her old American dresses "seem like things I wore in some prehistoric age— 'When wild in woods the noble savage ran'" (152). Giving Eveleth a line from Dryden's 1671 play *The Conquest of Grenada* (probably the first use of the phrase "noble savage"), Howells uses Eurocentrism as a weapon against itself. Here the noble savage is the ignorant American, still governed by retrograde capitalist standards.

As for the content of the advanced utopian society, a critical consensus presents Altruria as a pleasant place but one that Howells failed to realize fully, a failure that is often attributed to his lack of training in economics. In fact, though, it is more fully realized and less pleasant than that general assessment holds, complex to the extent that a hidden undercurrent of violence ensures its characteristic altruism. As it turns out, a nearly invisible state enforces through violence the apparently universal preference for honest labor over parasitic dependence; and it disguises that violence through Orwellian language reform. When an American yacht runs aground just off the Altrurian shore, the Altrurians capture its crew with "the flexible steel nets which are their only means of defense" (197). Those are not as nonviolent a means as may appear, since "when they attempted to break out, and their shipmates attempted to break in, a light current of electricity was sent through the wires and the thing was done." It can only be for reasons of nomenclature that this forceful abduction fails to dismay either Eveleth or the reader. As Eveleth continues,

> Those who were rescued—the Altrurians will not say captured—had hoes put into their hands the next morning, and were led into the fields and set to work. . . . As an extra precaution with the 'rescued,' when they were put to work, each of them with a kind of shirt of mail, work over his coat, which could easily be electrized by a metallic filament connecting with the communal dynamo, and under these conditions they each did a full day's work during the Obligatories.

Even if the ever-polite Altrurians will not *say* captured, the coercive reality is immediately obvious—though it seems to be just as quickly obscured by the Altrurians' semantic trick. Appropriately, the energy source for the captured prisoners' electrified armor is the "communal dynamo," another totalitarian, industrial aspect overlooked by critics convinced that they will see a pastoral scene. This passage directly follows the proud claim by Eveleth that "the principles of the Altrurians did not allow them to use violence in bringing them to subjection." Apparently, when not human hands but human-made technology enacts the violence, readers will disregard both the technology and the violence, allowing Altruria eternally to appear both peaceful and Luddite. The trick worked on every generation of *Needle*'s admittedly small group of readers, who describe the commonwealth not as sinister or hypocritical, but only as unrealistically idyllic.[40] The reality of labor enforced through electric shocks, after all, is a far cry from the conclusion that "for the Altrurians the primary motivation for doing work was 'the pleasure of doing a thing beautifully,'" as Howells has managed to convince the respected utopian specialist Kenneth Roemer.[41] Similarly, Kenneth Eble in his Twayne Series introduction to Howells describes *Through the Eye of the Needle* as having a "dreamlike aura," and Howells's biographer Edwin Cady calls Altruria a "lovely . . . pastoral idyll"—both assessments at odds with Eveleth's account.[42] Although this is not one of the utopian novels disparaged as a precursor to totalitarianism, as More's and Bellamy's occasionally are, this baneful version of pleasure in labor chillingly anticipates the Nazi promise that "work shall set you free."

For Howells, development is an ongoing process even in utopia. As in *Herland* (as we will see), and against the static perfection of More's utopia, the evolved society accepts the possibility of further change. In *Traveler*'s long lecture Homos assures his audience, "We are still far from thinking our civilization perfect" (206). And in another similarity to *Herland*, improvement takes the form not of technophobia, as readers assume, but of a limited and judicious use of technology. This is as regulated and regularized a land as Bellamy's twenty-first-century America. Horses have been banned from residential areas "because of their filthiness," and have been replaced by electric trains, cars, and buses (135). In terms of foreign relations, the commonwealth of Altruria has evolved into an entity that is, like Bellamy's America, bordered but also imperialistic. After an initial defensive war, "we were never afterward molested by our neighbors, who finally yielded to the spectacle of our civilization and united their political and social fate with ours. At present, our whole continent is Altrurian" (198–9). Not only the individual and the internal society have evolved, but also the outermost circumference of the nation; that evolution involves swallowing up its neighbors in a way that anticipates what Geir Lundestad would later call "empire by integration."[43]

By putting America's present in the dustbin of Altrurian history, Howells finds a way to create a future setting while remaining within a single time frame. Like *News from Nowhere*, his allegedly nostalgic utopia in fact attests to the power of a new teleological view of history. The turn-of-the-century utopian novels rely as heavily upon the ideology of developmentalism as their sixteenth- and seventeenth-century predecessors did upon the fantasy of empty oceans and fertile lands. In the case of Bellamy and Morris, a concern with evolution leads the author to insert a new device to ensure narrative motion: namely, the female romantic interest. Anti-colonial thinkers would later benefit both from the new attention to the possibilities of the utopian genre, and to the new formal element of the personifying female. However, these evolutionary utopias were also limited in their uses, precisely because of their reliance on a central doctrine of nineteenth-century imperialism. Bellamy's Boston, Morris's England, and Howells's Altruria, even if texturally quite different, all present a racially homogenized nation on the vanguard of global development. The connection between developmentalism and race purification will become even more apparent in Charlotte Perkins Gilman's 1915 utopia *Herland* as the concept of evolution evolves, itself, into a new pseudo-scientific avatar: eugenics.

II. Eugenics: Charlotte Perkins Gilman

Gilman follows Howells in choosing to employ the anachronistic structure of utopia removed in space rather than time—but for a very different motivation. While Howells sets his utopia on a "civilized," Europe-like peninsula and offers no explanation for its low profile, Gilman locates hers on an uncharted plateau set deep in a savage continent. As *Herland* opens, three college friends have joined a scientific expedition in an unspecified continent, "up among the thousand tributaries and enormous hinterland of a great river, up where all the maps had to be made" and "savage dialects studied."[44]

If Howells makes use of a genteel epistolary form, Gilman wraps her utopian fiction in a Conradian yarn. She acknowledges the anachronism of the
plot: as narrator Vandyke Jennings says, his fellow adventurer "used to make
all kinds of a row because there was nothing left to explore now, only patch-
work and filling in" (1–2). But despite its historically impossible prologue,
the Conradian expedition serves Gilman's purposes perfectly. When told by
their "savage" guides of "a strange and terrible Woman Land"—in tribute to
More's original utopian pun, several characters call it "no place for men"—the
intrepid explorers expect to find a quaint and backward community (2, 3, 5).
As Terry, the requisite misogynist among the three, predicts, "We mustn't
look for inventions and progress; it'll be awfully primitive" (8). Instead, they
find admirable achievements, including schools, roads, factory-like orchards,
and even "some kind of swift-moving vehicles" (29): in short, all the trappings of civilization. The resulting contrast between expectation and outcome, for the reader as well as the explorers, demonstrates why Gilman
chose to revert to the by-then-outdated form of spatial utopia: to highlight
the vast difference between her civilized women and the primitive males
who surround their island of managed productivity.

Indeed, the premise of *Herland* rests upon an underlying distinction
between civilized and savage, categories whose borders shimmer throughout the text. Like so many late-nineteenth and early-twentieth-century
authors, Gilman obsessively marks the difference between "primitive" and
"advanced" states. In *Herland* that obsession takes form through the ritual-
istic repetition of the terms "civilized" and "civilization" on the one hand,
which appear no fewer than thirty-two times in the novel, and "savage" on
the other (seventeen times). Gilman emphasizes the crucial difference
even before the men make it into Herland. Their first proof of the legendary land's existence is a scrap of cloth floating in the river. Examining it, the
sociologist narrator declares that "There is no such cloth made by any of
these local tribes . . . Somewhere up yonder they spin and weave and dye—
as well as we do" (5). That evidence of civilizational accomplishment spurs
the men on to abandon their expedition and venture further on their own.
Even with counterevidence in hand, Terry makes the guess that "it'll be
awfully primitive." But far from that initial supposition, "it looked like any
other country—a civilized one, I mean" (10). Gilman may contest the idea
that only men can produce civilization, but unlike Morris she accepts
wholesale that category of civilization itself. She employs the hostile voice

of the male explorers as a usefully ironic device to force readers to question all received knowledge, but the Conradian model is not ironic. Gilman gives her readers the option of stumbling upon a continental heart of civilized female whiteness instead of Conrad's option, the colonizer gone native and mad.

As in the case of Howells, the fact that Gilman rejects the new genre of science fiction should not be taken to imply that she has no interest in development. In fact, Herland has depended as heavily as Bellamy's United States on the angel of progress. Like Howells, Gilman makes use of the conceptual model that Fabian identifies, which by her time was far more firmly entrenched. But where Howells's use was ironic, Gilman's is typically and uncritically imperial. The only difference from the model that Fabian and McClintock study is that she places on the top of the developmental hierarchy not her own existing society, but—as in Rokeya Sakhawat Hossain's 1905 utopian sketch "Sultana's Dream"—an even better imaginary settlement made up exclusively of people just like her.[45] By contrasting Herland with its backward surroundings, she claims advanced civilization as the province of white women. The Conradian opening starkly illustrates the progress that her women have made all on their own. Gilman's choice of form accommodates her obsession with racial purity, which will become still more apparent below. Unlike Morris, Gilman truly departs from the Bellamy model in terms of how the story is told, motivated by the pressing need to demonstrate the superiority of white women to colored men.

In the area of content, however, Gilman's utopia has many significant if not immediately obvious similarities with Bellamy's rationalized future—even though Gilman rejects the plot outlines that Morris so astonishingly retained, and reverts to the by-then anachronistic model of the utopia in space. As in the case of Morris, extreme differences in appearance and texture obscure some underlying commonalities. Like those of Bellamy, Morris, and Howells, Gilman's utopia is tightly bordered. The futurists Bellamy and Morris simply retain the present-day borders of the United States and England; free to invent the terrain as well as the social structure of her utopia, Gilman follows Howells in depicting a political decision in geological terms. Even more isolated than Altruria, Herland sits happily atop a formidable plateau. More importantly, the entire society's relentless self-improvement places *Herland* squarely (even more so than Morris or Howells) in the camp of anti-nostalgist, progress-oriented utopianism. Its economy may be nonindustrial on the most superficial level; but where Bellamy imagines new machines, Gilman transforms trees, animals, and most significantly women's bodies into venues for efficient and constantly improving production. Bellamy's hyperdeveloped industrial state reappears here as hyperproductive nature. The men's first impression is of "a land in a state of perfect cultivation, where even the forests looked as if they were cared for . . . an enormous garden" (11). As the explorers immediately notice while navigating the outskirts of Herland, every bough is "trained" and every plant productive. Quickly revising their initial skepticism about the women's control over their surroundings, the men realize that biological manipulation has made plants into machines.

Like Herland's mode of production, its cultural values evince a Bellamyite developmentalism. Even if, unlike Morris, Gilman manages to depart entirely from Bellamy on the level of narrative, she shares entirely one of the most central parts of Bellamy's philosophy: a pure and unquestioned faith in progress. Despite its title, as mentioned, *Looking Backward* never looks backward for positive models, but only views that past in visceral disgust. Nor is there any inkling of nostalgia in Herland. The women look back to a mythic mother but certainly not to any social structures worthy of imitation. Rather, as the elder historians tell it, Herland's near-perfection developed gradually over generations. Herland's tranquillity leads Van to wonder whether the women even have a history; in fact, they revere the skill of historiography, and celebrate in particular the single immaculate birth that ushered in the "new race" and the "Era of Motherhood." In a strange departure from the novel's otherwise colloquial tone, Van appears to channel the Herland historians as he ends four successive paragraphs with the words "new race," so that prose history mutates into ballad (56–7). But despite that balladic history, the emphasis of this society is on the future, not the past. To Van's incredulous question "Have you no respect for the past? For what was thought and believed by your foremothers?" his lover Ellador replies easily "Why, no . . . why should we?" (111) She attributes such freedom to Herland's genesis, which rested upon a miraculous virgin birth many generations ago. Having begun in "a new way," Herland has no further need for the past. Paradoxically, history serves to justify its own irrelevance—but regardless of the paradox, the overall effect is of a society even more oriented toward the future than Bellamy's more stable and complacent United States. As opposed to the general lull that characterizes Bellamy's future, here collective self-improvement continues. "We are at work, slowly and carefully, develop-ing our whole people," Van's tutor Somel tells him. "It is glorious work—splendid!" (105)

That "glorious work" is essentially eugenics, the cornerstone of Herland's ever-improving society. Gilman's application of eugenic techniques is both a product of her times and also a logical outcome of the utopian tradition. Taking a theme common to almost all utopian fiction, she extends it further than any previous author due both to the racist pseudoscience available to her and also to her own white supremacist proclivities. Gilman's preoccupa-tion with overpopulation and selective reproduction is by no means without precedent within the utopian tradition, for all utopian authors address those issues in one way or another. In constructing the original utopia, More has his state intervene heavily in regulating its population, in the sense of making it regular. In one of *Utopia*'s more notorious details, narrator Raphael Hythlodae reports on the land's various measures of population control. The passage is well-known but still worth repeating given the enduring shock of the disjunction between its matter-of-fact tone and the extreme measures it conveys. More writes:

> that the city neither be depopulated nor grow beyond measure, provision is made that no household shall have fewer than ten or more than sixteen adults. . . . This limit is easily observed by transferring those who exceed the number in larger families into those that are under the prescribed number. Whenever all the families of a city reach their full quota, the extra persons help to make up the deficient population of other cities.
>
> And if the population throughout the island should happen to swell above the fixed quotas, they enroll citizens out of every city and, on the mainland nearest them, wherever the natives have much unoccupied and uncultivated land, they found a colony under their own laws. . . . The inhabitants who refuse to live according to their laws, they drive from the territory which they carve out from themselves. If they resist, they wage war against them.[46]

As so many subsequent utopian writers would do as well, More views popu-lation as raw material to be managed by the state in order to avoid scarcity or glut. Later authors, of course, could not be so extraordinarily blithe in the assumption that "unoccupied and uncultivated land" would be perennially available for utopian annexation. The topic of population control gives us an opportunity to witness in microcosm the transition from a first wave of uto-pianism based on the myth of empty land to a second wave based on the myth of progress: More's approach is perfectly typical of the first, expansion-ist wave of utopian fiction, while Bellamy's version of population engineer-ing, too, neatly reflects both the author and his time. In keeping with his developmentalist outlook, Bellamy portrays change in population as a pro-cess that is just as conveniently conflict-free as every other aspect of social change. Social Darwinism provides both the mechanism and the vocabulary for Bellamy to apply his ideal of passive evolution to human biology. The new prevalence of marriages based on love instead of economic necessity means that "for perhaps the first time in human history the principle of sexual selection, with its tendency to preserve and transmit the better types of the race, and let the inferior types drop out, finally has unhindered opera-tion" (191). Class inequality had hindered the operation of the same effortless improvement that benefits the animal world, but Nationalism merely allows nature to take its course. Despite his claim that his characters might be "black, brown, or yellow," Bellamy's definitions of superiority and inferiority are explicitly racialized. Following the quote above, Dr. Leete goes on to tell West that "You were speaking, a day or two ago, of the physical superiority of our people to your contemporaries. Perhaps more important than any of the causes I mentioned then as tending to race purification has been the effect of untrammeled sexual selection." "Physical superiority" and "race purifica-tion" are synonymous to Leete.

In the case of Morris, some embedded Darwinist phrasing provides yet another unremarked similarity with Bellamy, as the alleged nostalgist fol-lows Bellamy's sanguine view of human evolution. In an only slightly ironic nod to Bellamyite Social Darwinism, Dick Hammond explains that "In the early days of our epoch there were a good many people who were hereditarily afflicted with a disease called Idleness, because they were direct descendents of those who in the bad times used to force other people to work for them" (75). The intervening centuries have rooted out that hereditary trait. Again, closer examination of *News from Nowhere* reveals Morris's romance to depend more heavily on an evolutionary outlook than most readers generally perceive. To read Howells, on the other hand, would lead one to believe that Darwin had never made his seminal observations, for the vocabulary and concepts of heredity are utterly absent from the Altrurian series. Like so many utopian authors, Howells does invent some measures of population control, but they more closely recall More's interventions than those of any more recent author. In Altruria, as Eveleth writes in *Needle*, "the families are generally small, only two or three children at the most, so that the parents can devote themselves to them the more fully; and as there is no fear of want here, the state interferes only when the parents are manifestly unfit to bring the little ones up" (160). Here none are deemed unfit for reproduction (as opposed to Herland, as we shall soon see), but some for child-rearing.

Writing in 1915, Gilman had far more material to apply as she adapted and magnified the intrinsic utopian propensity to mold and beautify populations. Like social evolution, eugenics represents another misapplication of Darwin to the human species. Its adherents sought societal improvement not through civilizational development over time, but through reproductive control. Coined by Francis Galton in 1883, the term "eugenics" rapidly gained currency, especially after the turn of the century. Based on its linguistic provenance in Galton's and Darwin's England, historians of science identify eugenics as an import to United States, though one could also trace its origin to the antebellum U.S. South and the conscious and forced "breeding" of slaves for particular inheritable qualities.[47] But unlike the later incarnation of the genetic pseudo-science, this common practice had no written, codified literature. As Marouf Hasian points out, only the eyewitness narratives of slaves themselves attest to their owners' quasi-scientific approach to increasing and improving human stock. Certainly the literature of eugenics first took form in England, where its earliest proponents were "an odd assortment of noblemen, literary figures, and Fabian socialists."[48] But even if born in England, eugenics gained immeasurably in force and complexity in the United States, which is not surprising given the country's concern with race and heredity. One historian marks the doctrine's "period of greatest influence" as the years from 1905 to 1930.[49] That period saw the founding of several eugenic societies and research institutions: the National Eugenics Laboratory in 1904; J. H. Kellogg's Race Betterment Foundation in 1906; the Eugenics Education Society in 1908; the extremely influential Eugenics Record Office in 1910; and the Eugenics Research Association in 1913. Worldwide conferences proliferated as well, such as the 1912 First International Congress of Eugenics in London; the 1913 First National Conference on Race

Betterment in Battle Creek, Michigan, attended by Booker T. Washington and Jacob Riis; and the still larger 1915 National Conference on Race Betterment at the San Francisco Exposition. Where in England it had been a fairly elite and esoteric field, eugenics in its stateside version took on more popular-cultural forms, including college courses and "Fitter Family" contests at state fairs.[50] Not until revealed as genocidal by their extreme application in the hands of the Nazis—according to some accounts, not even then—did the growing legitimacy and implementation of eugenic methods begin to wane.[51]

On both sides of the Atlantic the eugenics movement crossed political ideologies and encompassed a wide range of specific objectives, meeting with support from feminists, freethinkers, and white supremacists alike. In England, Fabian Socialists like George Bernard Shaw (most notably in *Man and Superman*), the Webbs, and H. G. Wells, as well as the pioneering sexologist Havelock Ellis, preached eugenics even though Galton himself disapproved of their sexual radicalism. Victoria Woodhull made her contribution to the literature with the racist and classist 1891 tract *The Rapid Multiplication of the Unfit*. The various objectives of the movement ranged from much-requested birth control (another neologism, invented by Margaret Sanger in 1914) to immigration restrictions and forced sterilization. The different components of a eugenics platform are particularly difficult to separate both because of their deceptive umbrella term and also because of the real alliances between the various strands of the movement. Sanger, in trying to make common methods of contraception available to working-class women, strategically employed the rhetoric of race betterment and lectured in front of such anti-black organizations as the Ku Klux Klan in order to spread her message. (She also found an audience in the Indian nationalists who are the subjects of the following chapter, though they gave her little support. *Young India*'s associate editor writes skeptically, "We listened to her speeches, though we could not fully follow her philosophy on the subject."[52] Despite Sanger's observation that "Internationalism was in the air, and I wanted that outlook brought into the movement in the United States," both birth control and its cousin eugenics remained limited to transatlantic Anglo circles.[53]) Meanwhile, the central, conservative flank of American eugenicists— like New York's prestigious Galton Society, which hosted the masters of race paranoia Lothrop Stoddard and Madison Grant—disassociated themselves from Sanger and the birth control movement.

Historians commonly divide the multiple strands of eugenic thought into "positive eugenics," which encourages the better classes to reproduce more quickly, and "negative eugenics," which attempts to restrict reproduction of unwanteds like alcoholics, prostitutes, and the "feeble-minded."[54] Most utopian authors tend to apply only one or the other of those categories. Bellamy and Morris optimistically assume that a more transparent and egalitarian process of choosing mates will lead painlessly to an improved national stock (though both begin with an inventory mysteriously purged of non-Anglo elements). Howells, on the other hand, allows the state to determine who may raise children. Tellingly, the first utopian author to implement both negative and positive eugenics is Charlotte Perkins Gilman. Empowered by the prevailing climate and equipped with new vocabulary and methodologies, she expands a perennial utopian concern with reproduction to previously unseen dimensions. She uses the term "negative eugenics" outright, identifying it as the solution to a past crisis of overpopulation, and also employs other elements of both negative and positive eugenics (69). Early on in Herland's history the women, having determined to limit their population, "set to work to improve that population in quality—since they were restricted in quantity" (71). This is positive eugenics—but we learn later from Somel that "We have, of course, made it our first business to train out, to breed out, when possible, the lowest types. . . . If a girl showing the bad qualities had still the power to appreciate social duty, we appealed to her, by that, to renounce motherhood" (82). Such social pressure against reproduction is not far from the compulsory sterilization that various American states were just then debating or enacting.[55]

The Herlanders need not resort to compulsory measures; rather, Gilman converts her own eugenic wish-fulfillment into an unprecedented form of reproduction that she names "parthogenesis." Ever since its founding era (discussed below), the women of Herland have spontaneously become pregnant with girl children at just the right time. In Alys Weinbaum's description, this is an asexual and genealogically "pure" form of reproduction that allows the women of Herland to "produce perfect citizens modeled on themselves."[56] Motivated by both her disgust with miscegenation and also her critique of men, Gilman invents a biologically impossible but metaphorically appealing solution. When combined with the social pressure "to renounce motherhood," parthogenesis brings not only continuity but even progress. Situating her utopia firmly in the realm of eugenic fantasy, Gilman eschews force, wistfully creating a place in which "Some of the few worst types were, fortunately, unable to reproduce."

Negative and positive eugenics combine to assure Herland consistency in the quantity and quality of its population. To the extent that the population changes at all, the change is only in the direction of improvement. Like Bellamy, Gilman both applies and adapts existing generic conventions as she happily controls her small and stable population. Thomas More had endorsed internal redistribution and expansion; Gilman invokes More by bringing up the possibility of the latter, but specifically rejects expansion as a solution to overpopulation. Their little plateau having become overcrowded, the women opt against "predatory excursions to get more land from somebody else, or to get more food from somebody else, to maintain their struggling mass" (68). Instead, Gilman borrows and elaborates upon Howell's idea of state intervention against "manifestly unfit" parents. In the case of the eugeni-cally minded Herland, instead of repossessing the neglected "little ones," the state precludes their very existence by encouraging antisocial types not to reproduce.

As a result, the women are "tall, strong, healthy, and beautiful" (77–8). Reflecting the upper-class concern with neurasthenia that runs through all the utopian texts of this period, the Herlanders boast a perfect synthesis of lower-class strength, health, and calm with upper-class intellect. Their suc-cess rests on their reconciliation of qualities that the explorers had previ-ously believed incompatible. As Van marvels, "Never, anywhere before, had I seen women of precisely this quality. Fishwives and market women might show similar strength, but it was coarse and heavy. These were merely athletic—light and powerful. College professors, teachers, writers—many women showed similar intelligence but wore a strained nervous look" (22). As in other utopian texts, health comes through the repudiation of patholog-ical dependence; but Gilman adds to that common theme a new emphasis on breeding. With Van's training in sociology as a convenient reason to employ all the latest social-biology jargon, Gilman has him observe that the population "lacked all morbid or excessive types," forcing her readers to view complete conformity as a general benefit (77).

Even before receiving the benefit of eugenics, the "tall, strong, healthy, and beautiful" women sprang from the finest raw material. Van concludes that "there is no doubt in my mind that these people were of Aryan stock, and were once in contact with the best civilization of the old world" (54).

Like Bellamy, Gilman responds to the vagaries of Reconstruction by excising the presence of nonwhites—but in a more overt and violent manner. The founding of Herland came in reaction to a slave rebellion centuries ago. Following the "volcanic outburst" that sealed off the plateau from all surrounding land,

> Very few men were left alive, save the slaves; and these now seized
> their opportunity, rose in revolt, killed their remaining masters
> even to the youngest boy, killed the old women too, and the
> mothers, intending to take possession of the country with the
> remaining young women and girls. But this succession of
> misfortunes was too much for those infuriated virgins. There were
> many of them, and but few of these would-be masters, so the
> young women, instead of submitting, rose in sheer desperation
> and slew their brutal conquerors. (55)

Unlike William Dean Howells, Gilman never equates Herland's past with America's present—but if Herland's history recalls any element of America, it would be the recently departed agrarian slaveholding South. Through the counterrevolt that founded Herland, Gilman enacts the revenge of the South, embodied according to its own favored imagery as an "infuriated virgin." This feminist version of *Birth of a Nation* (released in the same year that Gilman serialized *Herland*) reconfigures its gender roles so that the imperiled damsels can also be the avengers. Gilman, like Bellamy, uses her racially purified utopia to heal the wounds that the Civil War and Reconstruction had inflicted on white America. Her industrial garden reconciles the values and production systems of mechanized North and plantation South. As in *Looking Backward*, the welcome cost of that reconciliation is the banishment of all immigrants and native nonwhites.

Far from being limited to human reproduction, eugenics is nothing short of Herland's guiding philosophy, determining the character of all its plants and animals. Eugenics allows the Herlanders to root out any unpleasant realities: irritated by the loud meowing of their pets, "by the most prolonged and careful selection and exclusion they had developed a race of cats that did not sing!" The policy of selective breeding has been carried out in a thoroughly utilitarian manner, so that the cats "had ceased to kill birds," but would still "destroy mice and moles and all enemies of the food supply," and even "make the various mother-noises to their kittens" (49). Their analogue

in terms of flora are the trees whose maximized productivity, a perfect meld-
ing of nature and culture, so astonish the men on their initial arrival. In
every arena, selective breeding is the solution that merges opposites and creates perfect specimens, whether of women, plants, cats, or even language.
The Herlanders' language, for example, is "smooth and pleasant to the ear"
but also "as scientific as Esperanto" (31). Gilman's first order of business had
been to impress upon the reader the contrast between the civilized women
and their primitive surroundings, and thus early on she has Van describe
their language as "no savage sing-song, but clear musical fluent speech" (15).
That having been accomplished, she may go on to show that all elements of
Herland are not only civilized but in fact superior to our own version of civilization, all due to the wonders of controlled reproduction.

In comparison with Bellamy's and Morris's attempts to naturalize their
utopian orders, Gilman's vision of ongoing improvement relies on a far
more active notion of state control. Both Bellamy and Morris portray their
utopias as the result of social relations allowed to take their own unimpeded
course. For Gilman, conversely, only a high degree of manipulation can
ensure continual progress. Though cultivation is so engrained as to appear
natural, in each instance Gilman later reveals such appearance to be carefully manufactured. Within the perfectly arranged woods, for example, the
men find "birds, some gorgeous, some musical, all so tame that it *seemed*
almost to contradict our theory of cultivation, until we came upon occasional
little glades, where carved stone seats and tables stood in the shade beside
clear fountains, with shallow bird baths always added" (14). More than any
previous utopia, this pleasing land has been carefully engineered by human
manipulation, through controlled breeding, of all aspects of the natural
world. Indeed, eugenics infiltrates all aspects of Herland life. In contrast
with the several competing central beliefs that Eveleth Strange ascribes to
Altruria, here there is only one: improvement through selective reproduction.

Herland's eugenic philosophy ensures a lack of stasis in Gilman's utopian society. As in *Looking Backward,* we can see Gilman's commitment to
motion and progress in the form as well as the content of her utopia; and in
this area too Gilman extends that commitment even further than Bellamy
had. Her written place is not meant to be a "last word"; rather, it is deliberately and self-evidently incomplete. Gilman chooses to address head-on the
issue of social stasis that Bellamy assiduously avoids in *Looking Backward.*
In this she follows Howells, who in *Through the Eye of the Needle* briefly

acknowledges the literary allure of social conflict, and the dramatic problem presented by peace and tranquility. Early on, Eveleth remarks impassively that "there is usually nothing like news" in Altruria (128); several months later, the neutral comment reemerges as her abashed admission that

> I do long for a little American news! Do you still keep on
> murdering and divorcing, and drowning, and burning, and
> mommicking, and maiming people by sea and land?[57] Has
> there been any war since I left? Is the financial panic as great
> as ever, and is there much hunger and cold? . . . It is no use to
> pretend that in little over a year I can have become accustomed
> to the eventlessness of life in Altruria." (218)

A similar complaint on Van's part explicitly connects Herland's success in biological manipulation with a lack of narrative drive in his own story. As he apologizes, "It is no use for me to try to piece out this account with adventures. . . . There were no adventures because there was nothing to fight" (49). From here he turns for evidence to the utilitarian supremacy of Herland's cats, who as mentioned earlier "by the most prolonged and careful selection and exclusion" have been bred to purr but not meow, and kill mice but not birds. Uncomfortable with that level of perfection, Van looks everywhere for faults; in response, his informants assure him that "of course we have faults—all of us . . . our standard of perfection seems to get farther and farther away" (82). If perfection achieved through consciously manufactured evolution can become a problem, then still more evolution is the only solution.

With Van's lament that "there were no adventures," Gilman acknowledges and even incorporates the generic shortcomings of utopian literature. The result is a utopia with a deeper sense of process than any earlier one: in comparison with any of the others, the land is constantly in flux, and there is far more at stake in the story. This holds true on every level, from social structure to plot to narrator. As shown, Herland itself stays new by continually revising its standard of perfection. Van's skeptical presence points to another way in which Gilman injects process into her utopian novel: namely, by appointing a potentially antagonistic outsider to narrate it. Gilman's choice of a male narrator means that Herland as such ("no place for men") no longer exists from the moment we see it. The society is in a state of flux beginning with their, and our, arrival. Gilman creates further narrative tension by giving the story over to that outsider, who is by definition both alien and also unsympathetic. The result is that his voice creates and conveys tension merely in its relation to his new environment. Van's skepticism far exceeds that of West, Guest, and née Strange; and since the writing makes the world, to have a narrator who is sexually predetermined to be antagonistic is a bolder move than Bellamy, Morris, or Howells were willing to make. Even the name "Herland" is an imposition from without, coined by the most belligerent of the three explorers. Not only is this society always improving, but the way that Gilman presents it disallows any sort of stasis from the outset.

Gilman's commitment to narrative motion ultimately destroys her utopia. Like Bellamy, she uses love stories to power her narrative: here, not one but three. But where Julian and Edith's union pulls the narrator in and thus strengthens the utopia, the romances in Herland threaten its very foundation. The three explorers—misogynist Terry, chivalrous Jeff, and condescending narrator Van—together represent a full gamut of the forms that sexism can take; each meets his match in one of the local beauties. Their triple marriage to fiery Alima, vapid Celis, and measured Ellador "is the dawn of a new era" in Herland (119). These visitors introduce far more change to the utopian society than Julian West, William Guest, or Eveleth Homos did to theirs, with both Terry and Jeff precipitating separate crises. Terry and Alima's "tempestuous courtship" ends with Terry accused of rape and banished from Herland (142). Van and Ellador make no waves, but simply determine to accompany Terry home, thus allowing Gilman to track Ellador's reactions to America in the 1916 sequel *With Her in Ourland*. But most significantly for the survival of the utopia, Jeff elects to stay there permanently, thus ushering in a new practice of nonparthogenic reproduction that could alter the social order forever. After a hundred-odd pages of praise for Herland's accomplishments, Gilman follows Morris in denying her readers the certainty of utopia.

With *Herland*, Gilman contributed several formal innovations to utopian fiction: an unsympathetic narrator; a hostile and unassimilable character; a social structure that tolerates change; and a possible abandonment of the underlying utopian premise. Those innovations lead toward the "critical utopias" of the 1960s and 1970s, which, according to Tom Moylan, recognize the limitations of utopia and respond by embedding an ongoing process of social change.[58] Thus Gilman's work anticipates at once the recuperation of utopianism into a new, self-critical subgenre, and also the association that made that recuperation necessary: namely, the sullying of utopianism's reputation through its equation with totalitarian aims. With the rise of fascism—a movement that united utopian rhetoric and genocidal methods—the connection between utopianism and race purification that haunts *Herland* comes undeniably to the surface.

Like *Looking Backward*, *Herland* offers a mixed legacy to the anti-colonial writers who took up its utopian tactic. Gilman's thoroughgoing racism—something her critics have only recently begun to confront—manifests itself as a belief in social betterment through eugenic breeding. On the other hand, on a formal level *Herland* evinces a valuable capacity for self-critique. With both the author and the utopian citizens willing to risk the society's stability for the sake of possible improvement, both the book and the place have a helpfully unfinished or provisional quality. This is another element of Gilman's legacy: the idea of utopia as an ongoing endeavor rather than a finished product.

Herland marks the end of the turn-of-the-century utopian resurgence that I examined in this chapter. The next wave of canonical utopian fiction (as opposed to the unacknowledged anti-colonial utopias that make up my subsequent chapters) merely borrows a utopian form, but uses it to argue against the very premise of utopianism. If the turn-of-the-century period saw the popular renewal of utopian fiction into a future-oriented optimism, it also saw the emergence of the related subgenres of anti-utopia and dystopia.[59] I would contend that it is largely in response to the ominous promises of the eugenics movement, along with other spurious claims made by ideologies of progress, that these quintessentially twentieth-century genres emerged. In order to demonstrate this causal relation, it will be necessary to digress one final time (following the two previous excursions, to William Morris's surprisingly developmentalist England and through the history of eugenics) to run briefly through a few key examples of the critique of eugenics found in twentieth-century anti-utopian and dystopian fiction. In fact, dystopia took on social biology even as early as 1884, with Edwin Abbott Abbott's brilliant satire in his caustic gem *Flatland* of the Victorian obsession with breeding that predated the formally identified movement for eugenics. The mathematical romance tells of a two-dimensional land inhabited by shapes organized into a strict social hierarchy based on their number of sides. But every new generation automatically receives an extra side, so that even a lowly triangle's "posterity may ultimately rise above his degraded condition."[60] Consistently and pointedly parodying the vocabulary of developmentalism, Abbott ironically terms such a phenomenon alternately "development" and "Evolution," and shows how such a doctrine serves to justify present-day inequality.

The first anti-utopia, or deliberately negative utopia, appeared less than a decade into the twentieth century. Like its many successors, E. M. Forster's 1909 short story "The Machine Stops" ties eugenics to other forms of oppressive state control. In an infinitely regularized future, every individual lives in a single room where all of his or her needs are met by an omnipotent and apparently benevolent machine. That machine engages in positive eugenics by granting or denying permission to bear children, whom it then places in public nurseries; negative eugenics takes the form of infant euthanasia.[61] Like *Flatland*, "The Machine Stops" uses the language of developmentalism— "the advance of science," "civilization," "progress," "atavism," "savage type"—to expose the potential viciousness of that ideology. An indictment of industrial modernity, the story never made it into the modernist canon—unlike its more fully realized offspring, Eugene Zamyatin's *We*, which became a minor classic during the Cold War. Zamyatin's 1921 novel, a response to the early excesses of overly statist Soviet rule, delivers a pointed critique of developmentalism in all the forms I have discussed in this chapter: namely, linear understandings of progress; increased regularization of human activity; state control of reproduction; and the perception of the "primitive" as a benighted and long-vanished condition. As the jacket of a 1952 paperback edition proclaims, "*We* is a powerful challenge to all Socialist Utopias." Not as useful from a Cold War point of view (and therefore unmentioned on any book jacket) is the work's more direct challenge to all ideologies of progress, regardless of economic orientation. The first-person narrator of *We* matches *Herland*'s Van in the obsessive need to differentiate between the advanced society and a primitive state—i.e., at least eleven uses of "primitive" to *Herland*'s seventeen uses of "savage"—with the crucial variation that Zamyatin's motives are satiric. His nightmare society resonates with developmentalist utopias in many other ways, all of which reflect unfavorably on the earlier texts. Almost every page of *We* exhibits some social Darwinist vocabulary. As in Altruria, a museum of the degraded twentieth century showcases that progress. And as in *Herland*, progress depends upon eugenics. Where in the past "like beasts they blindly gave birth to children!" who "in those days were also private property," the state now raises its young in a "Child-Educational Refinery."[62] Much like Aldous Huxley's *Brave New World* a decade later, *We* connects eugenics and mass production, crediting Taylor— "this prophet who saw ten centuries ahead"—as the new society's guiding genius.[63]

Opposition to eugenics is even more central to *Brave New World*. While Zamyatin criticizes eugenics as merely one part of a reductive and destructive statist philosophy, Huxley uses it as the pivot to turn the utopian genre against itself. Significantly, Huxley opens his dark fantasy in the "Hatchery and Conditioning Centre" that ensures "progress" and "social stability" through "the principle of mass production at last applied to biology."[64] *Brave New World* goes on to provide a valuable critique of developmentalist social engineering through reproductive control, even if its prognostications are motivated primarily by Huxley's profound fear of female sexual emancipation. In the novel, women's liberation from the burden of reproducing the nation causes the dissolution of male identity. According to the logic of *Brave New World*, there is no way for romantic male individuals to coexist with nonreproducing women. The novel is far from anti-racist—as in *Herland*, the fear that dark-skinned men might ravage white women underlies many of its premises—but, unlike *Herland*, it deeply mistrusts the aims and methods of eugenics.

The eugenic practices that Huxley and Zamyatin reacted against were merely a logical extension of developmentalist utopianism, and even of developmentalism more generally. The works of Bellamy, Morris, Howells, and Gilman exemplify one strand of utopian fiction, in which national welfare depends on the excising of internal racialized minorities as well as uneven development across the globe. The close connection between development ideology and colonialism, in which "social evolutionism made it possible to legitimate the new wave of colonialism," is one that observers like Du Bois and Lajpat Rai were quick to perceive. Yet the utopian undertaking would not prove irremediably tainted, for those same observers would find ways to divorce it from its developmentalist elements and adapt it for their own uses. After all, Bellamy, Morris, Howells, and Gilman also brought an enormous amount of energy to a dying genre. By locating utopia in the future (or, in the case of Howells, moving our own inferior civilization into the past), they suggest to their readers that we can get there without the aid of a compass and sextant, and despite a dearth of conveniently colonizable land.

In showing how utopia grows out of inequality and disorder, they add an element of human agency absent from the works of More and his immediate followers. This is rich material for eager anti-colonialists to apply and appropriate. However, it is flawed material as well: developmentalism has obvious racist elements, even without its particular incarnation as eugenics, but all the more so with it. The bordered nation, further, presents limitations for any anti-colonial movement with global aims. As we will see in the subsequent chapters, Lajpat Rai, Coomaraswamy, Hopkins, and Du Bois found many ways of rising to these challenges, creating new utopias that replace a bordered nation with a loose network of transnational solidarity, developmentalism with nostalgia, and utilitarianism with romance.

2

A Periodical Nation

> I still have hope not that the wrecks will be mended
> but that a new world will arise.
> —Rabindranath Tagore, "Give Power to Suffer"

Only rarely has the literature of national liberation been considered under the purview of utopian fiction.[1] Yet in many ways the documents of Indian nationalism from the early part of the twentieth century are just that. In the period before Gandhi's Civil Disobedience campaigns of the 1930s, the disparate leaders of Indian nationalism largely agreed on what they opposed—the extraction by England of India's material resources without commensurate political representation—but not necessarily on the best alternative to the colonial system. The most obvious points to be determined were the desired form of governance and the future relationship to the British Empire, with nationalist leaders disagreeing on whether to seek Home Rule or complete independence. But even among that majority for whom Home Rule was the definitive goal, important areas such as education and production had yet to be specified. The free India of the future was a clean slate—and filling in that slate is of course a classically utopian project.

In that case, one might expect to see a flowering of utopian fiction, the imaginative works that, like More's *Utopia*, help their readers to negotiate their changing place in history by embodying a new order in a concrete form. Yet Rokeya Sakhawat Hossain's 1905 short story "Sultana's Dream" is the

only work from the anti-colonial period that would qualify as utopian according to a conventional definition—and in that feminist fantasy of reverse
purdah, colonialism is conspicuously absent except for the philosophical
statement that "we do not covet other people's land."[2] However, if we revisit
our definition of utopian fiction, further possibilities arise. A work of utopian writing—I will now refrain from "fiction" in order to expand our formal
possibilities—illustrates a coherent and sustainable social system that is
based on an oppositional philosophy, and that is presented as preferable to
that of the author. Thus manifestos, too, are utopian, and we may readily
classify Mohandas Gandhi's treatise *Hind Swaraj* as a utopian text.[3] Taking
the definition further, I propose that the nationalist periodicals that flourished in early-twentieth-century India provide an analogous sort of imaginative space and readerly experience of community. How can a periodical function
as utopian literature? Quite simply, it does so if it proposes and enacts a
better order that does not yet exist anywhere.

Like utopian fiction, nationalist periodicals provided an opportunity to
write India's future. In fact, they operate in the same conditional realm as
Looking Backward, Herland, Of One Blood, and *Dark Princess*. As in those
novels, the content is more often than not counterfactual. Sandhya Shukla
writes of late-twentieth-century Indian diaspora periodicals that they function as "sites . . . for constructing new Indias."[4] This is even more true during
that elastic period before India itself existed as a sovereign state. Before 1947
and independence, as Manu Goswami is only the most recent to demonstrate, India proper was very much under construction.[5] Despite its colonial
roots, periodical publishing contributed immeasurably to that construction.
Until late in the nineteenth century, the only Indian periodicals were those
of the colonial establishment. It was Sir William Jones, father of academic
Indology and a member of the Bengal Supreme Court, who founded India's
first periodical—the transactions of his Asiatic Society—in 1788. But the first
decades of the twentieth century saw the founding of an unprecedented
number of Indian-run periodicals on subjects as wide-ranging as botany,
archaeology, Ayurvedic medicine, and library science. Many of these, notably
Ramananda Chatterjee's *Modern Review,* were anti-colonial in their outlook
and frankly advocated Home Rule. In fact, by 1947, many of the luminaries
of Indian nationalism had made periodical publishing one of their primary
avenues for activism. Tilak had *The Kesari,* founded in 1881, Bipin Chandra
Pal had *Indian Student* (1911), Abul Kalam Azad *Al-Hilal* (1912), Annie Besant

New India (1914), and Gandhi the Ahmedabad-based *Young India* (1919). Whether in English or an indigenous language, each of those periodicals resembles a Victorian political weekly, complete with opening editorials, book reviews, and reprinted "gleanings" from other journals. Like nationalism itself, the nationalist periodical takes on a derivative form and fills it with anti-colonial content.[6]

The New York–based *Young India* is doubly utopian in that it does the work of imagining a future India from a position of exile. If we can generally classify utopian fiction as relying upon either spatial or temporal remove, this set of utopian writings does both; it is therefore more audacious in its utopian undertakings than either domestic periodicals of the pre-independence period, or diasporic periodicals of the late twentieth century. Published only from 1918 to 1920, *Young India* owes its existence to England's banishment of Lala Lajpat Rai from both India and England during World War I. Born in 1865, Lajpat Rai by the time of his death at British hands in 1929 had become legendary in patriotic lore both as "the Lion of the Punjab" and as the first syllable of the euphonic nationalist trilogy "Lal-Bal-Pal," which also included Bal Gangadhar Tilak and Bipin Chandra Pal. Trained as a lawyer, Lajpat Rai made his mark as a prolific writer, founder of schools, and delegate to the Indian National Congress. Less well-known are his exile years in New York from 1914 to 1919, when he worked as "Indian Nationalist ambassador to America."[7] The self-granted appellation wonderfully encapsulates the complex dynamic by which an individual comes to represent an inchoate polity that can only take concrete form in the body of that individual. As ambassador for an idea, Lajpat Rai had a similarly unprecedented and improvised job description that entailed founding and running the India Home Rule League of America; lecturing in front of labor unions, Unitarian congregations, Theosophical lodges, Irish home-rulers, and anyone else who would listen; and publishing *Young India* every month out of a small office on Broadway. After founding the nationalist periodical and overseeing its publication for two years, Lajpat Rai turned *Young India*'s editorship over to Unitarian minister J. T. Sunderland for its final year in 1920. Thus from its topmost level, the magazine was a transnational product. Mirroring its staff, the magazine's audience was also a dual one: Indians living in the United States, and also interested Americans. Thus we have several, overlapping utopian entities: the man himself, as official representative of a nonexistent state; his community of writers, readers, and supporters; and finally, the periodical they so implausibly produced together. The resulting product is a periodical nation: a pluralist entity, at once theoretical and actual, that appeared every month in printed form.

Young India comes during a perfect inchoate moment in India's history, one in which its anti-colonial nationalists had to work out details of governance, education, culture, and foreign relations, at a time when statehood was far from immanent. The periodical addresses questions that all utopian thinkers must consider. Should the ideal society's educational system value vocational or academic learning? Should its mode of production be craft-based or industrial? Should it prioritize cultural or political freedom? Should it embrace nationalism on the European model? Can it look to the past for successful social arrangements? In a February 1919 article entitled "Suggestions to Hindu Students," Lajpat Rai reminds Indians studying in the United States of "the work of reconstruction—political, economical, social as well as educational—which awaits them at home." Those wide-ranging categories indicate that Lajpat Rai envisions the future India not as a predetermined structure, but rather as a full-scale imaginative project. As preparation for that vast undertaking, he recommends that Indian students make good use of their time abroad by studying the following:

1. The co-operative movement
2. Co-operative education
3. Labor organization
4. The organization of recreation centers
5. The organization and workings of public forums
6. The organization of private popular education
7. Public and semi-public libraries
8. The machinery for the improvement of agriculture and its cooperative use
9. Publicity work in connection with *every kind of organization*
10. Industrial and commercial organization.[8]

In anticipating all of those as areas of possible future intervention, Lajpat Rai makes clear that independence will entail a complete reinvention of civil society. As Goswami and others have shown, the ongoing tension between secular and sectarian conceptions of national identity dates to this inchoate period.[9] So does the tension between a primarily agrarian nation rooted in village life—a vision primarily associated with Mohandas Gandhi—and the modernizing industrial force promoted by Jawaharlal Nehru. As Sumit Sarkar notes in his definitive survey *Modern India,* during the "Non-Cooperation" period of 1919–1920 the concept of Swaraj, or self-rule, was "left, quite deliberately, undefined" and "vague."[10] As a result, it could encompass myriad activities, from promoting local crafts to developing large-scale industry, from encouraging interfaith cooperation, to promoting an exclusively Hindu idiom of emancipation. All the tensions inherent to domestic nationalism play out in the pages of *Young India.* Whereas *Looking Backward* provides for Bellamy an opportunity to cast his lot with bourgeois state socialism over anarchism, whereas *News from Nowhere* allows Morris to illustrate the benefit of craft-based over industrial production, *Young India* too weighs in implicitly and illustratively regarding the central debates within Indian nationalism.

Each month *Young India* rendered and circulated an ideal version of India. The periodical's task was at once descriptive and prescriptive, describing its present and past glories, while advocating for the free nation of the future. It carried out that creative task through a collage of contents, assembled by editors Lajpat Rai and Sunderland from contributors both willing and unwitting. Each issue consists of news dispatches, book reviews, poems, art reproductions, pirated notes from the English and Indian press, and new India Home Rule League of America member lists. Toward its goal of conceptualizing a nation from abroad, *Young India* makes heavy use of cultural materials, reproducing summaries of the *Mahabharata,* the latest works of Rabindranath Tagore and Sarojini Naidu, and a variety of American poems intended to draw parallels between American and Indian patriotism. With hardly any paying advertisers competing for space (Hammond typewriters, on behalf of its Hindi-capable typewriter shuttle, the publishers of mystic convert Sister Nivedita, and the Theosophical Society of America being among the very few), promotions for the periodical itself occupy all the remaining pages. Like a utopian novel, *Young India* is self-referential and self-contained, asserting a cohesive community that exists only in print.

At the same time that it rendered an ideal, transnational India in print, *Young India* also enacted that theorized nation through the coming together of writers and readers. As one of its self-advertisements pleads, "Our Friends Are Requested" most immediately "to remit their membership and subscription dues at the earliest possible moment," but also and perhaps just as importantly "to create live centers to carry on India's work."[11] *Young India* itself functioned as just such a "live center" in both its production and its reception. Its editorial collective included Indians living in the United States on a more or less permanent basis, as well as various radical hyphenated and unhyphenated Americans, like the Irish immigrant novelist Francis Hackett, the British-born Sunderland, and the native daughter Agnes Smedley, born in Missouri and in our own time a heroine of working-class feminism. (Lajpat Rai appears in Smedley's fictionalized autobiography *Daughter of Earth* as wise and charismatic Sardar Ranjit Singh, a reference to the early-nineteenth-century Sikh leader who attempted to consolidate an independent Punjab.) Contributors ranged from Nobel laureate Rabindranath Tagore to Norman Thomas, unknown at the time but later a perennial Socialist candidate for president. Tagore's contributions were numerous and prominent but, given his distance and stature, presumably unauthorized; the periodical also reprinted statements, poems, and lectures by Gandhi, Naidu, Indian National Congress president Annie Besant, and other homeland luminaries. At the same time, Lajpat Rai solicited original articles from local academics (Arthur Upham Pope), politicians (Dudley Field Malone), labor organizers (Scott Nearing), and bohemians (Henrietta Rodman). Those contributors also served on the board of the India Home Rule League of America and spoke at its fund-raising dinners. *Young India* then reported extensively on those dinners and lectures, so that the periodical both created a unique local community and also reproduced and disseminated that community for its readers.

The idea that periodicals can help to consolidate national identity is of course a familiar one to students of political theory. *Young India* carries out a function similar to that of the early modern newspapers that Benedict Anderson examines in *Imagined Communities*: namely, creating and mobilizing new reading publics.[12] In Anderson's description, the nation has the utopian qualities of being imaginary and communally determined, qualities shared by *Young India*. However, the periodical departs from Anderson's model in many important ways. First, creating community is a conscious objective rather than an unforeseen outcome. As Partha Chatterjee has noted, Anderson's determinism fails to account for "the working of the imagination."[13] Anderson treats effect but not cause; his actors wish merely to convey shipping schedules. Equally important, *Young India* differs from Anderson's periodicals in its exile position. *Imagined Communities*, justifiably enough, never considers the possibility of a nation being formulated from abroad. Because *Young India*'s readership and its perceived homeland are far from synonymous, its imagined nation is an even more fictive one than that of Anderson's nationally constitutive periodicals. Anderson does come to the phenomenon of "long-distance nationalism" later, in his 1992 essay of that name. But because his focus there is the contemporary world, Anderson portrays long-distance nationalism as exclusivist, "menacing," and unaccountable.[14] Real nations change over time, Anderson claims, while nations imagined from abroad by immigrants to wealthy countries become mired in fictive stasis. Naturally the nation will always look different and more whole from afar; but where Anderson's exile nations exclude, *Young India* creates a utopia of pluralism.

Indeed, *Young India*'s imaginary nation is surprisingly transnational, dynamic, and diverse. Even its title is a transnational product, borrowed from another work of exile nationalism: Mazzini's *Young Italy*. Mazzini, one of Lajpat Rai's early heroes, was only one of the many extra-Indian influences on the periodical's formulation of its goals. The United States milieu, especially the New York–based nationalist organizing that accompanied the Versailles conference, was the most significant of these. By including many pieces on Ireland, Egypt, Turkey, Persia, Japan, and China, as well as on the labor movement in the United States, *Young India* creates a new imagined community based on solidarity among colonized and other working people. Even if we look exclusively at the "India" of the title, that seemingly concrete entity becomes geographically indeterminate. Not limited to South Asia, it bleeds out across the globe to Fiji and Africa as well as the United States. As I will discuss further in this chapter, the new polity that *Young India* constructed was a transnational one whose contours depend more on solidarity than on geography. Its range comes across well in its book reviews: *Young India*'s final volume, for example, contains reviews of Du Bois's *Darkwater*; several books on Ireland; *The Opium Monopoly*, a muckraking account from East Asia; the *Letters from China and Japan* of John Dewey and his wife; as well as a scathing rebuttal to Lothrop Stoddard's notorious *The Rising Tide of Color*. The periodical's self-promotions evince the same global field: readers could choose subscription packages with bonus copies of Lajpat Rai's own book *Young India* as well as Hackett's *Ireland*, Tagore's *Nationalism*, Kawakami's *Japan and World Politics*, *The Opium Monopoly*, and several New York–based Leftist magazines.

Young India belongs among the countercultural periodicals that were then proliferating in New York. In using the phrase "little magazine," another internal advertisement places the organ of exile nationalism within the new constellation of socialist, feminist, and generally avant-garde journals that included Margaret Anderson's *Little Review*, Max Eastman and John Reed's iconoclastic socialist review *The Masses*, and the short-lived literary magazine *The Seven Arts*.[15] As in *Young India*, the politics of these "little magazines" took form less through direct analysis than through cultural offerings; like *Young India*, each created periodical worlds of real depth. "Reading these publications of the teens," Christine Stansell writes, "you could find a map of bohemia."[16] *Young India* belongs on that map even though its main purpose was to represent a nation thousands of miles away. Lajpat Rai made use of writers who frequently appeared in the other "little magazines"; his own and *Young India*'s publisher, Ben Huebsch, also printed new works by Chekhov, Strindberg, Joyce, D. H. Lawrence, Maxim Gorky, Romain Rolland, and Sherwood Anderson. Rai himself had written for *The Masses* and *The Seven Arts* before *Young India*'s launch in 1918.[17] His contribution to the *Seven Arts* may even have prompted his own periodical's Mazzini-inspired name: his 1917 article "Young India" was part of a two-year series on romantic nationalisms, for which Van Wyck Brooks provided "Young America" and John Dos Passos "Young Spain."[18] Once up and running, *Young India* recognized the other periodicals that shared its radical world by advertising discounts on the *New Republic*, *The Nation*, *Freeman*, *Socialist Review*, and the antiwar Fellowship of Reconciliation's magazine *The World Tomorrow*. *The Nation* even allowed *Young India* to use its presses for several months during one period of extreme financial hardship.[19] In short, *Young India* was only one component of a loose but coherent print community. Lajpat Rai, like other editors in New York as well as across India, viewed periodical publishing as a utopian venture in its ability to bring new possibilities into being, simply by circulating them in writing. He recognized that utopian aspect of periodical publishing when he announced at his own farewell dinner in 1919 that by allowing him space in the *New York Evening Post* back in 1916, Oswald Garrison Villard had ushered in "the dawn of a new day for India."[20] If a few editorials comprised the dawn, then a whole periodical must represent a new age.

In order to create its idealized nation, *Young India* had to begin by dismantling the existing version of India manufactured, as Lajpat Rai claims, by the biased "British sources" he mentions in his opening editorial. Rai is practicing a version of the utopian technique of defamiliarization. This technique of severing readers from our deep-seated ideological assumptions goes by several names, including displacement and cognitive estrangement as well as defamiliarization; I prefer the latter term because of its implicit link to the political function of realist fiction, as outlined by the Russian formalists.[21] In Marxian terms, defamiliarization results in the exorcism of false consciousness. Utopian fiction abounds with examples of defamiliarization, as its authors usher their readers into utopia by helping them unlearn what they already know—or think they know. In More's *Utopia*, for example, gold chamber pots and jeweled baby toys force readers to recognize the arbitrariness of an emerging practice of commodity fetishism.[22] In *Looking Backward* and *Herland*, Bellamy and Gilman defamiliarize multiple commonplaces of class and gender, respectively. Through the device of an imagined twenty-first-century audience's reactions, Bellamy highlights the ridiculousness and inappropriateness of social inequality, investment income, redundant retail establishments, and many other elements that his readers would have taken fully for granted. The dream sequence discussed in chapter 1 allows Bellamy's nineteenth-century reader to observe how far he has come in the course of reading the novel. Similarly, Gilman carefully separates her readers from their unacknowledged preconceptions regarding the cult of domesticity, the systematic disempowerment of women as a precondition of romantic love, the bourgeois need to mark children as possessions through family names, and other mainstays of early-twentieth-century gender ideology.

Appropriately, *Young India* aims its defamiliarization at American readers' preconceptions regarding India's capacity for self-rule. British lore holds India to be incapable of governing itself for several reasons, especially barbarism, insularity, and fragmentation or infighting. Accordingly, *Young India* presents its periodical nation in direct opposition to the received picture: it is not barbaric but civilized, not grateful but rebellious, not insular but cosmopolitan, not fragmented but unified. Many of its articles situate themselves directly against the historiographical claims that undergird British colonialism. Even the "gleanings" are critical, often correcting portrayals of India in the *New York Times* or the English press. *Young India*'s anti-colonialism, in other words, is at once political and cultural: in addition to advocating directly for Home Rule, the periodical also lays the groundwork for cultural sovereignty by refuting colonialist claims of inferiority and dependency.

In historiographical terms, we could call this revisionism. Almost an etymo-
logical synonym to defamiliarization, revisionism also forces its readers to
see anew, to reexamine widely held and ideologically rooted ideas about how
past societies functioned. As one American contributor wrote, "We had
taken Kipling's India for what it was not, a political and social reality, instead
of for what it was, a brilliant product of Mr. Kipling's imagination, real only
in an artistic sense."[23] In response, and as part of its larger project of revisionism, the periodical employed the same tools of the imagination in order
to convey a different India that it could then present as real. In his opening
editorial, Lajpat Rai bemoans the fact that "the Americans derive their knowledge of India from British sources"; accordingly, his primary goals are to
wrest from British hands the right to represent India, and to reclaim that
right for Indians, in the person of himself.[24]

In *Young India,* as in conventional utopian fiction, defamiliarization is
followed by naturalization, the process by which a text replaces unmoored
assumptions with a new set of values and relationships. In other words,
Young India's historical revisionism had both a negative valence (challenging
the picture of India set out within colonial sources) and a positive one (replacing that picture with a new one of its own creation). Toward that dual objective, the periodical portrayed not only India's present, but its past—and,
specifically, revised the particular readings of Indian history that had been
wielded as justifications of colonial rule. For us, the clearest entry into the
topic of defamiliarization or revisionism in *Young India* will be through the
periodical's treatment of a central myth of colonial historiography: the infamous episode of the "Black Hole of Calcutta." As the now-disputed story
goes, the nawab of Bengal, Siraj ud-Daulah, imprisoned 146 British soldiers
in a small dungeon following a battle in 1756. According to the British East
India Company's John Zephaniah Holwell, 123 of them died overnight. The
incident outraged the British public, producing both a surge in support for
the East India Company and also an enduring association between India and
barbaric cruelty. Not surprisingly, given Edward Bellamy's colonial outlook,
Looking Backward is one of the texts that perpetuates the myth. As Bellamy
puts it, through the voice of the twenty-first-century minister Mr. Barton,

> an act of barbarity was committed in India, which, though the
> number of lives destroyed was but a few score, was attended by such
> peculiar horrors that its memory is likely to be perpetual. A number

of English prisoners were shut up in a room containing not enough
air to supply one-tenth their number. . . . to us the Black Hole of
Calcutta, with its press of maddened men tearing and trampling
one another in the struggle to win a place at the breathing holes,
would seem a striking type of the society of their age.[25]

The incident was alleged to have occurred in 1756; writing in 1887, Bellamy
assumes that the story would endure for another century or more. *Young
India* devotes two 1920 editorials to openly refuting the "Black Hole of
Calcutta" legend and unseating it from its comfortable place in popular
understandings of Indian history. As the first editorial points out, the story
handily serves the purposes of imperial justification. It "has been used time
and again to expose the essential cruelty and barbarity of the Indian people.
It is, therefore, with undisguised joy that we welcome the disclosure by a
Bengali scholar that the entire story is a myth, invented by British historians
to create prejudice against . . . one of the reigning princes."[26] In the following
issue, *Young India* goes even further in assigning the debunked myth a central role in the ideology of British rule: "Perhaps nothing in the entire modern
history of India is cited so often as an evidence of the barbarity of the Indian
people, of the inferiority of their civilization to that of the British, of their
unfitness to govern themselves, and of the great boon that British rule is to
them, as the story of the 'Black Hole' of Calcutta."[27] *Looking Backward* demonstrates how the story functioned as a commonplace, even a cliché, of
imperial history; *Young India* carefully overturns that commonplace. This is
historiographical revisionism in the purest and most obvious sense: investi-
gating what the past looks like when history is not written by the victors,
while exposing the political uses of the old, mythic history.

Elsewhere in *Young India*, the goal of revisionism is simply implicit. In
the guise of a disinterested historical account, Benoy Kumar Sarkar's
"International India" counters the image of an insular subcontinent that had
been a commonplace of colonial historiography. Sarkar carefully subdivides
India's history into stages of commercial, intellectual, and cultural interaction, from "intercourse with the Egyptians" through "the Aegeans," "the
Semitic Empires," "the Hebrews," "the Zoroastrians," "the Hellenistic king-
doms," "the Roman Empire," "the Chinese," "the Saracens," "Europe during
the Later-Middle Ages," and "Europe since the Renaissance."[28] This catalog,
which reads history as a sequence of contacts, contradicts the idea that

nationalism must necessarily create a mythological Golden Age in which the nation is pure and untouched. Here, instead, *Young India* presents a nation's history as a whole succession of hybrid Golden Ages, which perhaps might better be called high-quality alloy ages. Sarkar labels the last period in India's history as "the only Dark Age of India," in which "India's contribution . . . has been, first, a vast market for the industrial powers of the Western World, and secondly, a land of raw materials. She has thus been in touch with the modern world-forces . . . though mainly as a passive agent." Sarkar inverts the label of insularity, accusing England of ruining a paragon of cosmopolitanism rather than rescuing an isolated region.

Within its revisionist campaign, the colonial commonplace that *Young India* most frequently attempts is the claim of Indian fragmentation. As hard as the periodical works to erase from India's history the qualities of barbarism and insularity, it works doubly hard to characterize both India's past and its present as comfortably and sustainably diverse. In drawing from the cultural treasures of many centuries, *Young India*'s art editor A. K. Coomaraswamy takes care not to privilege any single period of Indian art, but reproduces images from Hindu, Buddhist, and Muslim schools, not only from all over India but also from Java and Ceylon. Applying the same objective to the representation of the present, assistant editor N. S. Hardiker opens his 1918 article "United We Stand" with the claim that "The people of India are united and fully determined to manage their own affairs," continuing rather optimistically that "the Brahmin and the non-Brahmin question is the creation of British bureaucracy."[29] Similarly, one 1920 article hails as "inspiring" "the achievement of a unity and cooperation between the two great elements of the population—the Hindus and Mohammedans," while another asserts that "to-day their unity and harmony are complete."[30] These are only a few of many such examples; throughout its three years, *Young India* makes constant gestures toward unity in diversity. The imaginary India consists of many constituencies, who have only one thing in common: the desire to see Home Rule.

This is a far more catholic vision than we are accustomed to associating with nationalism. Rather than suppressing the voices of its minorities, *Young India* mobilizes those voices toward its own ends. Its inaugural issue contains a column called "What Do Prominent Indians Say?," apparently intended as an ongoing feature though it never appeared again. Significantly, the first and in fact the only "prominent Indian" is a Muslim—Hasan

Imam—presumably by deliberate choice on the part of the predominantly Hindu editors.[31] What this particular prominent Indian says, of course, accords neatly with what all other Indians and their sympathizers say regarding India's desired future. As a capitalized section heading in the column reads, "OUR ONE GOAL/HOME-RULE FOR INDIA." *Young India's* picture of unanimity is as rosy, and as fictional, as its claims toward religious harmony. In fact, the nationalist movement enjoyed no such consensus; many nationalists both at home and abroad advocated for total independence. That reality comes to light only through occasional cracks in *Young India's* façade, like the warning against the "sneaking methods" of those U.S.-based nationalists "who want complete independence"—presumably the California-based Ghadar Party.[32] Aside from the few mentions of more radical elements, *Young India* effectively manufactures a consensus on the goal of Home Rule.

All of Lajpat Rai's strenuous efforts toward defamiliarization have a single intent: to promote an image of a unified India, specifically as counter to British claims of fragmentation and incapacity for self-rule. Inevitably, Rai allows British representations of India to set the terms of his response. *Young India* thus exhibits the quality of derivativeness that has been so convincingly shown to haunt Indian nationalism at large. Even within the United States, arguing for an apparently neutral audience, Rai finds that colonial discourse has preceded and exceeded what he and his periodical are able to do. One of the periodical's many advertisements for itself sets out testimonies from prominent American readers. In a sadly incomplete version of Julian's aborted nineteenth-century nightmare, these testimonials attempt to demonstrate that the periodical has succeeded in defamiliarizing its American readers from the racist ideologies to which they have been exposed through British propaganda. Nebraska Senator G. W. Norris praises the magazine for its efforts toward "more enlightenment and a better education," continuing that "the magazine throws great light into the dark places of civilization"; *World Tomorrow* editor Norman Thomas announces that "I wish it long life"—a hope that *Young India* itself, with its historically specific purpose, could not share. [33] Despite the inappropriateness of the comments, Lajpat Rai chose to include them, showing how important it was to register that Americans in high places had noticed his product. As India itself sought recognition of its sovereignty, *Young India* also staked out a claim by demonstrating an effect, however insufficient, on its readers. As I will discuss later, in relation to the shape of *Young India*'s transnationalism, they have the effect of endorsing American public opinion as a legitimate arbiter of national worthiness. At the same time, the unintentionally humorous compilation reveals American readers' enduring ignorance regarding *Young India*'s content.

Such internal inconsistency is perhaps *Young India*'s prime characteristic. Read as the utopian fiction that it is, the periodical provides us with a fundamentally new kind of utopia, one not governed by a single, individual vision. Because of its collective and periodic form, *Young India* never falls victim to the kind of stasis that plagues the classical utopias from More's to Howells's. In the areas of education, production, and international relations, the periodical offers divergent and sometimes directly contradictory visions for India. Where Tom Moylan finds redemption in the ability of the "critical utopia" of the 1970s to represent ongoing dissent within the utopian society, *Young India* intrinsically conveys the same equivocality. Perhaps the most important of *Young India*'s consistent characteristics is its ability to represent divergent points of view in some of the critical areas for utopian intervention. Fully realized in some respects, in other areas the imaginary nation has ongoing paradoxes still unresolved at the end of its run. From Moylan's reading, these are *Young India*'s real strength, in contrast to the static and potentially totalitarian fictional utopia.

These paradoxes tend to crystallize around individual contributors. The sections that follow, therefore, will continue to center on the work of a single author or editor. As mentioned above, Lajpat Rai's contributions attest to *Young India*'s only partially successful defamiliarizing function. Toward his goal of undermining a received image of India as fractious and fragmented, Rai is aided by the young art historian Ananda Kentish Coomaraswamy, who had recently arrived in Boston to curate the India collection for the Museum of Fine Arts there. Coomaraswamy's many *Young India* articles on art, aesthetics, literature, and culture, along with his role as *Young India*'s art editor, demonstrate the importance the periodical places on cultural production as an intrinsic part of nation-building, despite its primarily political objectives. Similarly, many of the debates on nationalism and the desirability of the nation as a political form coalesce around the person of Tagore, whom I examine as a second key contributor. By reading the Tagore poems that appeared in *Young India* alongside his contemporaneous works that it chose not to include, we can see how the periodical manipulates Tagore's writing to mute his anti-nationalist message. Tagore, Lajpat Rai himself, and especially Sarojini Naidu composed poems that represent India as a tragically wronged mother. The third section, on Naidu's work, will track the simultaneously symbolic and actual role of women in the nationalist movement. Within *Young India*, potentially debilitating personification coexists incongruously with active and vocal participation. Finally, J. T. Sunderland and his eclectic 1920 volume of *Young India* illustrate how the periodical, even while endorsing the nation model, creates something different—namely, an organ for evolving forms of transnationalism that include diaspora, solidarity, and correspondence. Those four important contributors alter the shape of *Young India*'s utopia; Coomaraswamy endorses multiple and equally valid forms of cultural expression, Tagore insists on the need to come together without excluding, Naidu develops women's symbolic and actual presence, and Sunderland shows how India's goals match those of other communities.

Even at the end of its three years, the imagined nation remains inchoate, accommodating seemingly incompatible visions in many areas. Nationalism and internationalism, cultural and political emancipation, industrial ambitions and craft nostalgia coexist on the pages of the periodical. In other areas, however, Lajpat Rai exercises significant editorial control, carefully managing the periodical's content in order to shape the utopia that is the free India of the future. Across the thirty-six issues, significant areas of divergence with some of his most frequent contributors seem to vanish—as we will see especially in *Young India*'s selective inclusion of the writing of Coomaraswamy and Tagore.

I. Culture: A. K. Coomaraswamy

From its opening issue, *Young India* exhibits a belief in the importance of cultural expression as an essential component of nationalism. Along with worldwide news briefs, progress reports on League membership, and academic book reviews, nearly every issue contains at least one poem. *Young India* assiduously reprinted practically every new composition by Rabindranath Tagore and Sarojini Naidu, reviewed productions of Tagore's plays, and even included an abolitionist lyric by James Russell Lowell under the rubric of "Why America Should Sympathize," leaving no doubt that poetry can function as political doctrine. As I showed above in my discussion of Lajpat Rai's revisionism, the editor and his staff understood the gravity of literature and culture in forming public opinion. In that valued category, the most frequent and varied contributions came from two sources in particular: first, Tagore; and second, the art historian and Boston Museum curator Ananda Kentish Coomaraswamy, who provided essays on art, literature, and aesthetic theory, and ultimately served as the periodical's art editor. Though established by Lajpat Rai, *Young India*'s commitment to culture grew even stronger following his departure—for it was in the periodical's last year, under Sunderland's tenure, that Coomaraswamy assumed an editorial position and began sending in monthly art dispatches from Boston.

Such a consistent emphasis on culture would by no means have been taken for granted as having a place in a nationalist periodical. *Young India*'s closest successor, *The Voice of India*, began publication out of Washington, D.C., in 1944. As opposed to *Young India*'s bizarrely rich and eclectic cultural offerings, one sees in *The Voice of India* a complete absence of any cultural references at all. The latter publication's omission was so complete that Coomaraswamy, twenty-five years older and still committed to the nationalist uses of art, wrote to the editors that

> We hear nowadays almost exclusively of India's right to a political
> and economic freedom. . . . There are, nevertheless, other and
> perhaps even more important freedoms to be considered, which
> may be called collectively a cultural freedom. . . . There are cultural
> and religious as well as political Imperialisms; and if we are to be
> free in any more real sense than that in which the 'economically
> determined' Western man is free, then our whole system of
> education must be liberated not only from direct or indirect
> control by any foreign government.[34]

This was one entry, as Coomaraswamy's pieces in *Young India* had also been, in the ongoing debate within nationalism regarding which type of emancipation should take priority. With its consistent inclusion of art and poetry, *Young India* was declaring at least a partial allegiance. Certainly culture mattered, declared Lajpat Rai in word and deed, toward the project of recuperating India's image from British control. Tagore's poems and Coomaraswamy's critical essays helped to round out the imaginary India, to give it substance and texture. By comparison with the flatter and more single-minded *Voice of India*, we can see how *Young India*'s cultural offerings helped to convert the periodical from simply an advocational periodical into a utopian one.

Outside the pages of the periodical, however, both Tagore and Coomaraswamy departed radically from Lajpat Rai on several questions of culture and nationalism. Tagore's anti-nationalism will be the topic of the following chapter; here I examine Coomaraswamy's role in *Young India* and the many areas of divergence between him and the rest of the periodical's editorial board. For one, Lajpat Rai agreed with Coomaraswamy on the importance of cultural freedom, but certainly not on its primacy. Writing in *Art and Swadeshi,* his anti-colonial treatise of 1912, Coomaraswamy clearly pronounced cultural freedom more meaningful than its political counterpart: "The kingdom of heaven is within; so also is the freedom of nations. The Pole adhering to his language and traditions, preserving in himself something of character and individuality, is more free despite his fetters, than Indians would be tomorrow if every foreigner left their shores forever."[35] Here, Coomaraswamy not only includes art and literature as part of the project of nationalism, but even prioritizes them, declaring a ranking of importance that Lajpat Rai could not have endorsed. Such sentiments on Coomaraswamy's part appear nowhere in *Young India,* so that the periodical's nuggets of culture may supplement its objective of statehood rather than undermining or obviating that objective.

Coomaraswamy's own opinions differed from those of *Young India* at large on several other important matters, none of them represented within the periodical. Most notably absent from *Young India* was the anti-industrialism that colored his four decades of work. Coomaraswamy was one of three men, along with E. B. Havell and Abanindranath Tagore (Rabindranath's nephew), who helped apply the ideas of William Morris to India. In the latter part of the nineteenth century, Morris's Arts and Crafts movement articulated one of England's most powerful and concrete critiques of Victorian industrialism. The movement sought to restore meaning to labor by resuscitating craft production; it espoused guild socialism and only tangentially engaged with colonialism. Coomaraswamy recognized and developed the anti-colonial potential latent in Morris's campaign, providing the theory that the teachers and artists of the Bengal Renaissance then put into practice. While *Young India* allows Coomaraswamy to praise Havell and Abanindranath Tagore, the primary contemporary practitioners of the Arts and Crafts movement's anti-colonial incarnation, it never accompanies that praise with the anti-industrial critique that undergirds it. The Arts and Crafts stance, which eschews mass production, was never part of *Young India*'s philosophy.

Rather, as seen in Lajpat Rai's advice to Indian students, reproduced above, *Young India*'s editor approves wholeheartedly of the industrialization and mechanization that Coomaraswamy and his Arts and Crafts kin so despise. Thus *Young India* replicates in miniature a larger debate within Indian nationalism, with Coomaraswamy advocating a Gandhian and Lajpat Rai a Nehruvian approach. On the related problem of imitation, Lajpat Rai and Coomaraswamy differ accordingly. Whereas Lajpat Rai encourages his readers not even to adapt U.S. institutions to Indian needs but simply to copy them outright, Coomaraswamy uses words like "vulgarisation," "prostitution," and "caricature" to describe India's imitation of the West.[36] Not surprisingly, such terms never make it to the pages of *Young India*. As with Rabindranath Tagore, the periodical includes Coomaraswamy's writing but incorporates his strategy and his vision only selectively.

Raised in England and trained as a geologist, Coomaraswamy awakened into nationalism only through an appreciation of the threatened artisanal traditions of South Asia. Charged with preparing Ceylon's mineralogical survey, he not only did an exemplary job—in the process discovering a previously unknown mineral—but also applied the same research skills to cataloging another threatened natural resource, that of arts and crafts. Coomaraswamy's first book, *Medieval Sinhalese Art*, attests to Morris's heavy influence on his aesthetic and political formation. The affiliation was quite self-conscious: Coomaraswamy printed *Medieval Sinhalese Art* on Morris's own Kelmscott Press, which he had purchased for that purpose. Despite its title, *Medieval Sinhalese Art* in fact examines contemporary art, or at least that which Coomaraswamy deemed to have survived the industrializing, hostile onslaught of colonialism. The designation of "medieval" indicates quality rather than chronology; that high quality was not naturally time-bound, but had been forcibly extinguished. As Coomaraswamy writes, "Medieval Sinhalese Art was the art of a people for whom husbandry was the most honorable of all occupations . . . and whose ploughmen spoke as elegantly as courtiers"; "Medieval conditions survived in full force until the British occupation."[37] Just as it does for Morris (along with Ruskin and Carlyle), "medieval" designates not a historical period as much as a state of absolute harmony between individuals and their labor, which would have continued indefinitely had it not been sundered by unwelcome and avoidable new developments. If the young art historian did not confine himself to the medieval period as defined chronologically, neither did he address only art. Rather, as its subtitle "With an Account of the Structure of Society and the Status of the Craftsman" indicates, his book is a Morris-influenced inquiry into conditions of production, making it a quite appropriate if unprecedented product for the Kelmscott Press.

Morris would have hailed Coomaraswamy's contribution, even if his Arts and Crafts forebear, John Ruskin, would not have. Speaking just after the Sepoy Rebellion of 1857, Ruskin had declared that "the art of India . . . either forms its compositions out of meaningless fragments of colour and flowings of line or if it represents any living creature it represents that creature under some distorted and monstrous form. To all the facts and forms of nature it willfully and resolutely opposes itself."[38] Half a generation their elder, Ruskin functioned as guiding spirit for the conceptualizers of the Arts and Crafts movement, who invariably deferred to his opinion on entire schools of art. It is therefore quite significant that Morris in his 1879 lecture "The Art of the People" reversed Ruskin's earlier judgment. Digressing from his main argument, Morris declares the need to "speak also of another piece of discouragement before I go further." That piece of discouragement is the rapid decline of Asian art, which had only recently been "at once beautiful, orderly, living in our own day, and above all, popular."[39] For Morris, there is no question that colonial occupation is to blame: "It is a grievous result of the sickness of civilization that this art is fast disappearing before the advance of western conquest and commerce—fast, and every day faster."[40] Within the Arts and Crafts movement, this was a step toward overcoming Ruskin's legacy of disgust towards Indian art; it also opened the door to what became a very productive application of Arts and Crafts doctrine to colonial concerns. That Morris later not only declared Indian design beautiful but cited it as a model for English pattern makers, as he did in "The Art of the People," allowed art-based nationalists like Coomaraswamy and Abanindranath Tagore to apply his analysis without the taint of disapproval.

Like Morris, Coomaraswamy developed his politics through his aesthetics—specifically, through his belief in the superiority and the vibrancy of medieval, blessedly pre-industrial art. But while making use of Morris's terms, Coomaraswamy departed from him by considering colonialism a far more important factor in artistic production than class relations. In the lecture quoted above, Morris returns to the subject at hand—art education in England—by reminding his audience that "neither on this side, nor on any other, can art be amended, until the countries that lead civilization are themselves in a healthy state about it."[41] Morris, inevitably a product of his times in certain ways, could not help but accept England's role as a leader of civilization, if only it would do a better job of performing that role. It was up to Coomaraswamy then to apply the most useful of Morris's insights—the insistence that production must spiritually elevate its participants, the taking of art as a measure of social health—to the colonial system as seen by Tagore. Indeed Coomaraswamy himself saw his early mission as extending Morris's dicta to a wider field of analysis. As he wrote in the foreword to *Medieval Sinhalese Art*, "This book has been printed by hand, upon the press used by William Morris for printing the Kelmscott Chaucer. . . . I cannot help seeing in [this] an illustration of the way in which East and West may be united in an endeavor to restore the true Art of Living which has for so long been neglected by humanity."[42]

Here, Coomaraswamy employs the language of his second major influence and his primary mentor in nationalism: namely, Rabindranath Tagore. Coomaraswamy's formative stay in Ceylon coincided with the height of the Swadeshi movement, the far-reaching boycott of British goods that had begun in reaction to Viceroy Curzon's 1905 partition of Bengal. As we will see in the following section, Tagore disavowed the movement during its later violent and exclusionary phase; but in its early, heady days, the poet was heralded as its bard. Traveling in India, Coomaraswamy not only met Tagore but became immersed in his milieu: the salon-like Calcutta home, the school at Santiniketan, and Abanindranath's art studio. He became one of the earliest translators of Tagore's poetry into English, and the first whose translations received attention in the West.[43] Coomaraswamy's interest in art—and his conviction that colonialism was slowly killing it—fed his nationalism, which then took on the contours of Tagore's own. During this formative period, Coomaraswamy founded the Ceylon Social Reform Society in 1905 and launched its journal the following year.[44] According to its utopian manifesto, the Society's purpose was "to encourage and initiate reform in social customs amongst the Ceylonese, and to discourage the thoughtless imitation of unsuitable European habits and customs."[45] By the time of his involvement with *Young India*, then, he was no stranger to periodical publishing—nor to utopian imaginings. From early in his new career, Coomaraswamy understood the utility of art in building a new world; this is what he most admired about Tagore and what he strove for, in various ways, in his own work. Introducing Tagore's poems, Coomaraswamy places their author in the visionary company of those artists who articulate the collective needs of a nation. He writes, "The painters of our visions—the makers of our songs—the builders of our houses—the weavers of our garments, these all are a touchstone, that . . . if we could let them, could lead us back to a world we have lost, the world to which our real greatness belongs."[46] Here, too, Coomaraswamy affiliates himself at once with Tagore and with Morris, who also built his literary and artistic utopias by looking back to a mythic past.

Coomaraswamy's expressions of nationalism never strayed far from the Morrisian preoccupation with artistic production. As he wrote in the preface to his first book on nationalism per se, the 1911 collection *Essays in National Idealism*, "it may appear strange that in a book devoted to the ends of Indian nationalism, so much space should be given to art and so little to nationalism. It is because nations are made by artists and poets, not by traders and politicians."[47] Indeed, Lajpat Rai would enlist artists and poets—most frequently Coomaraswamy and Tagore—to help make his imaginary nation. When, seven years after writing those words, Coomaraswamy arrived in the United States at almost the same time as Lajpat Rai, it made perfect sense to include him as part of the *Young India* collective.

Even while contributing to *Young India*, Coomaraswamy presided over a different kind of idealized nation of his own. He had moved to the United States to become curator of Indian art at Boston's Museum of Fine Arts, a position originated by pan-Asian theorist Kakuzo Okakura. The Indian collection grew prodigiously under his tenure, ultimately forming another exile nation. As one biographer writes,

> this India which Coomaraswamy assembled at Boston was the
> India of his liking and making. It was bereft of human beings,
> flora and fauna belonging to contemporary India. Nor was there
> any trace of the India bustling with nationalist activity, non-
> cooperation, riots, lathi charges and firings. In Coomaraswamy's
> India carefully and methodically displayed in the huge halls and
> corridors of the Boston Museum were extant pieces of Indian art
> that spoke with 'voices of silence.'[48]

But his was not an apolitical project. The mere act of gathering artworks and artifacts was a revisionist one in that, like *Young India*, it formed the perception of India in the eyes of this new imperial power. Like that of periodical publishing, the history of museum collecting is linked to the growth of empire. In fact, the first organized display of Indian art belonged to none other than the East India Company, which in 1858 founded a museum in London. The purpose of that collection, the East India House Museum, was "to give information about the life and manners, the arts and industry of [India's] inhabitants."[49] If, as Thomas Metcalf has argued, the East India House Museum and its kin allowed the English to invent and then preserve a constructed India, Coomaraswamy's collection reclaimed for Indians the right to represent their nation. By 1923, the collection in Boston far surpassed any other outside India; over the four years that followed, Coomaraswamy presented his idealized India in print form as the magisterial five-volume catalog of the museum's collection.

Coomaraswamy's revisionism suited Lajpat Rai's purposes, even if the editor then mixed the perfectly static archival India back in with the modern, resisting nation. Beginning in March 1920, *Young India* featured an ongoing column by Coomaraswamy entitled "Our Art Section." It consisted of a new reproduction each month of a national treasure, always accompanied by a page-long commentary on the significance of the piece. If the costly inclusion of art reproductions demonstrates the periodical's strong commitment to art, the artworks themselves demonstrate what sort of nation *Young India* aimed to create. As in *Looking Backward* and *Herland,* it is a simple matter to gauge the overall values of a utopia through its imagined aesthetics. In *Looking Backward,* music and literature serve to reflect and bolster the prevailing sense of bourgeois conformity; in *Herland,* art and folklore are geared directly toward early childhood education and thus toward ideological reproduction. Coomaraswamy's "Our Art Section" helps *Young India* to consolidate the image of unity-in-diversity that is so central to its self-presentation.

Like everything else in *Young India,* "Our Art Section" caters to a dual readership. At the level of the title alone, the indeterminate first-person plural possessive allows Indian readers to take pride in their art; meanwhile, the descriptions, intended for a reader with no familiarity with Indian art, pull the American audience in so that the art, or at least the art section, belongs to them as well. Most important, rather than privileging any particular artistic tradition, Coomaraswamy carefully chose objects that bridged genre, period, region, and religion. They are even more varied than Coomaraswamy's own objects of academic study—which themselves are North and South Indian, Sinhalese and Tamil, Hindu and Buddhist. Over the course of a year, the selections in *Young India* range from the eighth to the twentieth centuries and include Rajput painting, North Indian Brahmanical temple sculpture, Ceylonese bronze Buddhist sculpture, Mughal painting, contemporary painting, South Indian copper sculpture, Himalayan painting, and Javanese Buddhist relief. In other words, Coomaraswamy drew his offerings from all over South Asia, from several religious traditions, and from not one but multiple Golden Ages.

According to the detailed captions, each individual work holds national value for various reasons; Coomaraswamy consistently manages to state those reasons in superlatives, somehow without contradicting himself. He writes of Rajput paintings that no school "uses more unmistakably the pure idiom of Indian art";[50] Buddhist sculptures "represent the period of finest achievement in Indian art";[51] the Mughal period is a "brilliant episode in the history of Indian art";[52] Buddhist reliefs in Java "illustrate every aspect of Indian life with a peculiar grace and dignity;"[53] and a contemporary Bengal Renaissance painting "has been able to give genuine expression to a theme still infinitely dear to Indian Vaisnavas."[54] Each work appears both for its particular aesthetic quality and also for its ability to embody the values of a nation. Never does Coomaraswamy give any sense of ranking or preference, or even comparison; each work offers something specific to the cultural construction of a nation. This is far from true in his other writing, in which Rajput painting occupies a vastly elevated position. Whereas Coomaraswamy as *Young India*'s art editor betrays no preference for any particular artistic school, Coomaraswamy in his own academic writing holds the eighteenth-century Hindu miniatures as the pinnacle of artistic achievement. As early as *Art and Swadeshi,* Coomaraswamy expresses his preference for that period over the better-known, Muslim, and, to him, overrated Mughal school of painting. "Rajput painting," he writes, "has a range of content and a depth of passion foreign to the sentimental Persian idylls and battle and hunting scenes, and rarely touched in the Mughal studies of individual character."[55] By the time of his *Young India* contributions, Coomaraswamy had published several books on the Rajput period and was making its paintings the primary focus of his collecting efforts. The preference comes across starkly in Coomaraswamy's Boston Museum catalogs, which contain 131 plates in the Rajput volume, compared with 74 in the Mughal volume and a total of 86 of all types of sculpture. Elsewhere he indirectly justifies the imbalance. In the posthumously published *Introduction to Indian Art,* Rajput painting tops the hierarchy of Indianness as well as that of quality. Whereas Mughal art appears in *Young India* as thoroughly Indian, *Introduction to Indian Art* finds Rajput art even more so. "A first glance at these paintings will suffice to convince the observer that they belong, and could only belong, to a pure Indian tradition: they are totally unlike Persian art of any period," Coomaraswamy writes in the chapter titled "Rajput Painting."[56] Coomaraswamy here employs an exclusivist idiom that is absent from the more catholic *Young India*; Mughal painting, meanwhile, merits no corresponding chapter in the survey. Nowhere in "Our Art Section" is such a preference at all apparent. While Coomaraswamy's own oeuvre—both his writing and his collection—holds out a single school as the most perfect and most Indian, his work for *Young India* identifies several schools as worthy of representing the nation.

Even while explaining what makes each component of "Our Art Section" particularly and superlatively Indian, Coomaraswamy also endows each piece with some universal value. In a wonderfully modernist phrase, he characterizes a twelfth-century South Indian copper sculpture as "the ultimate energy revealed in the movement of the world process."[57] An eighth-century Ceylonese bronze exhibits "high aesthetic qualities combined with an ethically sympathetic motif, and the appeal of grace and elegance."[58] In the Mughal example, "the reality of life and death is nakedly delineated, without any touch of sentimentality."[59] With such descriptions, Coomaraswamy uses his ongoing art section to carry out goals articulated earlier in *Young India*. An essay from *Young India*'s first year details European understandings of Indian art, or lack thereof; in it, he identifies himself as one of "those who from the standpoint of national pride seek for a just recognition of Indian achievement."[60] That recognition has been denied because the likes of Ruskin misunderstood Indian art, judging solely its mimetic achievements. Even "highly educated Indians," Coomaraswamy continues, are unable to comprehend the ideas contained in Indian artworks, "largely because they have come to look upon art as essentially a process of representation and to test its merit by verisimilitude . . . partly due to a misunderstanding of European aesthetic." In response to detractors of Indian art, Coomaraswamy calls for new ways of perceiving it. Just as the editorials debunking the "Black Hole of Calcutta" myth revise the commonplaces of imperial historiography in order to defamiliarize their readers from their ideological assumptions, his descriptions serve to overturn the commonplaces of imperial aesthetics. Coomaraswamy's commentary on the Mughal miniature serves as a pointed rejoinder to Ruskin in particular: "One realizes, what is apt to be forgotten, that it is not the idealistic method or the realistic method in itself that makes a work of art supreme, but the intensity of vision, the vitality or the clarity of intuition."[61] Judged as such, Coomaraswamy insists every month, Indian art both helps to define the nation out of which it arose, and also offers a larger world insight into human experience. Like so many of *Young India*'s contributors, Coomaraswamy engages in the eternal balancing act of nationalism, at once asserting the particularity of Indian art and also insisting on its universal value.

"Our Art Section" conforms to *Young India*'s larger purpose by demonstrating that India can be both pluralist and unified. Appropriately to Coomaraswamy's myriad talents, he conveys that same thesis through poetry as well. His rendition of a Mohammad Iqbal poem conveys the same sense of religious harmony that prevails through "Our Art Section." An original translation of Iqbal's "Naya Shivala" appeared in the April 1919 issue. As the introduction explains, "the following poem, which was translated by the Editor, and put into poetry form by Dr. Ananda Coomaraswamy, has a direct application to the modern problems of Indian and Religious unity."[62] That application is an optimistic one. The poem anticipates the 1920 articles hailing the new "unity and cooperation" and "unity and harmony" between Hindus and Muslims, quoted above in my discussion of Lajpat Rai. Similarly, *Young India*'s version of Iqbal's poem has religious communities uniting to produce a nation. In their joint effort to render Iqbal in English, Lajpat Rai and Coomaraswamy made several significant alterations to form the poem more closely to their own purposes—beginning with the title itself. *Young India* drops the "shivala," or Siva-temple, of Iqbal's title, calling the poem simply "The New Temple." This version serves two uses: it is comprehensible to the American part of the periodical's dual audience, and it also makes the poem's promised new edifice a universalist one. The poem itself, in *Young India*'s rendition, maintains that same universalism. Where Iqbal's original enacts religious cooperation, Lajpat Rai's and Coomaraswamy's version goes even further to present Hinduism and Islam as absolutely equivalent forces. Holding back from full-blown syncretism, the poem enacts the temporary merging of these two equivalent forces, which still remain identifiably distinct.

Of Lajpat Rai's and Coomaraswamy's several alterations to the original poem, the most striking is its new arrangement into three numbered stanzas. In their version the poem moves forcefully from a problem (religious

strife), to a scene of rebuilding, to a utopian solution (interfaith collaboration). Both the first and the last stanzas present Hinduism and Islam as
exact equivalents even on the level of syntax—another of Lajpat Rai's and
Coomaraswamy's interventions. As translated, the poem opens with the failure of institutionalized religion in any form. Iqbal's original speaker had
been a Hindu criticizing his own faith from within, but the voice in the
Young India version rejects both religions at once, and therefore cannot be
identified as a practitioner of either. The speaker announces: "because I am
sick to the heart of our mutual strife, I have deserted both mosque and
temple./I heed no longer the Mullah's sermons, I heed no longer your
ancient tales, oh Brahman." Here, every Muslim reference is balanced by a
Hindu one; mosque and temple, Mullah and Brahman have each failed. This
sense of balance, the simultaneous and equal failure of both Hinduism and
Islam, is essentially an imposition on the part of the translators.

The parallels continue in the poem's utopian conclusion. The last stanza
begins: "With the rosary in our hand and the sacred thread upon our shoul-
ders/We shall unite the glory of the mosque to the beauty of the temple."
Again, it is Lajpat Rai and Coomaraswamy who force the precise correspondence of rosary and sacred thread, mosque and temple. Placed between strife
and cooperation, allowing the negative parallels of the first section to become
the positive ones of the last, is a vision of unity through a Whitmanesque
nationalistic pantheism. As the opening stanza concludes, the disenchanted
speaker has already discovered the alternative to religion: "But every atom of
my country's dust is God to me." Lajpat Rai and Coomaraswamy pay tribute
to India in the language of Whitman's *Song of Myself,* whose third line reads
"For every atom belonging to me as good belongs to you." The next stanza,
which inaugurates the process of rebuilding, also employs language familiar
to students of American writing. In Coomaraswamy's words, Iqbal enjoins
his listeners, "Let us join hands and tear down the veils that keep brothers
strangers." Here we must remember W. E. B. Du Bois's promise in his
"Forethought" to *The Souls of Black Folk* to reveal "the two worlds within and
without the Veil," a central trope of his meditation on race and progress. The
poem uses that same trope, stripped of its original sense of enclosure, to
represent the barriers between Hindus and Muslims in India. With those
barriers destroyed, the speaker proposes to construct a new house of worship: "The city of my heart has long been empty;/Come, let us build up a
place of peace together, a towering shrine,/The pinnacles of which shall

extend to the sky:/Let us establish it in the sanctuary of our hearts." For an exile periodical, this is a perfect image of nationalism: a capacious edifice, large enough to accommodate previously fractured communities, that can be shrunken down and carried "in the sanctuary of our hearts." From there, the poem proceeds to the positive parallels of the third stanza, as quoted above. In their translation of Iqbal, Lajpat Rai and Coomaraswamy carefully place Hinduism and Islam on equal ground. The poem sets out to build a new edifice; Lajpat Rai and Coomaraswamy subtly but deliberately alter the nature of that imaginary place and the experience of their readers upon entering it.

Translating a contemporary poem is quite an uncharacteristic undertaking for Coomaraswamy, whom biographers would invariably describe as a nostalgic. Just as *Young India*'s Coomaraswamy shows no preference for any single school of art, he shows none of the distaste for all things modern that runs through so much of his other work. Despite his apparent modernist tendencies—the friendships with George Bernard Shaw, Ezra Pound, and Alfred Stieglitz; marriages to no fewer than four avant-garde artists; and the aesthetic hierarchy of "intensity of vision" and "vitality . . . of intuition" over realism, as quoted above—he generally found his ideal art objects in the distant past rather than the present. His characteristic anti-modernism finds no outlet in *Young India*, with its insistence on the promise of youth and modernity. Rather, one of his priorities there is to assert a continuity between ancient and modern India. His column "Our Art Section," with its diverse selections not only spanning centuries but also appearing nonchronologically, has the effect of erasing time difference while emphasizing a common culture. It gives substance to the term "Indian" over vast gaps in space and especially in time. To give one example, Coomaraswamy writes of one of the Rajput paintings featured in "Our Art Section" that "the foliage of the trees outlined against the dark forest background is treated in a manner almost impressionistic and modern."[63] His writings on literature in *Young India* achieve the same end; he begins one essay on the *Bhagavad Gita* by crediting the epic with raising "an intensely interesting and very 'modern' problem in ethics," and later identifies Arjuna with conscientious objectors to the current war.[64] Even more surprising considering Coomaraswamy's reputation as an anti-modern nostalgist is his choice to include contemporary artworks in "Our Art Section," a gesture that presents modern Indian art as a national resource on par with the Rajput works to which Coomaraswamy devoted so much of his academic attention.

Within *Young India,* Coomaraswamy depicts India as an almost mythical place in which the ancient and the modern are in harmony; several compatible versions of a perfect national art form coexist, and each period of history earns some sort of superlative. Absent from the periodical are Coomaraswamy's fierce anti-industrialism and his nostalgia, the aspects of his thinking that would contradict *Young India*'s overall mission. Under Lajpat Rai's guidance, he alters his own aesthetic hierarchy to accord with *Young India*'s vision of pluralism, and tempers his anti-modernity to accord with its future-oriented optimism. Like Sarkar in "International India," he represents India's history as a series of successful episodes: in his case, periods of artistic achievement whose products are diverse in form but unified in their expression of Indianness. His contributions help *Young India* to create an idealized world populated by only the best elements of the past.

II. Nationalism: Rabindranath Tagore

In the arena of contemporary culture, *Young India* turns to one artist more frequently than any other: Rabindranath Tagore, who effectively becomes the poet laureate of the periodical nation. As published in *Young India,* Tagore barely resembles the poet as we have come to see him. Beginning in the 1990s, perhaps in response to the post-Soviet fragmentation riddling Eastern Europe, historians and philosophers with little else in common began turning to Tagore as the ultimate model of a nonsectarian humanism utterly immune to the allure of the nation-state.[65] Within *Young India,* conversely, Tagore is a nationalist poet. The many reprints of his work converge to convey a collectivity united in love for the motherland. The distinction between *Young India*'s nationalist Tagore and our inherited anti-nationalist is not one of chronology, but rather of selective republication. When *Young India* began its brief run, Tagore had already gone public as an enemy of the nation—any nation. He had retracted his earlier support, which had always been highly conditional, for both Indian and Japanese nationalism. In his 1917 book of lectures on nationalism, Tagore describes Western nationalism—which he fears both India and Japan will imitate—as variously "mechanistic," "impersonal," "lifeless," "monotonous," "carnivorous," "cannibalistic," "false," "selfish," "materialist," "competitive," "exclusionary," and "a great menace."[66] Nor is such an incarnation limited to the West. For Tagore, there is no good nationalism; it can only be what he calls "the fierce self-idolatry of nation-worship."[67] India is at a crucial juncture, he believes; it can and must resist the temptation toward nationalism. "The moment is arriving when you also must find a basis of unity which is not political," Tagore told his American audience in the first lecture. "If India can offer to the world her solution, it will be a contribution to humanity."[68] He goes on: "Even though from childhood I had been taught that the idolatry of Nation is almost better than reverence for God and humanity, I believe I have outgrown that thinking, and it is my conviction that my countrymen will gain truly their India by fighting against that education which teaches them that a country is greater than the ideals of humanity."[69]

Given its goal of advocating from afar for Indian independence, *Young India* can hardly agree. Indeed, an unattributed book review calls the *Nationalism* collection "a curious blend of truth and sophistry, of sense and no-sense. . . . There is much in the essays that is beautiful and sublime, specially in the first essay, but much also which seems to us to be fundamentally wrong."[70] The anonymous reviewer (who we can presume is probably Lajpat Rai, given his multiple roles as primary contributor, publicity manager, and chief fund-raiser as well as editor) finds Tagore correct in his criticism of Western nationalism, but mistaken in his wholesale rejection of the nation form as a worthy goal. "Tagore confuses 'the nation' idea with its Militaristic and Imperialistic manifestations," claims the review.[71] As for Indian and Japanese nationalists, "we have nothing but admiration for them, in spite of what Tagore says."[72] Other *Young India* contributors concur. Several articles argue that healthy nationalism can in fact coexist with "brotherhood of nations" (a favorite phrase throughout the periodical), that nationalism need not imply exclusivity or claimed superiority, and even that India will be able to provide the West with a new and better model of nationalism—all claims that directly contradict Tagore. In one instance, again anonymous, *Young India* uses poetry to rebut Tagore's blanket repudiation of nationalism. Lajpat Rai himself wrote the unfortunate prose poem "At the Mother's Feet," which ran in *Young India*'s inaugural issue under the pseudonym "Thy Humble Son." As in his review of Tagore's essays, Lajpat Rai again defends nationalism as compatible with philanthropy:

> Some critics find fault with me because sometimes I so act and
> speak as to hold you above humanity. They don't like it because

they say it narrows one's sympathies and breeds international
hatred and jealousy. But I don't agree with them. I see humanity in
you and through you. . . . My love for you, my mother, is not
narrowing, because through you I can serve the whole universe.[73]

The category of "some critics" seems designed to refer obliquely to Tagore, and the poem, therefore, to rebut his criticisms of narrowness and jealousy.

Despite their stark differences on the desirability of the "nation" form, *Young India* consistently featured Tagore's work throughout its thirty-six issues. It even offered Tagore's book on nationalism—including the "fundamentally wrong" segments—as an incentive for subscription. The poet's heavy presence culminates in a special 1920 Tagore issue, with ten poems, two profiles, a report on his school, a report on New York productions of his plays, plus his own essay on "India's Struggle for Freedom." To some degree, the effect is one of a deliberate equivocality regarding nationalism, wherein the periodical chose to absorb dissent and thereby transform itself into something more complex and rounded. However, much of Tagore's work in *Young India* was carefully selected to mesh with the periodical's project of imagining a nation—a flexible and diverse one, perhaps, but incontrovertibly a nation nonetheless. The Tagore selections demonstrate both the periodical's ability to absorb dissent, as well as its tendency to reshape contributor opinion.

By the time that Lajpat Rai launched publication of *Young India*, the cult of Tagore was already in full swing. Before winning the Nobel Prize in 1913, he had been a favorite of modernists like Yeats and Pound. The prize, awarded largely on the basis of the poetry collection *Gitanjali*, came as a surprise to Tagore as well as to his few devoted Western readers. But during the four years that followed the Nobel, his several lecture tours of Europe and America enhanced his reputation to the point where it could hardly be sustained. He drew huge crowds who hailed him as nothing short of mystic and prophet. Pound, unsurprisingly, turned against him with the accusation that he had become "commercial property" and a "popular fad."[74] Among those other than the most vindictive and punishing of the avant-garde, though, Tagore retained his status as the preeminent literary interpreter of Asia to the West. The Nobel was awarded partially on that basis: the physical prize itself reads "For reason of . . . the brilliant way in which he translates the beauty and freshness of his Oriental thought into the accepted forms of Western belles-lettres."[75] From that time on, Tagore bore the burden of speaking, if not for his entire region, then at least for his country. In a study of his own father's complicated relationship with Tagore, E. P. Thompson writes perceptively of "the impossible pressures under which the poet had been placed by his world reputation—a reputation not only as a poet but as an embodiment in the world's eyes of Indian culture and national identity."[76]

By including Tagore's writing, the *Young India* collective evidently hopes to capitalize on that reputation. Never does Tagore appear in the periodical's pages without some adjectival reminder of his greatness. His decision in 1919 to renounce his knighthood following the British massacre of protesters in Amritsar's Jallianwala Bagh garden, *Young India*'s editorialist writes, "will shed even greater luster on his otherwise immortal name."[77] That immortal name often serves as a touchstone to identify or vouch for others; for example, W. W. Pearson, a teacher and writer associated closely with both Gandhi and Tagore, appears in the headline of a news brief simply as "Tagore's Secretary."[78] More specifically, *Young India* makes use of Tagore's acknowledged role as regional and national spokesman. In fact, despite his own vocal stance against nationalism, Tagore's work in *Young India* cannot be characterized as anything but that of a nationalist poet. Ashis Nandy points to the fine distinction between nationalism and anti-colonialism, writing that "Tagore rejected the idea of nationalism but practised anti-imperialist politics all his life . . . at a time when nationalism, patriotism, and anti-imperialism were a single concept for most Indians."[79] Tagore's work elucidates that distinction; in particular, his fictional portrait in *The Home and the World* of Bengal during the Swadeshi movement dramatizes how reductive iconography can transform an organic, open-ended anti-imperialism into a closed, exclusive, and ultimately violent nationalism. *Young India* deliberately obscures that critical distinction between anti-imperialism and nationalism, emphasizing a nationalist Tagore while excluding some of his most anti-nationalist writings. In some ways, *Young India*'s is a fundamentally new kind of utopia, one not governed by a single, individual vision. However, in order for it still to function as a cohesive, comprehensible entity, is must still be subject to a governing vision.

During its first year of publication, *Young India* reprinted three Tagore poems from the Calcutta-based *The Modern Review*, a far more catholic disseminator of all things Tagorean. *The Modern Review* published thirteen of his poems that year, most of which were typically languid, reflective lyrics.

Out of those thirteen, *Young India* borrowed "The Day Is Come," "India's Prayer," and "National Education." The titles alone point to a millennial vision of nationalism. Lest their political relevance be missed, *Young India* prefaces two of the three poems by pointedly specifying the institutional context of their initial delivery. "India's Prayer," the periodical explains parenthetically, was "*Offered at the opening of one of the sessions of the Indian National Congress.*" Similarly, "National Education" was "*Sent as a message by Mr. Tagore to the Society for the Promotion of National Education in India.*"[80] Far from the individual, private meditations that make up more of Tagore's work (especially the *Gitanjali* series so beloved by Pound, Yeats, and the Nobel Committee), these are poems that salute the institutions of nation-building. If *Young India* differs from the later *Voice of India* in claiming cultural production as an essential component of nationalism, until its very last issue it incorporates only cultural material whose message is overtly nationalistic. Not only with Tagore but also with Sarojini Naidu—as we will see later—*Young India* rejects private, personal lyrics in favor of poems that openly declare a political allegiance.

In terms of content as well as context, the reprinted Tagore poems perfectly serve *Young India*'s larger purpose. "The Day Is Come," which appeared in *Young India*'s first issue along with Lajpat Rai's nationalist prose-poem "At the Mother's Feet," opens with an image of the globe as made up of discrete national units all worshipping the same deity: "Thy call has spread over all countries of the world and men have gathered around thy seat."[81] The refrain insistently asks whether India will have a place in that exercise of national worship: "The day is come./But where is India?" Whatever Tagore's own sentiment on the appropriateness of India's imitating Western forms of nationalism, his reprinted poetry endows India with the responsibility of joining "all countries of the world" in an identical quest. Unlike the vast majority of Tagore's poems, "The Day Is Come" springs from no particular voice or persona, but simply calls out to its unnamed deity from an unidentified source.

Not one of the three poems reprinted in *Young India*'s 1918 volume, in fact, uses an individual speaker. If nationalism is a collective endeavor, its most effective poetry must feature a collective voice. As in "The Day Is Come," the poetical voice of "National Education" lacks a specific origin. Here, the objective voice addresses itself not to "Thou" but to "Comrades"— presumably, from the poem's specified context, Indian educators. As in

"The Day Is Come," the scene is one of millennial promise. The poem opens:

> The lamp is trimmed.
> Comrades, bring your own fire to light it,
> For the call comes again to you to join the star pilgrims
> Crossing the dark to the shrine of sunshine.

Lacking the overt nationalistic air of the earlier poem, "National Education" shares with it the sense that a communal task must immediately be undertaken. "Sleepers, arise from your stupor of dim desolation!" the poem continues, echoing the second refrain of "The Day Is Come": "O Lord ever awake!"

With their unidentified, objective voice irresistibly issuing commands, "The Day Is Come" and "National Education" fit well into a nationalist periodical. The third Tagore reprint from 1918, "India's Prayer," makes its collectivist goal even more explicit by using another technique that was fairly unusual for Tagore: namely, the first-person plural. Once again the addressee is "Thou"; as opposed to "The Day is Come," that addressee may now be identified as an ungendered but personified India. Whereas the other two poems stem from an objective voice, we now have a identified speaker, for almost every line contains "us" or "our." The poem asserts Tagore's own version of humanistic patriotism: even though "Thou hast given us to live," at the same time "Thy glory rests upon the glory that we are." If India is a god, as the personification certainly implies, then that god is one of man's making. The poem may be dedicated to India and presented to the Indian National Congress—but the poet insists, along with the essayist of *Nationalism,* that the nation be viewed not as an abstract notion but as an entity that depends upon its constituents. Amid an explicit prayer for country, Tagore carefully embeds a critique of the exclusivist nationalism he so despised: "They fight and kill for self-love, giving it thy name." Despite such barbs, however, the poem is well suited for nationalist purposes by its overall tone and especially its consistently collective voice.

Evidently, the *Young India* editors carefully culled the Tagore poems that most closely complemented their own collective task, rejecting ten out of the thirteen that had appeared that year in the Calcutta-based *Modern Review.* *Young India*'s strategic use of Tagore becomes clearer in contrast with a quick look at the range of the poet's writing in *The Modern Review.* Its acclaimed editor Ramananda Chatterjee, born in 1861, belongs to the same utopian generation as Lajpat Rai and Tagore. He launched *The Modern Review* in 1908, having already made his name with the Bengali-language journal of cultural nationalism *Prabasi*, whose first cover depicted Hindu, Buddhist, Muslim, and Sikh monuments from India and Burma. In other words, he was another proponent of unity in diversity. Despite *Prabasi*'s success, Chatterjee felt that an English-language journal would have a wider effect, and began *The Modern Review* in order to encourage the same revolutionary fervor among a larger public.[82] Indeed, *The Modern Review* circulated throughout India as well as Europe and the United States. A significant venue for Bengal Renaissance aesthetics, it was the prime English-language vehicle for Tagore's work, just as *Prabasi* had been for the Bengali originals. Whereas *Young India* reprinted three Tagore poems during its first year of publication, *The Modern Review* had featured thirteen in the same year, along with several essays and lectures as well as excerpts from his novel *The Home and the World*.

Given the similarity in tone and outlook of *Young India*'s selections, and how exceptional they were within his oeuvre, it is worth examining which poems the exile periodical omitted. As opposed to the first-person plural driving "India's Prayer" and the objective voice of "National Education" and "The Day Is Come," many of the omitted poems originate from an isolated and often alienated "I." "The Captain Will Come to His Helm," which *The Modern Review* featured on the first page of its April 1918 issue, not only uses the first-person singular entirely absent in the *Young India* poems, but also draws that "I" apart from others around it. "I have sat on the bank in idle contentment and not yet stepped into the boat to launch it for the farther shore," reads the poem's much more languorous opening; it continues, "Others proudly travel to the King's house across the far away dimness, but my call does not sound in the rumbling of their wheels."[83] As opposed to the deliberate instructions and collective voice of the poems reprinted by *Young India,* this poem evokes a sense of isolation and silence.

Until its last issue, the Tagore special issue, *Young India* in fact ignored all of Tagore's poems that were not overtly political. The ten poems in that December 1920 issue are divided into two sections, "Poems of Life" and "Poems of Patriotism." The latter category includes "India's Prayer" and "National Education," despite the fact that both had already run in 1918. Like most of the poems printed during the same years in *The Modern Review,* all but two of *Young India*'s seven "Poems of Life" are in the first-person singular, confirming nicely that life must be an individual undertaking, and patriotism a collective one. Like the omitted *Modern Review* selections, too, the "Poems of Life" present a speaker who draws away from the din of society to spin self-indulgently long lines of Romantic-influenced poetry, as "In the stillness I hear in every blade of grass, in every speck of dust, in every part of my own body, in the visible and invisible worlds, in the planets, the sun, and the stars, the joyous dance of the atoms through endless time—the myriad murmuring waves of rhythm surrounding Thy throne."[84] Only in *Young India*'s last issue do we finally see the solitary, contemplative Tagore—at least as a complement to the national spokesman who appears elsewhere in this issue and dominates the periodical as a whole.

During a single year—1919—two periodicals in effect manufacture and present two different versions of Tagore: *The Modern Review* a romantic individual, and *Young India* a collectively minded nationalist. The contrast becomes even clearer in the case of *The Home and the World*. Beyond one quite thoughtful book review, *Young India* makes no mention of the novel that so uncompromisingly portrays nationalism in its Swadeshi phase as violent, reductive, and ultimately dehumanizing. *The Modern Review*, on the other hand, serialized the novel's English translation over all its twelve issues in 1918. Like the omitted poems, the novel lends an insight into what aspects of Tagore's thinking *Young India* preferred to suppress, and it elucidates the way in which authorial identity can be manipulated by such publication choices.

The Home and the World (in Bengali, *Ghare Baire*) narrates the later days of the Swadeshi movement, depicting some of the internal conflicts of that seminal campaign for self-sufficiency. Initially a large-scale boycott of British goods, Swadeshi eventually took on several often contradictory incarnations, including craft initiatives, steel and hydroelectric projects, and revolutionary societies. *Ghare Baire* dramatizes Swadeshi's mutation from a positive force for economic and cultural decolonization, to a reactionary and punitive expression of cultural authenticity.[85] The novel's main theme is iconography, particularly its dangers. Tagore sets out the plot through the alternated diary-like impressions of three characters: Nikhil, an idealistic landowner and reformer whom many readers have equated with Tagore himself; Nikhil's old but untrustworthy friend Sandip, leader of a new and more violent Swadeshi; and Nikhil's wife Bimala, who must choose between the two men and their respective visions for India. Throughout their individual testimonials, Tagore carefully accumulates references to the symbols, phrases, and icons employed toward nationalist ends. Those emblems of nationalism include bonfires, the image of Bengal or India as a woman, and most frequently of all the phrase *Bande Mataram*, or "Hail, Motherland." Whereas the measured and reasonable Nikhil, echoing Tagore, doubts the value of nationalist symbolism, Sandip justifies such symbolism on the basis that it provides "an appeal to the imagination" and performs the necessary task of "realizing my country in a visible image."[86] Whether nationalist iconography in fact creates or destroys, gives energy to a movement or robs it of reason, is the central question of the novel.

Within *Ghare Baire*, reductive nationalist symbolism most frequently tales the form of nation-as-mother imagery. In what amounts to a mission statement for iconography, Sandip argues that "True patriotism will never be roused in our countrymen unless they can visualize the motherland. We must make a goddess of her" (120). Sandip justifies the need for such nation-worship in exactly the terms Tagore excoriates in his *Nationalism* lectures; in response, both Nikhil and his respected old teacher vocalize opinions that are unadulteratedly Tagore's. "To worship my country as a god is to bring a curse upon it," Nikhil remarks, anticipating Tagore's description of modern history, quoted earlier, as "the fierce self-idolatry of nation-worship" (29). Nikhil's teacher agrees with him that a country must not become an object of worship: "This making a fetish of one's country, won't do" (166). Yet *Ghare Baire* dramatizes the undeniable power of such fetishization. Tagore brilliantly boils the problem of nationalism down to the use and misuse of the phrase *Bande Mataram*, which throughout the novel serves to foreclose any kind of dialogue or exchange of ideas. From the outset, the precise danger of *Bande Mataram* lies in its ability to dominate any other forms of expression. On multiple occasions throughout the novel, the two words put an end to the possibility of exchange or compromise.

For a novelist and poet, to show that a single phrase can foreclose dialogue—even put a stop to language—is a powerful allegation. In leveling such an allegation, Tagore disavows his own earlier forms of activism. For he was in fact one of the two people who had done the most to popularize *Bande Mataram*. Bankimchandra Chatterjee, India's foremost nineteenth-century novelist, first circulated the expression through a poem that appeared in his 1882 novel *Anandamath;* Tagore himself then set the poem to music in 1896.

But once Tagore turned away from both nationalism and Swadeshi, he also began to distrust the phrases and icons that powered those movements. Though for a brief time iconographic language created possibility, Tagore represents it by 1915 as potentially foreclosing intellectual exchange. In his later years, Tagore understood nationalism and iconography as practically synonymous evils. Romain Rolland's recollection of the cordial debates between Tagore and Gandhi conveys the linkage between the two areas:

> The first subject of discussion was idols; Gandhi defended them,
> believing the masses incapable of raising themselves immediately
> to abstract ideas. Tagore cannot bear to see the people eternally
> treated as a child. . . . The second point of discussion was
> nationalism, which Gandhi defended. He said that one must go
> through nationalism to reach internationalism.[87]

This exchange took place in 1923; once again, as in both *Nationalism* and *The Home and the World*, Tagore found himself arguing against "an appeal to the imagination" that he found demeaning and dangerous. It should be noted, however, that Tagore's defamation of *Bande Mataram* in *The Home and the World* well predated this collegial difference with Gandhi, and in no way should be taken as evidence that he intended the character Sandip to be a "caricature of Gandhi," as Georg Lukács erroneously claimed.[88] In fact, Gandhi never uses the phrase in his anti-colonial manifesto *Hind Swaraj*, and only once in his entire *Autobiography*. [89] Further, the single use in the *Autobiography* comes in conjunction with *Allah-u-Akbar*, so that one potentially exclusivist phrase coexists with another, thus rendering each one partial as well as universalist. *Young India*, on the other hand, relies heavily upon the phrase *Bande Mataram* to convey its purpose. The periodical's first issue carried as its logo a map of India with lines radiating outward, topped with the phrase in italics. By March of 1918, *Young India* had replaced *Bande Mataram* with its English equivalent, "*Hail! Motherland*," still italicized. Faced with the task of recreating India from abroad and for a dual audience, *Young India* chose to translate the phrase for its American readers, while still retaining it as a central rallying call. As an exile periodical, *Young India* cannot afford to eschew "realizing my country in a visible image," to use Sandip's phrase. In New York, *Bande Mataram* reads as purely anti-colonial, whereas in Bengal it could too easily become anti-Muslim.

It should be unsurprising that Tagore later joined with some Muslim delegates in opposing the Indian National Congress's adoption of "Bande Mataram" as its anthem. Besides his commitment to interfaith harmony, one can also attribute the stance to a simple distaste for the work done by the anthem. Tagore's definitive biography contains a wonderful illustration of the poet's uncomfortable relationship to the national anthem he helped to produce. During Tagore's 1912–13 trip to England, "Rothenstein and Yeats arranged a small and convivial dinner in his honor. Afterwards they asked Rabindranath to sing 'Bande Mataram,' Bengal's nationalist song. He hummed the tune but could not remember more than a few words. Then, in succession, Yeats attempted the Irish anthem, Rhys the Welsh national anthem, and Rothenstein 'God Save the King.' Each stumbled. 'What a crew!' said Rothenstein."[90]

The anecdote shows the poets' ironic distance from the paraphernalia of nationalism. But Tagore in particular could never escape those trappings, for his own words worked too well in their service. After agreeing to abandon "Bande Mataram," the Congress chose another Tagore poem, "Jana Gana Mana"; today not only India but also Bangladesh uses his poems as national anthems.

The appropriation of his work toward nationalist ends may be the greatest irony of Tagore's career. Like other artists and myth-makers, Tagore is the victim of his own success. He may incessantly express his reservations about nationalism and its attendant symbolism, but his world prominence as well as the power and beauty of his words make him too valuable a tool for those who favor Western-style nationalism. *Young India* exploits Tagore in much the same way that India itself later would. Without *The Home and the World*, without the *Nationalism* essays, Tagore as reprinted in *Young India* appears to endorse the periodical's project outright. *The Home and the World* in particular offers a historiographically useful dramatization of the range of definitions that the single word *swadeshi* can contain: from promotion of village handicraft, all the way to armed rebellion. *Young India* loses that historiographical nuance; it also loses an aspect of Tagore's work that accords particularly well with the periodical's own structure and outlook. The use of a collective voice, after all, is central both to *Young India*'s form and to that of *The Home and the World*, with its three interwoven and often contradictory stories. As Ashis Nandy shows, the need for dialogism is one of Tagore's central points: "The novel suggests that a nationalism which steam-rollers society into making a uniform stand against colonialism, ignoring the unequal sacrifices imposed thereby on the poorer and the weaker, will tear apart the social fabric of the country, even if it helps to formally decolonize the country."[91] With its wide range of contributors and opinions, Young India avoids "making a uniform stand"; in this sense the periodical furthers Tagore's goal even if it omits the novel that most loudly insists on equivocality.

Ultimately, Young India's failure to include The Home and the World as part of the full spectrum of the writer's thought undermines its provisional equivocality. Given Young India's goals and content, though, that failure is hardly surprising. For one thing, The Home and the World gives the lie to Young India's sanguine pronouncements of interreligious harmony. Sandip states outright that "though we have shouted ourselves hoarse, proclaiming the Mussulmans to be our brethren, we have come to realize that we shall never be able to bring them wholly round to our side. So they must be suppressed altogether and made to understand that we are the masters" (120). The novel ends with a communalist riot that destroys Nikhil along with his moderate and ecumenical version of Swadeshi; Young India effectively suppresses Tagore's warning, instead using prose, poetry, and art to assert interreligious unity.[92] More importantly, Young India could not print The Home and the World because the periodical also participates in Sandip's project of "realizing my country in a visible image." To Tagore, that image can only be a dangerously reductive one. In omitting his novel, the periodical filters out Tagore's distrust of potentially static iconography.

One may be tempted to conclude that Young India, therefore, is creating a reductive image of the nation. But despite their partial censorship of Tagore, one would have to guess that the punctuated and collective form—a form that is definitionally not singular in voice or in time—is one of which Tagore himself would strongly approve, as it necessitates internal disagreement as well as development over time. In terms of form, it is necessarily anti-static. The very fact that Young India included so much of Tagore's work, registered its disagreement with his stance on nationalism, and initiated a dialogue in poetry, indicates a willingness to accommodate differing points of view within the theorized nation. At the same time, operating from outside India proper (as opposed to The Modern Review), Young India has a stronger need both for iconography and also for the nation form as a goal, in order to give shape to an otherwise abstract and removed entity. As an exile periodical, Young India cannot afford to aspire to the polyculturalism expressed in Dark

Princess; it needs a "visible image" for its imaginary nation. Thus, even while emphasizing "unity within diversity" as counter to British claims of Indian fragmentation, the periodical skirts the homogeneity of Bellamy's and Gilman's eugenic utopias. We can therefore locate *Young India*'s utopianism on a middle ground between the bordered nations of chapter 1 and the loose transnational network of *Dark Princess,* a model whose many conceptual strengths and weaknesses will occupy us in chapter 3.

III. Personification: Sarojini Naidu

We may use the example of *The Home and the World*'s Bimala as an entry into a topic discussed earlier in relation to Bellamy and Gilman, one that is crucial to revisit in connection to *Young India*. That is, what does utopia do to its women? As outlined in chapter 1, countless male-authored utopias relegate women to a less than secondary status, acknowledging their importance in biological reproduction and using them to ensure either stasis or motion, as the case may be, but denying them any meaningful participation in civic matters. In Jennifer Burwell's summary, both Bellamy and Morris deem women to be valuable inhabitants of utopia "only to the extent that they contribute to the happiness and well-being of the men," in the case of Bellamy, and "as aesthetic objects and . . . a titillating distraction to men," in the case of Morris.[93] In one of the many areas of overlap between utopian fiction and nationalism, both place an unwelcome burden of representation on women. Scholars in a wide range of disciplines have shown how nationalism, in consolidating and promoting its own reactive vision, tends to rely on women—as a collective and undifferentiated mass—to safeguard national identity and purity. A central part of that process involves relegating women to the space of the home and the role of mother. Thus, the argument goes, nationalist movements inflate women's symbolic value even as they diminish women's actual power.[94] We might expect this to be the case with *Young India,* but in fact the periodical presents a far more progressive picture of women's role toward and in the idealized nation. While *Young India* abounds with maternal symbolism, in this case such symbolism never precludes the real presence and action of women. Instead, paradoxically, we see both agency and also personification. The clearest way to observe the dynamic of that apparent contradiction is through *Young India*'s many mentions of the poet

Sarojini Naidu. Naidu's poetry perpetuates an anti-feminist symbolism, while the reports on her multiple modes of activism (as well as on a range of other feminist practices) undermine its disempowering quality.

In *The Home and the World*, Tagore denounces his nationalist straw man Sandip for, among other sins, exploitatively forming Bimala into a symbol of India. As Tagore demonstrates, such symbolism at once glorifies and reduces Bimala; either way, it transforms her from a human being into an abstraction. In his careful portrayal of that dehumanizing process, Tagore anticipates the important late-twentieth-century critique of anti-colonial nationalism's gender politics. It is largely for this reason that critics often characterize *The Home and the World* as Tagore's feminist novel: the novel presciently dramatizes the damaging effect on one woman of a crudely gendered nationalism. By characterizing Bimala variously as Bengal and as India, Sandip undermines her sense of self: "Listening to his allegories, I had forgotten that I was plain and simple Bimala"; "I was utterly unconscious of myself. I was . . . the sole representative of Bengal's womanhood" (31). With the example of Bimala, Tagore demonstrates from within the problem with being a symbol.

On the other hand, as Bruce Robbins correctly points out, Tagore's own reductive symbolism parallels that of Sandip.[95] For Tagore as for Sandip, Bimala functions as the figure for India, who must decide between a liberal, rationalist Swadeshi and its militant, revivalist counterpart. Ultimately, then, it is the anti-nationalist Tagore—as much as his deplorable character Sandip—who forces Bimala into the role of icon. In fact, despite its reliance on the language and iconography of nationalism, *Young India* takes a far more progressive view of women's role in the building of a modern nation than does Tagore. In a review of his plays, *Young India* accuses the great writer of exhibiting "the deplorable bias of an old fashioned Hindu" and "repeatedly harp[ing] on the old ideals of womanhood, now happily gone and dead forever."[96] This particular organ of nationalist utopianism, at least, refuses to participate in the reactionary revival of those "old ideals of womanhood." For even while including multiple examples of nation-as-woman symbolism, *Young India* simultaneously promotes a genuine presence and agency on the part of women.

Within *Young India*, the single author most guilty of the dehumanizing nation-as-woman equation is in fact a woman, namely the adored nationalist poet Sarojini Naidu. Naidu's poems rely heavily on the same reductive, sexist, potentially disempowering imagery as "At the Mother's Feet," even while her presence in *Young India* counteracts the silencing that such imagery might otherwise effect. *Young India* reprinted several of Naidu's new poems in 1918 and 1919, and also reported on the peregrinations of the visible and outspoken nationalist and feminist. A Cambridge-educated poet who had convinced her reformer parents to accept her quite unorthodox cross-caste love marriage, Naidu had just published her third volume of poetry, had founded the Women's India Association along with Margaret Cousins and Annie Besant, and would go on to serve as president of the Indian National Congress and the first woman governor of an Indian state. She participated in, and was jailed for, all the major campaigns of the late nationalist period: Satyagraha (arrested in 1930), Civil Disobedience (imprisoned, along with Gandhi, from 1932 to 1933), and "Quit India" (imprisoned from 1942 to 1943). In introducing her poems, *Young India* evinces pride in her multiple roles as artist, feminist, and nationalist. The brief descriptions that preface each poem invariably identify her first as "the poetess," "the noted poetess," or most poignantly "India's poetess," and then as a "prominent worker in the woman movement" or simply an "Indian leader."[97] Her poems are her most important contributions, the periodical implies; beyond that, it sees no contradiction between her nationalist and feminist activism.

As with its strategic reprinting of Tagore, *Young India* naturally gravitates toward Naidu's most overtly nationalistic compositions, those with titles like "India," "India to England," and "Panjab—1919." Their selection in no way represents her latest volume, *The Broken Wing*, in which love poems dominate. Just as it rejects Tagore's more contemplative works published in *The Modern Review*, *Young India* also passes by both the romantic and erotic lyrics that make up the bulk of Naidu's collection and also the purely personal compositions like her memorial poem "In Salutation to my Father's Spirit." The periodical also chose not to reprint her poems of worship. Naidu occupies an important position within Indian literary history as a conciliatory figure who pays tribute to Persian as well as Sanskrit literature, and makes reference to Muslim as well as Hindu ritual, a trait that most commentators attribute to her immersion in the heavily Muslim culture of Hyderabad. But unlike Iqbal in "Naya Shivala," who balanced and combined elements of Hinduism and Islam to produce a new patriotic faith, Naidu incorporates each religious tradition into separate short poems like the Hindu-themed "Temple" and "Lakshmi, the Lotus-Born," and the Muslim-themed

"Imam Bara" and "Prayer of Islam." None of those appear in *Young India*, for both its minority and majority representatives must exemplify the virtues of national pride and cultural pluralism, not religious faith.

The poems that do appear in *Young India* all address themselves directly to the fate of the nation. This is the same criterion that the periodical used for its Tagore selection, but in the case of Naidu one further commonality is even more striking. Out of the five reprinted poems, four depict India as a personified female. In two of those, the personified India is more specifically a mother. In short, *Young India* relies on Naidu to perpetuate the image of nation-as-woman. The most clear use of a generic motherland rhetoric can be seen in her poem "Awake." The short poem, which Naidu had premiered in front of an Indian National Congress meeting, uses "mother" five times, along with "queen" and "goddess" (once each for good measure). It begins "Waken, O mother! thy children implore thee," and closes with a many-voiced chorus united in their object of adoration:

Hindus: —Mother, the flowers of our worship have crowned thee!
Parsees: —Mother, the flame of our hope shall surround thee!
Mussalmans: —Mother, the sword of our love shall defend thee!
Christians: —Mother, the song of our faith shall attend thee!
All Creeds: —Shall not our dauntless devotion avail thee? Hearken,
    O queen and O goddess, we hail thee! [98]

Like Iqbal's "New Temple," "Awake" forms separate religious communities into perfectly equivalent forces on the level of syntax. The poem fits in effortlessly with *Young India*'s entire project, from its motherland imagery, to the language of awakening, to the poetic formulation of perfect equivalence. While Iqbal (via Coomaraswamy) used his poetry to merge Hindu and Muslim into a single edifice of nationalism, Naidu allows those two religions—and two more besides—to retain their own identity and traditions while worshipping a common nation-mother.

Elsewhere, Naidu repeats and complicates the motherland imagery that she broadcasts so insistently in "Awake." The first-person "India to England" opens with a generic figure of the bereaved mother, lamenting that she has "yielded the sons of my stricken womb/To the drum-beats of duty, the sabers of doom."[99] Using incongruous and derivative vocabulary for those brown-skinned sons, she details how they "lie with pale brows" and "are strewn like blossoms" across Europe's battlegrounds. The poem's unexpected ending explains their pallor, as India concludes forcefully by enjoining her addressee, England, to "Remember the blood of thy martyred sons!" Naidu ends the poem on a triumphant note of paradox: Is she endorsing the patriarchal model of empire, or characterizing the Indian Army as illegitimate offspring? Naidu had published the poem as "India's Gift"; by altering the title into "India to England," *Young India* emphasizes its dialogic aspect and helps to personify India.

In yet a third incarnation, India appears as another wronged woman, now not grieving mother but a ravished wife. The infamous 1919 massacre at Jallianwala Bagh prompted Tagore to renounce his knightship—a public act much celebrated in and out of *Young India*—and Naidu to compose "Panjab—1919." The brief two-stanza poem appears in *Young India* across from an editorial entitled "Bravo Tagore"; in it Naidu casts India, or at least the heartland province of the Punjab, as the mythic princess Draupadi. Among her many appearances in the epic *Mahabharata,* she is humiliatingly stripped by the villainous Dushasana but is saved by Krishna. In Naidu's formulation, Draupadi's modern protectors will convert her shame into new resolve:

> O beautiful! O broken and betrayed!
> Endure thou still, unconquered, unafraid,
> O mournful queen! O martyred Draupadi!
> The sacred rivers of thy stricken blood
> Shall prove the five-fold stream of Freedom's flood.
> And guard the watch-towers of our Liberty.[100]

Through all the mixed metaphor—rivers of blood guarding watchtowers—Naidu's governing image of the suffering but surviving woman comes across clearly, as does the poem's central and quintessentially anti-colonial conceit of oppression turning into strength. That motif of resistance, however, does not necessitate any action on the part of Draupadi herself; she does not perform any action within the poem other than to stand as the object of the imperative "endure" and (implicitly) to bleed.

The remaining two of Naidu's *Young India* poems also personify India, though not as wife or mother. "The Broken Wing," the title work of what was then her most recent collection, presents India as a female songbird. Its themes overlap with those of the other Naidu poems. As in "Awake," there is a process of awakening: "From her deep age-long sleep she wakes at last!"[101]

As in "Punjab—1919," the movement of the poem converts weakness into strength, with the first stanza ending with the question "Song-bird, why dost thou bear a broken wing?" and the second with the reply "Behold! I rise to meet the destined spring/And scale the stars upon my broken wing!" Here Naidu anticipates another poet who forged beauty out of oppression: Langston Hughes, who in 1923 would write the lines "Hold fast to dreams, for if dreams die,/Life is a broken-winged bird that cannot fly."[102] Finally, Naidu's short lyric "India" again personifies the region, but without gendering it. The poem renders India as an ancient, sexless child:

> Thou whose unaging eyes hast gazed upon
> The pageant of Time's splendour and decay
> Round thee have fragile centuries blown away
> Into the silence of primeval dawn;
> Thou hast outlived earth's empires and outshone
> The fabled grace and grandeur of their sway
> The far-famed rivals of thine yesterday
> Iran and Egypt, Greece and Babylon.
>
> Sealed in To-morrow's vast, abysmal womb,
> What do thy grave, prophetic eyes foresee?
> What sudden kingdoms that shall rise and fall
> While thou dost still survive, surpass them all,
> Secure, supreme in ageless ecstasy? [103]

Unlike India's other manifestations, this one is not at all embodied except for its "unaging eyes." Despite its advanced years, it remains in "To-morrow's vast, abysmal womb." In this one instance the future, rather than India, is the poem's mother figure. The unaging child has already "outlived earth's empires," but now waits to be reborn into history.

Taken together, the five Naidu poems present five different images for India: a generic mother; a bereaved mother of lost soldiers; the mythic figure Draupadi; a female bird; and an eternal child. The very range of personifications undermines the potential reductiveness of writing nation as woman. Without the forceful singularity of one recurring image, the feminizing rhetoric holds far less sway on the reader's imagination. Additionally, Naidu's own life attests to the fact that women can be an active, vocal force even when the rhetoric of woman as nation is not only present but central. James

Cousins, an Irish poet who was Naidu's contemporary, sensed this gap between poetry and biography when he wrote disapprovingly that "in her life she is feminist to a point, but in her poetry she is incorrigibly feminine; she sings, so far as Indian womanhood is concerned, the India that is, while she herself has passed on towards the India that is to be."[104] Reveling in her publicity, *Young India* helps to support the feminist India of the future, while in the present it refuses to relegate its female contributors to the role of mute supporter. In Naidu's case, its review of *The Broken Wing* departs from Cousin's disparaging assessment. In a deliberately transgendered description, the review gives her poems the maternal attributes of "life, pathos and beauty," but then adds that "they are besides quite virile."[105] Rather than being "incorrigibly feminine," her poetry spans all the gendered characteristics that the project of nationalism demands.

Naidu's vocabulary and imagery sets the terms for many of *Young India*'s other poets. As the periodical's focus became more international (a shift that I will discuss in the following section), poems by non-Indian sympathizers began to appear in its pages. *Young India*'s later issues feature several poems by American women who, like Naidu, tend to write either as Mother India herself or as one of her faithful children. As Kumari Jayawardena's fascinating and well-researched *The White Woman's Other Burden* documents (and as the 2001 Bollywood blockbuster *Lagaan* dramatizes), unorthodox white women frequently enlisted in the nationalist cause.[106] This is certainly the case with *Young India*. Agnes Smedley and others of her radical set volunteered in the *Young India* office and contributed to the periodical. Their feminized role appears to have been to provide office help and poetry; the women were far less likely to have a byline for a prose piece than were their American male counterparts. Amy Dudley, for example, contributed two poems under that name, but used the neutered "A. M. E. Dudley" for her article "American Labor and India." Smedley, a prolific writer who published in *The Modern Review* among many other venues, has no bylines.

These poems exhibit the strong influence of Naidu, making it clear that the female contributors had been reading *Young India* and had absorbed its preferred poetical vocabulary. Gertrude Boyle's "India Waking" translates Naidu's "Awake" into free verse. Boyle, a moderately successful sculptor married to the Japanese poet Takeshi Kanno, also worked with Smedley and Margaret Sanger on *The Birth Control Review* and *The Call*. Her reworking of Naidu's themes from "Awake" adds American elements: an Orientalist fascination with India's "mystic" quality, and an emphasis on India's potential contributions to the out-side world. Here is Boyle's poem, in its entirety despite the ellipses:

> Dusk-browed India . . .
>   Sealed in silence still,
> Wrapt in shadows,
> Swathed in mystic gloom,
> How long must thou dream on?
>
> The world is calling . . . calling . . .
> In bleeding need of subtle balm,
> Athirst for wisdom—thy eoned wine,
> In quest of spirit food . . .
> Secret of thy hidden might . . .
> O why slumber on?
> Come forth, India,
>   Forth from thy dream-wrought sepulchre,
> Into the day! Into the light![107]

This is a pure type of the affirmative Orientalism perfected by Gandhi and, as we will see in the following chapter, W. E. B. Du Bois; it also borrows from Naidu's themes and language. Where Naidu's reveille—"Waken, O mother! thy children implore thee"—comes from the children of the nation, Boyle speaks of a spiritually hungry larger world that is calling to India to wake up and feed it. "The world is calling" for India's gifts of "wisdom," "wine," "subtle balm," and "spirit food." While not portrayed here specifically as maternal, India still provides sustenance.

Amy Dudley's "Great India" reworks not one but two of Naidu's poems. Like "India to England," Dudley's poem speaks in the first person to render India as an angered mother. One of its eight stanzas reads:

> I have mothered the race from which nations
> Have risen and waxed great and strong
> *The Wheel of the Law is eternal—*
> *A Cycle of Time is not long*[108]

Here, the personified India has given birth not only to her own people but those of many more nations. As well as repeating the familiar maternity trope, Dudley also revisits Naidu's narrative of history in "India." Echoing

Naidu's contention that India "hast outlived earth's empires," Dudley forms that progression into a simultaneous appeal and threat. As in Naidu's poem, India remains the single stable factor in humanity's fickle history. Dudley's second poem, "Kali Mai," like Naidu's "Panjab—1919" personifies India through one of its mythic women. In the vein of Naidu's reference to Draupadi, Dudley addresses the goddess Kali as "O World Mother."[109]

Through the poems of Naidu and her acolytes Boyle and Dudley, *Young India* employs a romantic mode of personification that contrasts sharply with the personification found in *Looking Backward*. In both *Young India* and *Looking Backward* (as in *Utopia* and *New Atlantis*, as I explain in chapter 1), the symbolic weight of women speaks to a given utopia's sense of time and history. In a romantic text, the female figureheads have a very different function from that of their counterparts in a developmentalist one. Whereas Edith Leete exists to incorporate the hero into the utopia he has unwittingly awoken into—just as *News from Nowhere*'s Ellen exists to deny that incorporation—the romantic Mother India figure represents an origin, the place we all came from. It makes perfect sense that she would not be a nubile unmarried innocent, holder of the future, but rather a venerated matriarch, representative of the past. This use of a romantic mother figure is only one of the many areas in which Indian and Irish nationalisms converge: Naidu's Mother India belongs in the same category as the Mother Ireland whom Yeats celebrates in his 1902 play *Cathleen Ni Houlihan*.

However, despite that fairly consistent use of a romantic motherland rhetoric—whether by Naidu or her many imitators—Indian women in the periodical are not only symbols but often actors. As the periodical demonstrates, the nation-as-mother equation need not preclude women being agents in nationalism. More in keeping with Naidu's vocal presence than with her romanticizing rhetoric, *Young India* exhibits concern with the material rights of women. In his two-part series on "The Woman in India," Lajpat Rai spends a predictably lengthy time on the respect and honor accorded Indian women during various phases of history, citing the fact that "every woman is a potential mother" as the driving reason behind that honor.[110] However, he also details whether each phase granted women important rights such as property, movement, and marital choice, demonstrating a commendable awareness that women seek more than symbolic honor. Like Coomaraswamy, Lajpat Rai looks to the past for models; as opposed to Bellamy's strictly developmentalist approach, *Young India*'s nostalgic utopianism identifies elements of pre-colonial social organization that it deems worth reviving.

As it does in its coverage of other recurring topic areas, such as religious tolerance and cultural production, *Young India* extends its examination of women in India across past, present, and future. Even while Lajpat Rai and others narrate a roseate history, anonymous news briefs also tell of the activities of contemporary women nationalists. In those ongoing dispatches, women appear as individual authors or speakers; Naidu's poems run alongside Tagore's, Annie Besant's addresses as Indian National Congress president never fail to earn a reprint, and Madame Cama's goodwill tours of the United States are covered in detail. *Young India* also attributes to women the capacity to organize and build coalitions. As individuals and as groups, women appear as active participants in nationalism, though only rarely as a separate constituency whose interest may not coincide utterly with the men of their nascent nation.

In most instances, the women of *Young India*'s news reports are an undifferentiated mass in terms of class, religion, and experience, as exhibited in their bland and general titles: "Women of India," "The Woman in India," "Woman's Position in India," and not one but two articles entitled "The Woman Movement in India." The "woman movement" at that time had several different meanings: women's physical presence in nationalist gatherings; women's appeals to the British for equal rights in all proposed reforms; and finally, women's demands on the men of their own communities. *Young India* is more likely to cover the first type of activism, which simply supports its own goals without altering them. "One of the most encouraging features of Indian activities is that of the awakening of its women," reads one report; that awakening consists simply of "the presence of women, and their participation in political, social and other gatherings," within a predetermined form.[111] Elsewhere, however, *Young India* marks a change in the character of those gatherings due to women's participation. One of the two articles entitled "The Woman Movement in India" quotes Naidu as a spokeswoman for that movement. Not only has "the Indian woman" begun to join in with nationalist groups as already constituted, Naidu says, but she has also "not infrequently been called upon to guide their deliberations, direct their policies, harmonise their differences, and unite their ideals towards a common goal of self-realization."[112] In taking on the gendered roles of negotiator and conciliator, Naidu implies, women intervene to alter nationalism's content. In other cases, the "wakened" women go still further to demand their own rights, though most often simply as a mirror to those being granted to men. One reprinted dispatch from 1918, for example, reports that "the ladies' branch of the Home Rule for India League, Ahmedabad, firmly believes that all the rights that have been granted to men in the new scheme of reform should be granted to women also."[113] Here, the "woman movement" entails not simply being present at nationalist meetings or negotiating between warring nationalist factions, but demanding one's own rights. Accordingly, unlike in the United States or England, Indian women achieved universal suffrage at the same time as the men of their country through that "new scheme of reform," the 1919 Montague-Chelmsford Act.

As with its other recurring topics, *Young India* does broadcast some differences of opinion, occasionally acknowledging—unlike Naidu in the quote above—that there is no single "Indian woman." In reprinting letters from female leaders at odds with one another in terms of strategies and nationalist priorities, the periodical informs the attentive reader of the complexity of the new feminisms in India. *Young India* also recognizes the class dimensions of the new activisms, noting with disappointment that women's organizing has largely been limited to "the few educated women," while taking care to report on the exceptions to that limitation.[114] An article on indentured servitude by Indian migrant laborers in the Pacific Islands concludes proudly that "the horror of it was only halted when . . . the women of India, throwing aside their caste differences, came together in great meetings of protest."[115] In that example, women's organizing extends outside India; on a still more international scale, an account of the 1920 Conference of the International Woman's Suffrage Alliance shows the Indian delegates performing the same kind of coalition-building work that *Young India* advocates elsewhere. The report asserts that "the cause of women in India and women throughout the world was the same" and anticipates "a perfect understanding between the women of the West and those of the East."[116] As the following section will demonstrate, this international feminism is only one of the several forms of cross-national solidarity that *Young India* endorses.

Despite the prevalence of reductive Mother India imagery within its pages, *Young India* conveys a genuine agency on the part of women inside and outside India, as well as a wide range of feminist practices. From Naidu to Irish-born Annie Besant, from "the few educated women" to mass cross-caste gatherings, the periodical reports on not one but several varieties of feminism—or, to use more temporally appropriate terms, of woman movements. Whereas *Looking Backward* typifies male-authored utopias in combining a superficial nod toward equality with an undercurrent of condescending separation, in *Young India* we find a discrepancy in the opposite direction.

IV. Transnationalism: J. T. Sunderland

Along with its other intellectual allures, *Young India* provides a case study in the uneasy balance between nationalism and internationalism. In attempting to negotiate that balance, the exile periodical shares company with utopian discourses of its own period as well as later works. After all, the founding of the Comintern, or Communist International, comes midway through *Young India*'s brief print run. In our own time, Bruce Robbins, Martha Nussbaum, and most recently Kwame Anthony Appiah have weighed in on the possibilities for twenty-first-century cosmopolitan formations. *Young India* has its own favored phrase to encapsulate the compromise between nationalist and universalist values: "brotherhood of nations." But what that concept entails, in practical terms, varies from issue to issue. Like *Looking Backward*, the periodical incorporates potentially contradictory visions for how the utopian nation fits in with the larger world. In the case of *Young India*, those visions include solidarity among currently colonized populations; international labor socialism; and identification with the United States's own colonial history. Once again, the periodical in its three-year run manages to accommodate dissenting opinions regarding its desired nation. Between 1918 and 1920 *Young India* moves from disavowing organized socialism to openly endorsing labor internationalism. Similarly, it initially deploys "affirmative Orientalism" to present independent India as an cure to the ills of the West, but later simply depicts India as a younger United States, thus losing the quality of antimodern critique that characterizes its earlier issues.

Over the course of *Young India*'s three-year run, India's borders become more and more porous. Rather than existing only on the subcontinent of South Asia, the imagined India is geographically indeterminate. In addition to spanning the United States and India proper, *Young India* locates its constituency around the globe, paying consistent attention to the Indian experience of colonialism outside India. Ongoing reports from across the British

Empire demonstrate the formation of a diasporic consciousness, well before the word began to be used in that sense. For example, two articles from 1920, "A Labor Revolt in the Fiji Islands" and "Indians in British East Africa," allow "India" to function as a conceptual category instead of a geographical one.[117] One *Young India* cover shows how flexible a term "India" can be. The periodical's cover for February 1919 broadcasts the titles "India at Washington, D.C.," followed by "Famine and Grip Sweeping India." It is clear at first glance that two different Indias are operating on the same page. Indeed, the first of the two articles reports on the progress of peripatetic assistant editor N. S. Hardiker in his lobbying endeavors, implying that "India" can exist even in the body of one man. The second operates in a more literal manner, covering the recent influenza epidemic back in the subcontinent. Within the space of two lines, "India" changes from a political entity to the more conventionally understood geographical one.

In keeping with that diasporic model, *Young India* includes Indian-Americans as part of the porous nation it seeks to represent. One 1918 issue features photos of uniformed U.S. Army soldiers of Indian descent, under the title "Our Men with Uncle Sam."[118] Free of any accompanying commentary, the photos are meant to speak for themselves. As part of its general strategy of wartime conciliation, *Young India* puts ethnic America, willing or not, in service to a claimed homeland—and changes the contours of that homeland as a result. Unsurprisingly, *Young India* claims some Indians in America as its own while disavowing others—specifically, those accused in the notorious "Hindu Conspiracy Case" of 1918. That sensational trial found twenty-nine Indians, mostly members of California's Ghadar Party, guilty of violating U.S. neutrality laws by colluding with Germany to bring down British rule in India. In the words of the prosecutor, it was a conspiracy that "permeated and encircled the globe."[119] This was a transnationalism with which *Young India* could not afford to be associated, and indeed Lajpat Rai rushed to draw borders of his imaginary nation that would exclude the conspirators. The episode's "only redeeming feature," he writes, "is that the men guilty of these failings were in no sense representative of the Indian Nationalist Party."[120] Here *Young India*'s otherwise catholic constituency diminishes to the size of one political body.

Along with developing and refining the concept of diaspora, *Young India*'s reports from across the empire also allow for a generalized understanding of the character of colonialism. The Fiji dispatch, for example, casts its analytical net as far as "the whole system of indenture which for many years has prevailed not only in the Fiji Islands but throughout the colonies and dependencies of the British Empire."[121] The article on "Indians in British East Africa" generalizes even more widely, asserting that "It is a well-known fact that whenever European powers seek to govern uncivilized peoples they assume at once an attitude of intellectual, moral, and racial superiority over the conquered."[122] *Young India* anticipates theorists like Frantz Fanon and Edward Said in offering an abstract and near-universal picture of not only colonialism's material conditions, but the colonial mentality. Francis Hackett takes the task of pan-imperial analysis even further in a 1920 book review. Hackett frames his review of Ellen La Motte's *The Opium Monopoly* as a quarrel with the contention of Sir Auckland Geddes, the new British ambassador to the United States, that the aim of British policy has been "to bring order out of chaos, to extend the boundaries of freedom, to improve the lot of the oppressed, to increase the material prosperity of the world."[123] Now freed of the contingencies of wartime, Hackett writes that "the worst drug that the British monopolize is not opium, but the drug of Christian righteousness with which they lull the world." The review covers Japan, China, French Indo-China, Siam, Singapore, British North Borneo, British Guiana, and Mauritius; even with no mention of India, it is clear how the treatise on British hypocrisy helps *Young India*'s cause.

Such generalizations on British imperial behavior, in turn, help *Young India* to strategize on the forces that may resist empire. Writing under the pseudonym of "A Student of Revolutions," Lajpat Rai announces in a 1918 essay that "I have made it my business to acquaint myself the histories of revolutionary movements in the different parts of the world."[124] Within New York alone, *Young India* reported on the activities of the League of Oppressed Peoples ("a new organization formed to work for the freedom of all oppressed nationalities, India, Ireland, Egypt, Korea, Persia and China") and the Small and Subject Nations League.[125] Maps from the first pages of *Young India*'s 1918 and 1919 volumes graphically demonstrate the periodical's growing sense of its own mission as part of a world movement. The January 1918 issue opens with a crudely hand-drawn map of India alone, with its rivers, mountains, and provinces, but only the faintest hint of a world beyond in the cramped letters spelling out "Burma" and "Afghanistan." January 1919 leads off with a full world projection boldly titled "HERE ARE THE OPPRESSED NATIONS OF THE WORLD; WHAT WILL THE PEACE CONFERENCE DO FOR THEM?"[126] Shades of gray indicate the status of various regions, with India as well as Southeast Asia and most of Africa labeled as "dependencies." In only a year, the imaginary nation has changed from a singular and self-contained place to one instance of a larger political category.

At the same time, *Young India*'s landscape of solidarity leaves out some large territories. Not every "oppressed people" makes it into the club. The article cited above on "Indians in British East Africa," even while attempting to comprehend colonial rule globally, recognizes only its Indian victims. That article uncritically mentions Indian assistance in the African colonial project, using the fact that "British East Africa owes its very existence to the enterprise and initiative of the Indian settlers" and that "Indians fought in the British army to win for the empire the colonies of Africa" as reasons for better treatment of those settlers.[127] Within the same pages, solidarity vies with expedience. This is particularly true of the objects of the United States' new imperial adventures. Given the periodical's goal of gaining support from the United States, it can hardly risk including its host country in the category of colonizer. Rather, *Young India* cited with unfortunate approval the United States' governance of the Philippine Islands. Losing a valuable chance for anti-colonial solidarity, two 1920 articles praise the administration of those islands in comparison with British rule in India.[128] Similarly, a report on the deportations of about 2,000 undocumented Indian laborers lets the United States off easy for the same strategic reasons. Despite the clear agency of U.S. immigration policy, the article still blames England and flatters the United States: "They are Indian seamen who, tired of their miserable and slavish life on British steamers, where they feel most bitterly the venom of their British masters, deserted their ships and settled in the United States to find some liberty and happiness."[129] These 1920 articles represent the legacy of *Young India*'s postwar decision to accept the United States' neo-imperial role as arbiter of sovereignty.

The periodical's United States milieu and the time in which it appeared together determined the contours of *Young India*'s map of solidarity. Especially in the 1918 and 1919 volumes, *Young India* made frequent use of a Wilsonian vocabulary of sovereignty and self-determination. Its editorials cannily take the terms at face value, proposing not to alter them in any way but merely to universalize them. One of Lajpat Rai's longer pieces illustrates that process. Lajpat Rai gave "The New Internationalism" as a lecture for the Conference of Radical, Socialist and Labor Organizations. The lecture works carefully to do one thing only: namely, to standardize the meaning of the word "democracy." Lajpat Rai begins by introducing a word that has been emptied of meaning. He shows this in several ways: by placing "democracy" in quotation marks, by referring to "the so-called democracies of Europe," and by mentioning Germany's claims to democracy. However, Rai continues, the word is not without relevance. Despite the ironic introduction, he claims to believe in what it could ideally mean. The utopian concept of "real democracy" will come about only when no nation impinges on the rights of another to democracy—or, as Rai himself put it, "the truth that 'democracy at home cannot be safe without democracy abroad' is to my mind the perfection and the completion of the idea of democracy."[130] In short, Rai defines the titular "internationalism" as transferability of a word's meaning, or standardization of terms. If Hemingway in A Farewell to Arms shows words like "honor" and "courage" to be empty, Lajpat Rai's internationalism will restore their ability to signify. His utopia, here, is a place where words like "democracy" mean exactly what they were intended to mean.

Lajpat Rai goes on to develop a hierarchy of how closely various democracies have conformed to his ideal. Russia has come the closest, he claims, with Trotsky's liberation of Persia "a great step towards real world democracy."[131] Trotsky exemplifies a new brand of Eastern democracy, Rai explains in classically Orientalist terms. He is "a man who is more of the East than of the West. The other democracies of Europe were material. The democracy of Russia is spiritual. The former were narrow, selfish, national; the latter is broad, unselfish, international. . . . So far all spiritual light has come from the East, and it was in the fitness of things that this new light should also come from the East."[132] Though claiming it as indigenous to Asia, Rai hopes that the West will imitate this new model of internationalist democracy. Even in a moment of chauvinistic triumph, he imagines that the perfect democracy will look the same around the world. The triumph of anti-colonial nationalism will give flesh to "democracy," as yet a term that can only be used ironically. By following the lead of Asia, the world may find an empty concept restored to meaning. Again, of course, there is no mention of the United States' own failure to live up to the ideals of democracy; the new internationalism will simply make America even more American. Support of anti-colonial movements will revitalize democracy.

Toward its American readers, Young India attempts to elicit an involuntary response of identification. The assumptions are that Americans comprehend and encourage the desire for freedom, and that Indian nationalism's goal is precisely what America has already achieved. All that stands in the way of solidarity, then, is a lack of knowledge. That knowledge having been provided—by *Young India,* of course—the younger imperial power will simply rise as a body to assist the cause. In the language of *Young India's* reporting, the process is a natural and inevitable one. Here, one American sympathizer voices Lajpat Rai's idealized theory of solidarity: "It is wholly a question of education as to awakening American sympathy with India, in her struggle for freedom. We love liberty, justice and fair play, and so long as you present the facts as they are, in the temperate way that you do, you can't fail to enlist American sympathy."[133] This quote, from the secretary of the India Home Rule League of America's Rochester branch, comes as part of a report on IHRLA branches outside New York City. Remarkably, not only Rochester but Philadelphia, Louisville, Indianapolis, Columbus, and Cleveland all had branches, due in part to the efforts of N. S. Hardiker. With Lajpat Rai stationed in New York, Hardiker operated as a sort of satellite, bringing India around the country in person. The intrepid Hardiker lectured in twenty-five cities over three months, opening ten new branches of the IHRLA as he traveled. As *Young India* put it, "the object of his trip was to disseminate knowledge about the true political and economic condition of India."[134] His content is purely descriptive, and his goals, like *Young India's,* ideologically clean. Hardiker's lecture tour, the new cross-country IHRLA branches, and *Young India* itself work together to give India a presence within the United States. Indeed, many of *Young India's* U.S.-specific writings serve to situate the periodical within a landscape of institutions, with the ultimate hope of making it, as well as the nation it represented, more real.

Upon Lajpat Rai's departure at the end of 1919, *Young India's* editorship passed to the Unitarian minister and loyal India Home Rule League member Jabez Thomas Sunderland. Under his brief tenure, the periodical spent even more time developing solidarity ties. A Civil War veteran and shepherd of a radical church with strong abolitionist ties, Sunderland had been advocating for Indian Home Rule ever since he visited India as a missionary. Once he assumed the helm of *Young India,* the periodical began to move slowly but decisively past Lajpat Rai. January's opening editorial "Mr. Lajpat Rai Sails" (largely an extended account of his visa woes) and February's special Lajpat Rai issue gave way to ten more months of a periodical that focused far more strongly on various kinds of internationalism, especially of the feminist and socialist varieties. It is in this final volume that the poetry of Amy Dudley and Gertrude Boyle appeared, along with the report on the international meeting for women's suffrage, all discussed above in the previous section on Sarojini Naidu and the "women movements." Further, the 1920 *Young India* paid far more attention to socialism as a force for positive social change.

The periodical's early record on socialism is an uneven one. Lajpat Rai did organize the India Worker's Union of America, with night classes in English taught by the indefatigable Agnes Smedley, but he also avoided openly allying the India Home Rule League of America with any more organized labor movement.[135] This was a philosophical as well as a strategic decision. He wished to appeal to as broad a range of his American readers as possible; and like many other nationalist leaders, he had found only limited assistance from European socialism. English socialists in particular, with the exception of Lajpat Rai's close Fabian friends the Webbs, had often been openly hostile. Hoping that international socialism would prove more amenable to the anti-colonial cause, the Indian delegations to the International Socialist Congresses in the first decades of the century had met with little support. In *Young India*, that complicated history comes across in the form of constant hedging on Lajpat Rai's part. For example, the Conference of Radical, Socialist and Labor Organizations heard his explicit endorsement of Trotsky in his "New Internationalism" lecture quoted above; but *Young India* subscribers also saw an addendum rescinding that endorsement and replacing it with "appreciation."[136] Similarly, the report on Hardiker's Midwest publicity tour cannily avoids any appearance of affiliation: "With a desire to reach as large audiences as was possible, he accepted invitations from a great variety of organizations in this country. But, in so doing, he made it clearly understood that he did not belong to and had nothing to do with any American political party or organization and that he was speaking on behalf of India only."[137] That shrewd qualification in effect identifies socialism as American and anti-colonialism as Indian, implying that the twain have not already met. Such a characterization entirely disavows the American and Indian socialism of M. N. Roy and the Ghadar Party, drawing a false distinction for expediency's sake.

By May of 1920, Sunderland had completely surpassed Lajpat Rai's qualified alliance with the U.S. labor movement. In that month alone, *Young India* ran two pieces entitled "Workers in India: Greetings from America" and "American Labor and India," a third by a U.S. Labor Party functionary, and a fourth proclaiming that "collective ownership, by the workers, is the next stage in the process of liberation."[138] All four assert that worker solidarity will bring freedom both for India and for American labor. Scott Nearing, a regular in anti-war, vegetarian, Chautauqua, and socialist circles, used his article "America and India" to intervene in the specific type of future that India ought to work toward: "You are striving, today, as we did two centuries ago, for political liberty. Beware that, in securing it, you do not fasten upon yourselves economic slavery. Look to Russia! Study her experiments closely, for her people are striving to win political and economic self-government together. Upon your village life, as upon her village life, you may build the structure of a wholly new society."[139] In other words, India's only hope now is to follow the exact path of the Bolshevik revolution. Similarly, "Workers in India" ends with a solidarity message, but a fairly prescriptive one: "I am sure that if there is anything that the Labor Party of the United States can do to help India get freedom, it will do it cheerfully. . . . It hopes the workers of India will organize swiftly into labor unions and into a Labor Party."[140] Where Lajpat Rai's *Young India* only rarely described India's future in concrete terms, Sunderland's now does so multiple times within the same issue, portraying that future as identical to American labor's own fantasy. As opposed to Edward Bellamy's blanket condemnation of anarchism in *Looking Backward,* here we have a further reminder of the equivocal quality of *Young India*'s utopia.

With that May 1920 issue, Sunderland's *Young India* had begun making India over in the image of American labor. During that same year, the new editor initiated a new feature in the periodical that identified India with America even more strongly. Throughout the 1920 volume a collage of poems and quotes, some composed for that purpose and others pilfered from unexpected sources, form the two nations into equivalents. As we have already seen, from its outset the periodical made literature a central focal point. Under Lajpat Rai, though, the literary offerings were exclusively from Indian authors like Tagore, Naidu, and Iqbal. Their poems, as well as Coomaraswamy's critical pieces, came in service to *Young India*'s mission of revisionist representation. Though many of them—like the Iqbal poem translated by Coomaraswamy and Rai, as well as the three Tagore selections reprinted from *The Modern Review*—had overt political content, each also appeared as part of the category of Indian culture. The poetical selections in

Sunderland's *Young India* work very differently. These are expressions of solidarity, both genuine and imposed, by American poets past and present.

One of the new odes of solidarity, composed for *Young India*, is Mayce
Seymour's earnest "To Lajpat Rai." The poem appears across from a portrait
of a solemn and turbaned Rai at the opening of *Young India*'s February 1920
issue. Despite the visual accompaniment, Rai only enters the poem through
a general reference to the "seekers of freedom" who "come and come," presumably to America, to restore to the jaded ex-colony its original passion for
liberty. Seymour's poem serves primarily to remind its readers that America
can only sustain its own utopian values by assisting those who seek to apply
them elsewhere. She does so by making a parallel between the settlers of the
Great Migration and current seekers of self-determination elsewhere:

> They were brave hearts who crossed on exile path
> The wintry seas, long centuries ago,
> To seek asylum for their liberties.
> Their day is past; yet still, lest we lose
> Our vision and our quest, they come and come,
> Seekers of freedom, followers of the gleam.[141]

According to the logic of the poem, the new seekers come solely with the
purpose of renewing America's values. Whatever their real motivation, they
arrive in the poem as a response to the possibility that "we"—presumably,
Young India's American audience—may "lose/our vision and our quest."
Like Lajpat Rai in his "New Internationalism" address, Seymour offers
Americans an incentive for supporting Indian independence. But while
Lajpat Rai invented a superior Eastern democracy that the world has not yet
seen, Seymour includes no such sense of difference or innovation. Rather,
the new seekers ought simply to follow the path of those who went before.
Gone is Rai's affirmative Orientalism, into an iterative haze of assimilation.

The other Sunderland-selected poems even more explicitly force India
into the mold of American patriotism. In choosing poets to reprint, the
Unitarian and Civil War veteran gravitated naturally toward the bards of New
England abolitionism. Accordingly, the poets John Pierpont and James
Russell Lowell appear on behalf of India in the last few issues. Neither had
lived to see the start of the twentieth century; unlike Seymour and Boyle,
who contributed original compositions to *Young India*, these poets had no
choice but to endorse India's goal of independence through their appropriated

words. Pierpont, like Sunderland, was a Unitarian minister and social reformer (but also uncle to J. P. Morgan). His poem appears in the October 1920 issue of *Young India,* under the heading "What Does India Want?" The answer is simply the three couplets that make up Pierpont's "A Word from a Petitioner," first published in 1843 as part of his collection *Anti-Slavery Poems.* By way of introduction to the poem, Sunderland writes that Pierpont "has answered exactly" the title question. According to Sunderland,

> India wants:
> 'A weapon that comes down as still
> As snowflakes fall upon the sod,
> But executes a freeman's will
> As lightning does the will of God
> And from its force nor doors nor locks
> Can shield you—*'tis the ballot-box.'* [142]

Sunderland erases difference of time and circumstance to allow an American radical of the previous century to speak for India. Further, while nowhere in the rest of *Young India* had India's precise method of representation been specified, Sunderland now presupposes that the future state will be an electoral democracy. Setting aside that presumption, as well as the incongruity of a monotheistic God, it seems to pose no problem to Sunderland that the vast majority of the nation Pierpont posthumously speaks for has never seen "snowflakes fall upon the sod." Sunderland here extends Lajpat Rai's technique, in "The New Internationalism" and elsewhere, of defining transnationalism as the standardization of meaning. Lajpat Rai, in his lecture, sought to standardize the meaning of "democracy" across geographical distance and in different contexts. Similarly, Hardiker's trip presented pure facts in order to elicit an involuntary identification. In both cases, the key to solidarity is equivalence, whether of language or of facts. Here, too, Sunderland insists that the meaning of poems can be standardized: Pierpont's "Word from a Petitioner" can mean the same thing to India in 1920 that it did for America in 1847. Given the poem's specificity, though, Sunderland's attempts at consistency now appear so labored as to be absurd.

Two months later, in *Young India's* final issue of December 1920, Sunderland offers a James Russell Lowell poem, again as an answer to a question posed by the editor himself. Under the heading "Why America Should Sympathize," Sunderland writes: "Does any one ask why America should sympathize with India's struggle for freedom? Here is the answer."[143] Whereas Sunderland enlisted Pierpont to ventriloquize India's desires, he uses Lowell to create sympathy. In order to do so, he reprints two out of Lowell's "Stanzas on Freedom," also published in 1843. Like so much abolitionist literature, the poem originally intended to remind white Americans of slaves' humanity, and to draw a connection between physical and spiritual bondage. "If there be on earth a slave,/Are ye truly free and brave?" Lowell asks rhetorically. Through Lowell, Sunderland reinforces Lajpat Rai's and Mayce Seymour's contention that America will benefit if its own values achieve universal application.

Not restricted to poetry for the expression of solidarity, Sunderland also amassed a whole arsenal of quotations that apply either directly or tangentially to India. Several of these ran along with Pierpont's poem in the editorial section of the October 1920 issue. The first four of Sunderland's "Editorial Notes" for that month all use the title "x on India" or "x and India," but offer a whole range of relationships under that same rubric. In the order in which they appeared: "Daniel Webster on India" quotes the secretary of state decrying "the yoke of a foreign power"; "Andrew Carnegie and India" informs the reader of the industrialist's "distrust of the British government [of India] and sympathy with the Indian people in their struggle for freedom"; "Mr. Asquith and India" quotes the former prime minister on the importance of democracy and then accuses him of hypocrisy given democracy's suppression in India; and "Henry George on India" cites a passage from Progress and Poverty, George's 1879 treatise on economic injustice, describing India as "a great estate owned by an absentee and alien landlord."[144] The odd conjunction of the four, each conveying a different relationship between one man and a nation, demonstrates India's incursion into every facet of American life. By now, Sunderland sees India everywhere he looks, and attempts to persuade his readers to do the same.

Sunderland's campaign to identify India with the United States reaches maximum intensity in Young India's final issue, which contains a barrage of quotes from United States patriots of the eighteenth and nineteenth centuries. Unlike the October selection, none of these mention India specifically; rather, they are intended to demonstrate the equivalence of each nation's respective struggles for independence. If Young India of 1920 had been getting more and more American, that tendency culminates in this last issue, with the Lowell poem as well as quotes from Patrick Henry, Whitman, and

Emerson all on its first page. Whitman and Henry address "liberty"; Emerson and Lowell (as we have seen) address "freedom." The keywords for posthumous solidarity have not changed, but the effect of their constant accumulation is new. The dense collection of quotes collapses time, so that India is at once the colony and the slave.

The dominant mode of this entire last year is analogy, a technique that has the effect of erasing historical specificity. Lajpat Rai's original goal was for India to represent itself, to reveal its hidden truth. Transnationalism prevents India from representing itself, for now America's past represents it. When not a ghost from America's past, "India" functions as a metaphor for suffering, a figure for all that must change in order for the world to be right. Within three years, it has come far from being that identifiable and clearly delineated space on the hand-drawn map of January 1918. The imaginary India is now an abstract category characterized no longer by geography or even by race, but by a highly familiar (to American readers) yearning for freedom.

Young India ceased publication after 1920, out of funds following the death of one of its primary supporters, the far-sighted Indian National Congress leader Bal Gangadhar Tilak. (When Sunderland wrote Tilak's obituary, he characteristically balanced the nationally specific opening statement that "India loses one of her best known and most honored sons" with the contention that Tilak belongs "by the side of Mazzini and the leaders of America's struggle for independence."[145]) Its goal of Home Rule may not have been realized, and independence may yet have been a quarter-century away, but a shadow of Lajpat Rai's utopian India remained in the form of the "live centers" he had recommended. Many of *Young India*'s contributors continued to agitate on India's behalf, with Agnes Smedley, Norman Thomas, and Dudley Field Malone organizing Friends of Freedom for India, and J. T. Sunderland writing *India in Bondage: Her Right to Freedom*. Once we sift through the layers of equivocation, what *Young India* ultimately advocated for was something that could be realized even in New York: a reconciliation of nationalism and internationalism, but without a complete dissolution of national borders. This is not a rootless cosmopolitanism but rather, as Vijay Prashad would describe a later phase of radical solidarity, "a vibrant world of internationalism through nationality, in other words, of a *particular universalism*."[146]

Reading the exile periodical within the framework of American utopian fiction allows us to place *Young India* on a continuum between the bordered, racially homogenous turn-of-the-century developmentalist utopias and the loose transnational network of *Dark Princess*. *Young India* elaborates on Gilman's internal critique by accommodating divergent points of view regarding many central elements of anti-colonial planning. Coomaraswamy's cultural nationalism is included, but his nostalgia is toned down to accommodate Lajpat Rai's modernizing impulse. Tagore's anti-nationalism disappears, but his commitment to diversity becomes a guiding principle for the periodical. *Young India* countervenes Tagore's opposition to portraying the nation "in a visible image," but shockingly manages to carry out the resulting personification in a way that does not detract from female empowerment both within anti-colonial nationalism and as feminism per se. Under the tenures of Lajpat Rai and Sunderland, the periodical conveys vastly different pictures of the role of socialism within the global struggle against colonial rule. *Young India* enacts the function of utopian fiction in its use of literary language to negotiate all those divergences within anti-colonial practice. The fact that its imagined community lay so far from an actual India was secondary. As Homi Bhabha writes of Du Bois's novel *Dark Princess*, its apparent internal contradictions alert its readers to "the importance of the 'counterfactual' in the realm of political discourse and the desire for freedom."[147] The concept of the "counterfactual" is equally relevant here. The idealized India of *Young India* does not yet exist by the time of the periodical's demise in 1920—and in fact it never would—yet a community of writers and readers were able temporarily to will it into being.

Once resistance became dominance, and the utopian nation mutated into the postcolonial state, that realized state would differ from *Young India*'s vision in many important ways. Despite an ongoing debate regarding the merits of heavy industry, the craft nostalgia brought in by Coomaraswamy's albeit mediated presence indisputably succumbed by the early 1950s to the force of Nehru's industrializing mission. As Arundhati Roy, among others, has eloquently protested, the emphasis on massive projects like hydroelectric plants and nuclear energy—not to mention nuclear weapons—represents a wholesale betrayal of the village life that Gandhi and Coomaraswamy had identified as India's greatest resource.[148] Further, from the bloodshed of Partition, whose massive trauma was entirely unanticipated within the periodical's rosy picture of interfaith cooperation, to the 2002 massacre of Muslims in Gujarat, independent India would prove far from the comfortably diverse nation represented in the periodical. However, *Young India*'s focus on transnational solidarity, at least, would reappear in India's leader-ship of the Non-Aligned Movement, which I will revisit in my last chapter. Meanwhile, *Young India*'s utopian nation also lived on as an image in American eyes of a modern, resisting entity, varied but unified, with a signif-icant presence on the world stage. That image was crucial to W. E. B. Du Bois as he composed the liberation of the world's colonized peoples in his 1928 novel *Dark Princess*.

3

Worlds of Color

> The black belt of the Congo, the Nile, and the Ganges
> reaches, by way of Guiana, Haiti and Jamaica, like a
> red arrow, into the heart of white America.
> —W. E. B. Du Bois, *Dark Princess*

Though the black literary utopia has yet evaded serious study, African-American utopian fiction enriches our understanding of utopian fiction more generally by departing entirely from the territorial model that prevailed from More to Howells.[1] Two emblematic novels, Pauline Hopkins's *Of One Blood* (serialized in 1902–1903) and W. E. B. Du Bois's *Dark Princess* (published in 1928) oppose the rigidly circumscribed hothouse varieties of chapter 1 by presenting ideal societies predicated on cross-continental contact. Denied a specific territory on which to project their utopian desires, these writers merge their utopian fiction with concurrent notions of internationalism, taking the utopian genre beyond the nation as the goal of the new imagined space. Within their novels a "world of colored folk," to use a phrase that recurs throughout Du Bois's fiction and nonfiction alike, already exists but must grow into consciousness of itself as a unit. Unlike the nationalist, bordered utopias of chapter 1—but like the translational solidarity network proposed in parts of *Young India*—this utopian body is not primarily national but is instead at once local and global. In the case of *Dark Princess*, it is a room in Chicago as well as a worldwide movement; in *Of One Blood*, it is a small underground city whose cultural and scientific achievements will improve all humankind. Besides organizing their utopian geographies non-nationally, thus rejecting a previous utopian model of space, these two differ from the developmentalist fictions of chapter 1 in their reckoning of time as well. Replacing the evolutionary understanding of Bellamy and Gilman is a nostalgic vision that uses a recovered past to create a better future. Decades before the emergence of what Tom Moylan calls the "critical utopia," both of these novels anticipate his definition by portraying a provisional utopia still in conflict or flux—though neither has ever appeared in even the broadest surveys of utopian writing.

Unlike the idealized nation of *Young India*, these utopias confront head-on many of the central qualities that define what I have identified above, in chapter 1, as the developmentalist utopia. *Of One Blood* and *Dark Princess* belong to a utopian tradition that precedes, exceeds, and outlives the Bellamyite school—in large part because it escapes the totalitarian impulses of that canonical strain. This is not to romanticize, on my own part, these romantic utopias: they are subject to many other problems, but narrative and geographical closure are not among them. On the contrary, they derive much of their energy from being both unbounded and unfinished. While Bellamy asks of his readers simply that they sit back and allow a natural and inevitable evolution to take its course, both Hopkins and Du Bois present better futures that are far from assured, and indeed demand reader participation in order to come into being. And far more than Lajpat Rai in *Young India*, with its tentative and qualified gestures toward affirmative Orientalism, both Hopkins and Du Bois use their utopian fictions to resist the constraints of rationality and empiricism.

The story of black utopianism does not begin with Hopkins and Du Bois. Outside the realm of written literature, but within that of cultural expression, is the utopian strain conveyed in generations of plantation songs and stories that often disguise that utopian strain as religious longing for the Promised Land or the New Jerusalem. As Du Bois writes in *The Souls of Black Folk*, "through all the sorrow of the Sorrow Songs there breathes a hope—a faith in the ultimate justice of things. The minor cadences of despair change often to triumph and calm confidence."[2] One certainly perceives that dialectic of tragedy and hope in Martin Delaney's unfinished novel *Blake* (1861–62), the story of an intricately planned and massive-scale slave rebellion based in Cuba, and in Sutton Griggs's *Imperium in Imperio* (1899), which depicts a secret society within the United States. However, my investigation of the African-American literary utopia begins in 1903, the year that saw the publication of both *Souls* and *Of One Blood*. My interest is in the romantic utopias that situate themselves directly in response to Booker T. Washington's accommodationist philosophy—which, in turn, I see as conceptually allied to Edward Bellamy's utilitarian utopia. Hopkins and Du Bois oppose Washington's literary realism as well as his political realpolitik. Refusing to cast their buckets where they are, Hopkins and Du Bois instead partake in a wider internationalism then emerging in response to colonial rule. As such, both authors oppose the race supremacy and teleological developmentalism envisioned in the utopian novels of Edward Bellamy and Charlotte Perkins Gilman.

Though this chapter centers on *Dark Princess*, I will begin with the earlier work of Pauline Hopkins, the pioneering novelist who shares Du Bois's messianic utopianism as well as his desire to represent an undocumented world "within the Veil." Both Hopkins's and Du Bois's novels reacted against the dominant view of what colored Americans should want, a view encapsulated largely by that giant among spokesmen Booker T. Washington. Between his Atlanta Exposition address of 1895 and the publication in 1903 of Du Bois's *Souls of Black Folk*, Washington alone set the terms for Southern black education and the Northern white philanthropy that supported it. He shared the palliative approach of *Looking Backward*; like Bellamy, he located hope in a future defined by industrial progress and material prosperity. Washington's institutional autobiography *Up from Slavery* describes the Tuskegee student body in terms reminiscent of those used by Bellamy for his "industrial army," the backbone of the utopian state.[3]

But Washington is no utopian, despite his lingering attention to ideal spaces like the Hampton Institute. As he so frequently insists, he is a realist; indeed, not only his politics but his narrative style accords neatly with literary realism's aesthetic of limitation. Introducing his method in *Up from Slavery*, he is as dismissive of romance as James or Howells could ever be, announcing with vociferous modesty that "I have tried to tell a simple, straightforward story, with no attempts at embellishment" (xxv). Such a technique is far from simple. Many recent critics have shown how the realist novel, like Washington's nonfiction writing, restructures reality rather than objectively representing it. Amy Kaplan sums up the work of her poststructuralist generation when she describes in her introduction to *The Social*

Construction of American Realism how "from an objective reflection of contemporary social life, realism has become a fictional conceit, or deceit, packaging and naturalizing an official version of the ordinary. . . . from a progressive force exposing the condition of industrial society, realism has turned into a conservative force whose very act of exposure reveals its complicity with structures of power."[4] According to this new reading, the world of the realist novel is a kind of negative utopia: a closed, fictionalized system whose portrayal ultimately serves to reinforce prevailing conditions of inequality. Realism, with its emphasis on mimesis, sets out a familiar, self-contained world in which language works to foreclose possibility. Upton Sinclair's *The Jungle* may end with the prophetic cry, "Chicago will be ours," but the rest of the novel's three-hundred-odd pages mire their reader in a grim and incapacitating present.

Therefore, in the arena of fiction as opposed to overt politics, it makes sense that the best way to counter Washington would be with romance. Indeed Hopkins and Du Bois's novels experiment with and then reject Washington's pragmatic, utilitarian approach, fighting that approach with spirituality, insanity, or fantasy as the occasion demands. Each continues the nineteenth-century habit, as described by historian Cedric Robinson, of resisting oppressive systems through an "epistemology [that] granted supremacy to metaphysics not the material."[5] In response to Washington's radical materialism, both novelists turn to a romance mode that frees them from the constraints of realism. There is a further parallel between the two: each writer's novelistic career follows a similar course in that both wrote novels taking place exclusively in the United States before moving on to transnational utopias. Therefore, though Hopkins's two early U.S.-based novels, *Contending Forces* and *Hagar's Daughter,* have little utopian content, they are valuable to us as precursors to her international romance *Of One Blood,* just as Du Bois's *Quest of the Silver Fleece* illuminates his purpose in *Dark Princess.*

I. Resurrection: Pauline Hopkins

Pauline E. Hopkins used the novel form, as Du Bois would a decade later, to react against the limitations of realism. Though surveys of American literature invariably group her with Frances E. W. Harper—both women worked

for temperance, and Hopkins wrote an admiring biography of Harper—
Hopkins's vision of uplift is of a different order entirely. The elder writer
Harper's novels and poems, of which *Iola Leroy* is by far the most widely
read, depict impossibly virtuous heroines facing hardship with faith and per-
severance. Almost a literary analogue to Washington, Harper shows her most
fortunate characters moving up gratefully into respectability. *Iola Leroy's*
subtitle, "Shadow Uplifted," exemplifies her irony-free project; in this novel,
uplift can only be a good thing, and never involves the selling of birthrights.[6]
Hopkins, on the other hand, abandons Harper's trajectory of material rise in
favor of a more mystical form of collective improvement. The move from
Harper to Hopkins is one from genteel materialist realism to a spiritualist
mode that demands more than realistic explanations. Like Du Bois in *The
Souls of Black Folk*, Hopkins is less concerned with uplifting shadows than
with representing an unvoiced truth about what lies within those shadows.

Hopkins's best-known work, *Contending Forces*, complicates the uplift
model in many ways. Here, "rise" or "rising" may signify an improvement in
class status, but it might also indicate a slave revolt. Further, the author uses
one particularly mordant pun to remind us that either kind of rise may be
followed by a violent reaction that also qualifies as an ascent. An early chapter
recounting casual dockside conversation points to the conjunction between
kinds of rising. "Thar's been some talk 'bout a risin' among the niggers," one
worker tells another, "and so we jes tuk a few of them an' strun 'em up fer a
eggsample to the res.'"[7] According to the causality outlined here, an uprising
will produce the literal upward motion of hanging. And for a substantial portion of the novel it appears that Tuskegee-style uplift is the only alternative to
the brutal "rise" of lynching. Booker T. Washington finds an adept if fictional
mouthpiece in Dr. Arthur Lewis, who believes "that industrial education and
the exclusion of politics will cure all our race troubles" (124). Opposing Lewis
and thus Washington is Hopkins's independent, self-sufficient, and often
caustic heroine Sappho Clark, who insists that such an approach "will leave
us branded as cowards, not worthy a freeman's respect" (125). Withholding
judgment on her own behalf, Hopkins allows Sappho to demolish Arthur's
claims with no effort at all. "I see. The mess of pottage and the birthright,"
she comments wryly on hearing how Arthur has stayed in the good graces of
Southern whites (126). Hopkins herself refrains from condemning outright
Arthur's compromise; she allows Booker T.'s stand-in a happy and genuinely
useful life, married to Sappho's gentle friend Dora and of course directing a

"large industrial school" in the South (123). The novel's close sees the Lewises living in a pleasant cottage of student-made brick, surrounded by "flowers indigenous to the Southern clime"; Arthur has done well by casting down his bucket where he is (387). Hopkins creates for him a limited but pleasant, perfectly Washingtonian paradise, thus showing that there is room in her fictional world—unlike that of Du Bois—for a well-intentioned accommodationist.

However, in *Contending Forces* there is another kind of rise that proves more meaningful than uplift: the resurrection of Christ. Two life-changing events occur on Easter Sunday, the first being that the resolutely idealistic Will Smith—a Du Bois figure to Lewis's Washington—proposes to Sappho. "O Happy Easter Day!" Hopkins apostrophizes in a portentous one-sentence paragraph (313). Their marriage promises to unite two strains of radical politics, but their affianced bliss is temporary. A buried past and a disavowed child return to torment Sappho, who disappears after Will's wicked rival reveals that she was "ruined" as a young girl. Exactly four years later, Hopkins invents another Easter miracle in the form of the lovers' serendipitous convent-side reunion. For those with faith, rebirth is always possible. Hopkins shows through her plot that she values spiritual uplift over the material variety. *Contending Forces* ultimately forsakes Arthur Lewis, closing instead with the more dramatic episode of Sappho and Will's Easter-morning reunion. Between the mundane scene of vocational domesticity and the sublime romantic miracle, Hopkins offers two happy endings with conflicting political implications. But she predetermines her readers' preference by crafting one of those happy endings to be far more satisfying than the other.

Hopkins's next novel shares none of *Contending Forces'* spiritualized optimism. The 1901–02 serial *Hagar's Daughter* shows, like *Contending Forces* and later *Of One Blood,* how wrongs of the past linger in the present; and once again the past takes the form of secret maternity and severed families. *Hagar's Daughter* undoes the happy endings of *Contending Forces.* Once again Hopkins uses the device of death and rebirth: the daughter of the title, presumed drowned, returns to the story as society darling Jewel Bowen. But in this case, one miraculous rescue is not enough, for the rediscovered Jewel ultimately dies "abroad of Roman fever" in the attempt to escape her tainted origin.[8] After seven prefatory antebellum chapters, most of the story unfolds in 1880s Washington, D.C., alleged to be a site for new starts. "We do not inquire too closely into one's antecedents in Washington, you know; be beautiful and rich and you will be happy here," one anonymous gossip tells another (114). But Hopkins disproves that offhand claim in count-less ways. In fact, material wealth and physical beauty are not enough to exorcise the haunted capital, for plantation secrets inhabit Washington even twenty years later. The nation's capital turns out to be a completely hermetic environment, where every character is unmasked as someone else we met before the war.

In this cursed place, there can be no marriage, regeneration, or produc-tivity unless the injustices of the past are remedied, and ultimately not even then. No part of the United States is exempt, for the same dramas of incest and theft extend even as far as California. "The sin is the nation's," Hopkins concludes bitterly (283). In this landscape, Bellamy's thorough repudiation of the past seems utterly naïve. With *Hagar's Daughter*, Hopkins abandons the idea that there can be a happy ending—even one that depends upon an Easter miracle—within the tainted terrain that is the United States. After this point, the only way for Hopkins to write utopia is to pull her narrative out of the doomed continent. Will anticipates this eventuality when he pro-poses in *Contending Forces* to build a school abroad, earning from Arthur the label of "chimerical and quixotic" (389). After *Hagar's Daughter*, such imprac-ticality becomes for Hopkins an absolute necessity.

Contending Forces derives its romantic messianism from the tropes of Christianity; with *Of One Blood*, Hopkins would employ the discourse of Ethiopianism toward the same end. That novel, published in the same year as *The Souls of Black Folk*, shapes protagonist Reuel Briggs into a new Jesus who rises from the dead to lead an ancient African empire. Hopkins brings her fiction abroad to escape the confines of American realism and its accom-panying politics of compromise. *Of One Blood* carries its U.S.-born hero to Ethiopia's Hidden City, a romantic realization of the imaginary "someplace way off in de ocean where de black man is in power" that Janie's skeptical grandmother would later deride in Zora Neale Hurston's 1937 novel *Their Eyes Were Watching God*. Only four chapters of the novel's twenty-four take place inside that utopia, but the brief foray is critical. It pulls Reuel out of the morass of rape, incest, and cultural amnesia that defines the United States; it offers an Afrocentric alternative; and it recasts the past as positive. As an antidote to the pain of memory in America, Hopkins invents an ideal society that derives all its greatness from ancient tradition. According to Hopkins's premise, the glories of the past will rise again. In suggesting a new order, she employs not only Africa, but more specifically a living African past. Without that ancient and enduring heritage, there can be no way to move forward into a generative future.

Of One Blood has two main stories, which may appear not to cohere but in fact comment sharply upon each other. The hero, Reuel Briggs, leads the life of an independent white Bostonian until, like Sappho Clark and every *Hagar's Daughter* character, he finds himself haunted by his hideous Southern past. In Reuel's case, that history consists of a mother born to plantation concubinage; once it inevitably catches up with him, he joins an archaeological expedition to Meroe, Ethiopia. There he discovers not only that a magnificent and scientifically advanced civilization exists, but that he is its appointed heir. This cursory summary glosses over much of the novel's action, for— unlike the often prosaic utopian novels discussed in chapter 1—this one cannot be condensed in fewer than several tortured pages. A utopian novel on a classical prototype, after all, is far less likely to inform its hero that his wife "is your own sister, the half-sister of [villain] Aubrey Livingston, who is your half-brother."[9] Such is the legacy of slavery—though in fact Bellamy too made use of an implausible, incestuous resolution. Hopkins's serpentine story employs still more of the trappings of melodrama: amnesia, racial passing, mesmeric trance, international conspiracy, incest, and even a late revelation of babies switched at birth. As such it echoes *Contending Forces* and *Hagar's Daughter* in presenting the American past as a stifling, incestuous, degenerative force that utterly disallows productivity. Before escaping to Africa, Reuel marries his amnesiac and thus inadvertently passing sister, who like him is the child of parents who were half-siblings. Like *Hagar's Daughter, Of One Blood* recasts the liberal fantasy of universal brotherhood as universal incest; while Frances Harper's doggedly optimistic *Iola Leroy* fortuitously reunites lost family members, Hopkins's novels reveal apparent strangers unfortunately to be family members who, far from being lamented, were never acquainted in the first place. The United States, and especially the American South, appear here as places of repressive and still-present endogamy to an absurd degree. The novel's two plots, the American and the utopian, may frequently seem mismatched; but their coexistence in the same book shows how ancient glory has degenerated under the system of slavery "in this new continent," and why utopia is thus so necessary.

Our first indication that Hopkins will seriously challenge the values of her predecessor Frances Harper is her choice of protagonist. Like Matthew

Towns, the hero of Du Bois's *Dark Princess*, Reuel Briggs is a medical student who is spiritually sick. The noble doctors and nurses who grace Harper's uplift novels are uncomplicated saints, upwardly mobile healers who will cure their race through their skills as well as their social prestige. Lonely and isolated, passing for white, possessed by "morbid thoughts" like "Is suicide wrong?," Reuel stands in sharp contrast with those hale and hardworking professionals (441). His fruitless and frustrating quest is for a science that will reconcile body, mind, and spirit.

Accordingly, the novel's first form of utopianism is epistemological. Since he has found empirical science inadequate to explain all his fevered questions, Reuel experiments with other kinds of knowledge, thus allowing Hopkins to tap into the utopian legacy of spiritualism and especially Mesmerism. Ever since 1784, when a French Royal Commission discredited Anton Mesmer's theory of animal magnetism, the new doctrine that Mesmer intended to establish as a legitimate science instead "lived an underground existence" as an occult practice whose rhetoric of universal brotherhood united "all classes of society from aristocrats and statesmen to prostitutes and paupers," as well as future revolutionaries like the Girondists.[10] Crossing the Atlantic in the nineteenth century, Mesmerism shared its utopian outlook with several nascent American reform movements. Nathaniel Hawthorne's humbug Professor Westervelt from *The Blithedale Romance* draws on that affiliation when he disingenuously evokes "a new era that was dawning upon the world; an era that would link soul to soul, and the present life to what we call futurity, with a closeness that should finally convert both worlds into one great, mutually conscious brotherhood."[11] Hawthorne uses Westervelt primarily to parody phony spiritualism, but the professor's hyperbolic language also documents the connection between Mesmerism and movements for radical democracy. In portraying Reuel's experiments in supernatural phenomena, and later in writing of the modern world as "stiff-necked, haughty, no conscience but that of intellect, awed not by God's laws, worshipping Mammon, sensual, unbelieving," Hopkins allies herself with an anti-materialist corpus that stretches from Mesmer, Mary Baker Eddy, and Madame Blavatsky up to Du Bois (558).

Mesmerism supplies Reuel with an alternative way of thinking but not of living: as a creed it is anti-establishment but not fully utopian in that it lacks a geographical base and a social structure. Such a full-blown utopia Hopkins will provide only at the end of the novel. To get there, Reuel must learn to see differently, and thus to recognize Africa's importance to the world's past and future. In other words, he must undergo a parallel process of defamiliarization to that which Bellamy subjects Julian West in *Looking Backward*—though in this case it is a process of racial, rather than class, reeducation. For despite Reuel's apparent commitment to a new kind of knowledge, his Anglo-American education has left its predictable legacy of racial self-hate. Before leaving for Ethiopia, he calls it "that dark and unknown country to which Fate has doomed me" (496). Arriving near the ancient city of Meroe, he still believes Africa to be a continent devoid of progress. "His healthy American organization," Hopkins narrates wryly, "missed the march of progress attested by the sound of hammers on unfinished buildings that told of a busy future and cosy modern homeliness. Here there was no future . . . Nothing but the monotony of past centuries dead and forgotten save by a few learned savants." (526) From Hopkins's previous novels and even from her portrayal of Reuel's predicament in this one, we know that "march of progress" to be a lie. Both *Hagar's Daughter* and the American chapters in *Of One Blood* are utterly devoid of "busy future" and "cosy modern homeliness." The novelist knows, and the reader can guess, what Reuel is not ready to see: namely, that those "past centuries dead and forgotten" will in fact provide the basis for a more worthy modernity.

To understand that himself, Reuel must pass out of the realm of empirical observation, a mode he has been fighting all along but has not yet fully foresworn. After months of collecting data both in Boston and in Meroe, he finally walks out from his encampment one night not to fulfill any of his academic tasks but "to lose himself in the pyramids" (542). He does in effect get rid of the rational self that had prevented him from understanding Africa's power: losing consciousness on the walk, he wakes up in Telassar, the cloistered settlement housing all the descendents of Meroe. His first sight of the "Hidden City" demonstrates the change in perspective that utopia both necessitates and reinforces. As Reuel awakens to the sight of Telassar's great hall, "Gone were all evidences of ruin and decay, and in their place was bewildering beauty that filled him with dazzling awe" (545). Once "evidence" is gone, he moves quickly to bewilderment and awe; to comprehend utopia, Hopkins suggests, we must abandon reason. Indeed, Meroe's inhabitants are even "more unreal than the vast chamber," which has already itself been characterized by "a touch of fairyland" (545). This is the realm of the counterfactual, rendered in careful physical detail.

Once Reuel has accepted the existence of fairyland, he finds a place that is in fact very materially present. Hopkins's brief utopian section features many conventions common to the turn-of-the-century utopian novel: the individual male utopian host; the host's habit of calling our protagonist "the stranger"; the tour of public works; and the host's amusement at the stranger's "ill-concealed amazement" at the grandeur of all he sees (548). Just as the strangers of Bellamy, Morris, Howells, and Gilman receive new and socially exemplary clothes, Reuel too wakes to see "that his own clothing has been replaced by silken garments" (548). In fact, as in the earlier utopias, utopian clothes serve to exemplify the unfamiliar society's central values as well as those of the utopian author. Proving Bellamy's cultural conservatism, Julian West notes that "it did not appear that any very startling revolution on men's attire had been among the great changes my host had spoken of, for, barring a few details, my new habiliments did not puzzle me at all" (56). The clothes of Morris's utopians are hand-embroidered and "so handsome that I quite blushed when I got into it," according to the hapless and undeserving narrator (167). Gilman's Herlanders offer their visitors outfits that "were simple in the extreme, and absolutely comfortable" (26). Emphasizing both the opulence of the African past-into-future and also its classical ties, Hopkins creates utopian uniforms of "soft white drapery, Grecian in effect" with "golden clasps and belts" (545, 549).

Despite her aim of defeating empiricism, Hopkins renders the utopia itself in careful detail. Her representation, full of precise detail and romantic language, far more closely resembles that of Morris than that of Bellamy. In describing the "combination of Oriental and ancient luxury" that characterizes Telassar, Hopkins engages not only vision but all the senses:

> Overhead was the tinted glass through which the daylight fell in
> softened glow. In the air was the perfume and lustre of precious
> incense, the flash of azure and gold, the mingling of deep and
> delicate hues, the gorgeousness of waving plants in blossom
> and tall trees—palms, dates, orange, mingled with the gleaming
> statues that shone forth in brilliant contrast to the dark green
> foliage. (548)

Though attuned to spiritual truths, the utopian society has not neglected the construction of substantial monuments. Telassar—as Reuel learns on his obligatory guided tour—is "a city beautiful, built with an outer and inner wall," surrounded by "fertile fields" and complete with the requisite statues, fountains, stately avenue, "splendid square," and "great buildings" including a 12,000-seat temple (550–2, 561). To get to this opulent metropolis, Reuel had to leave the United States, and also had to abandon empiricism. Once having done so, he is rewarded by the new and better place and the new and better knowledge that he sought.

In writing the glorious but unknown Hidden City, Hopkins had the precedent of Sutton Griggs's *Imperium in Imperio*. That labyrinthine 1899 novel depicts the hidden achievement of "a race that dreams of freedom, equality, and empire": a black American shadow government with its own legislature, judiciary, treasury, capitol building near Waco, Texas, and loyal population of 7,250,000.[12] The mission of that secret body, "to secure the freedom of the enslaved negroes the world over," anticipates *Of One Blood* and even more so *Dark Princess* (191). But Griggs, unlike Hopkins, maintains that the New World still holds promise. In response to a white mob attack on a small-town South Carolina postmaster—an incident that Griggs adapted from the 1898 murder of Frazier Baker—the Imperium considers settlement in central Africa.[13] But although "the African Congo Free State . . . could be wrested from Belgium with the greatest ease," the body decides instead to organize and fight for a homeland in Texas (224). Further, the novel's moral center Belton Piedmont dies for his loyalty to an undivided United States. In Hopkins's case, there would be no way to house that shadow government, "well nigh perfect in every part," anywhere in the United States (199). But the two have in common the fantasy of a fully realized state whose discovery restores the psychic completeness of a troubled hero. The Imperium's new president, Bernard Belgrave, learns simultaneously of its existence and of his own supremacy, while Reuel's encounter with his own history emancipates him from inferiority and shame, so that he can become the "king who shall restore to the Ethiopian race its ancient glory" (546–7).

Africa ultimately becomes a place that reconciles material and spiritual knowledge, thus resolving the novel's opening dilemma. Reuel, constantly negotiating the material and spiritual realms, finally finds a science that accounts for both. "What would the professors of Harvard have said to this, he asked himself. In the heart of Africa was a knowledge of a science that all the wealth and learning of modern times could not emulate" (576). His own innate mysticism, within the United States a mark of strangeness and difference, now has both a filial and a geographical dimension as Hopkins

connects "the mystic within him" with "the spirit that had swayed his ancestors" as well as "the shadow of Ethiopia's power" (558). A closeted minority—
cast in spiritual as much as racial terms—has finally reached his proper home.
Hopkins carefully melds Telassar's mysticism with prophetic Christianity; as
in Utopia, the stranger introduces the Bible to the utopian natives, but finds
their belief system already to be perfectly compatible with it.

Despite her use of familiar generic conventions, Hopkins's portrayal of
the Hidden City reveals the vast difference between her view of the past and
that of the developmentalist utopians. Her aim, like that of Young India, is
openly revisionist. Like the periodical, her work represents disputes about the
past while showing the direct relevance of those disputes to present-day power
structures. Of One Blood's main figure for the practice of historiography is the
expedition, whose mission is "to unearth buried cities and treasures which
the shifting sands of the Sahara have buried for centuries" (494) and more
specifically to "establish the primal existence of the Negro as the most ancient
source of all that you value in modern life" (520). Even the novel's treacherous
degenerate aristocrat Aubrey Livingston understands the archaeological
undertaking as a form of race uplift, invoking to Reuel "the good it will do to
the Negro race" (494). We see here how Hopkins departs from a race novel
tradition that stretches from Stowe to Harper and beyond, namely of painting
racism as one character flaw among many. Stowe's good whites are kind to
Negroes, and her villains indiscriminately villainous; Hopkins's universe is
far more complex and unpredictable. The horrible Aubrey can still mouth the
vocabulary of tolerance, while on the other hand the kind and reliable Charlie
Vance responds to the glories of Ethiopia with a shocked "you don't mean to
tell me that all this was done by niggers?" (532). Neither Reuel nor Hopkins
punishes Charlie for this outburst, for he is only vocalizing the mainstream
view that the expedition intends to counter. Outwardly decent people, Hopkins
insists, are still products of a racist society and are marked as such. That mark
shows most clearly, as Charlie Vance demonstrates, in what they believe to be
accepted knowledge. Therein lies the significance of this dig, and its immediate and crucial bearing on the present. Then as now, "in connecting Egypt
with Ethiopia, one meets with most bitter resistance from most modern
scholars" (532).[14] Every member of Reuel's expedition, in other words, understands what is at stake in unearthing the past.

The result of that expedition is not a museum full of preserved, ossi-
fied artifacts, but rather a living archive. Like clothes, museums provide an

exemplary function within utopian (and other) fiction. More specifically, both the artifacts exhibited and the manner in which they are displayed speak directly to the ways in which a given utopian society views the past. In the case of Howells and Zamyatin, museums exemplify and reinforce a prevailing developmentalist ethos by archiving objects that provide a measure of progress through contrast. Howells's Altrurian museum, as discussed in chapter 1, exhibits primitive objects like "Esquimau kyaks," "Thlinkeet totems" and Eveleth's discarded French fashions in order to show how far the civilized nation has come from its anterior states (152). Reflecting anti-utopia's larger purpose of parodying and thus pillorying utopia, Zamyatin's developmentalist museum is a caricature of the one so earnestly presented by Howells. Zamyatin imitates Howells and others with his "Ancient House" museum, a relic of the bygone era of the family (as the narrator explains, "children in those days were also private property" rather than that of the state) that now appears "nonsensical" (26–7). In these developmentalist museums, the past provides a measure of how far we have come.

On the other side of the historiographical spectrum, Hopkins invents what we might call a romantic museum. Like Coomaraswamy both in the Boston Museum and in his *Young India* "Art Section," Hopkins converts the glories of the past into the basis for a better future. What was initially visually uncertain ends up amply documented, in the form of treasure that "rests today in the care of the Society of Geographical Research" in England (540). Both Hopkins and Coomaraswamy indulge their readers in the fantasy that a lost or stolen past may be both documentable and recuperable. This type of museum contains a living heritage that may yet metamorphose into a reborn civilization. If *Contending Forces* indicates the rewards of faith by resurrecting the body of Christ, *Of One Blood* resurrects a whole people's history.

In fact, for all its grandeur, the city of Telassar is only an interim dwelling for the descendents of Meroe as they await the return of their king—who turns out to be none other than Reuel. With his arrival, according to ancient prophecy, Ethiopia's "glory should again dazzle the world" (548). Thus Hopkins's utopianism lies not only in her portrait of a thoroughly realized if limited social system (if *Walden Two* is a utopian novel, this certainly is as well) but also in her prophecy of its future expansion. Renamed King Ergamenes, Reuel will "begin the restoration of Ethiopia" (555). He has a lesser partner in that process, for like Julian West in *Looking Backward*, Reuel becomes a utopian citizen through the vehicle of a willing female body.

Queen Candace had guarded Telassar as it awaited its male heir, with the help of the coterie of virgins who serve as a symbolic compensation for the centuries-long violation of African women in America. Like Edith Leete, Candace is happy to perform a communal service by marrying her strange-yet-familiar outsider. As in *Looking Backward,* the means of incorporating the stranger is quasi-incestuous—Reuel and Candace bear the same lotus-shaped birthmark indicating royal lineage—though for Reuel, marriage to a distant cousin constitutes a distinct improvement over marriage to his half-sister.

Unlike the completely realized and thus static utopian societies of chapter 1, this one is not fully realized but immanent, with the underground state providing the seat for millenarian expansion. Despite Hopkins's rhetoric of pure bloodlines, the new civilization that is produced will be a culturally hybrid one. Reuel improves on the ancient order by "teaching his people all that he has learned in years of contact with modern culture," thus creating a flexible, syncretic utopia (621). For Hopkins, resurrection and resettlement provide the bases for a counterfactual reform agenda that uses utopian romance to oppose the pragmatism and realism of Booker T. Washington. However, not even this dynamic, messianic world kingdom can stop colonialism. From the Hidden City, Reuel worriedly watches "the advance of mighty nations penetrating the dark, mysterious forests of his native land" (621). Here that incursion comes only as an aside, for the drama of the plot has by that point been resolved. Reuel watches the colonial advance while ruling his newfound kingdom, as comfortable in his discovered homeland as Julian West is in his accidental paradise. For Du Bois, on the other hand, colonialism's encroachment is no tangential observation, but rather the central organizing principle of his resistant utopianism. Far from allowing an underground kingdom to coexist with the colonial "advance," his vision demands a halt to that advance.

II. Romance: W. E. B. Du Bois

Like Pauline Hopkins, Du Bois edited a periodical and wrote biographies of great figures in African America. But also like Hopkins, Du Bois made some of his political interventions outside didactic nonfiction. Both writers turned to fiction, and particularly romance, to shape the way they thought the world ought to be. Against the aesthetics and politics of realism, Du Bois's writing continually asserts that the limits of possibility in fact lie outside the known, material world and its mimetic counterpart. Ever since *The Souls of Black Folk*, whose high-flown allegorical language came in quick and decisive response to Washington's eschewing of "ornamental geegaws," Du Bois consistently rejected the model of a closed realist system.

Taken as a whole, Du Bois's oeuvre offers an extended meditation on the nature of hope. *Souls* in particular abounds with examples of dreams disappointed. The passage of time, within the collection, brings about the loss of hope as "the bright ideals of the past" grow "dim and overcast" (6). Du Bois ties this ongoing process of disillusionment to language, showing how portentous words like "emancipation," "freedom" and "book-learning" have gradually lost meaning. "Emancipation," for example, "was the key to a promised land of sweeter beauty than ever stretched before the eyes of wearied Israelites" (4). But by the time Du Bois writes, the children of freed slaves have met more locked doors than that single key could open—and other promises, too, proved empty. The sequence of vision to disappointment, faith to despair, recurs throughout the book. "The ghost of an untrue dream"—a resonant phrase that Du Bois attaches to the city of Atlanta—could just as well apply to any aspect of the group experience he recounts (47). For Du Bois writes history not as what actually was but as what was hoped for, gauging the past through its own sense of futurity. Within these fourteen lyrical chapters, Du Bois's strong utopian urge remains frustrated and objectless. Only through fiction, in *The Quest of the Silver Fleece* and *Dark Princess*, does it find fruition. Only in those novels can his characteristic question "Is it the twilight of nightfall or the flush of some faint-dawning day?" be answered in favor of day (45).

The content of that new day varies according to each individual novel, with hope coming in the vastly divergent forms of first a small rural collective, in *Quest,* and later a global conspiracy of colonized people, in *Dark Princess*. As Hopkins did in *Contending Forces*, Du Bois used *Quest* to explore the possibilities of social betterment in the United States before giving up and moving his fiction abroad. In its broadest plot, the novel does for cotton (the titular "silver fleece") what Frank Norris's unfinished trilogy did for wheat: namely, dramatize the filthy inner workings of the industry. But unlike those bleak naturalist masterworks, *Quest* also conveys a resistant counternarrative. That plotline chronicles the efforts of a young country couple to wrest productivity and collectivism from the dark, sinful underside of slavery. In the aptly named Toomsville, Alabama, hometown girl Zora Cresswell and charismatic outsider Blessed Alwyn unite to create new life. With modest goals and lofty aspirations, the two convert a tiny piece of land into "the beginning of a free community."[15]

Appearing amid that early phase in Du Bois's career when he battled with the Tuskegee machine over the meaning of "the Negro problem," *Quest* bears easily legible marks of that legendary rivalry. Du Bois shows how Booker T. Washington's proscribed goals have come to dominate the terms of white philanthropy. In the words of wealthy, bored Mrs. Vanderpool, Negro education should consist of lessons in "how to handle a hoe and to sew and cook" (59–60). She answers the query "And culture and work?" with the wholesale judgment "Quite incompatible, I assure you" (60). Rather than summarily dismissing Booker T.'s demeaning vocationalism, Du Bois allows it free rein for a good portion of the novel. In a canny geographical pun, Du Bois sends his rural characters to Washington, D.C., to learn how Washingtonianism describes at once the Great Accommodator's philosophy of compromise and also the chosen way of the nation's capital. As it had for Hopkins in *Hagar's Daughter,* Washington serves as metonym for the sin of the nation. There, the cynical wheeler-dealer Caroline Wynn, exemplar of the capital, echoes Mrs. Vanderpool when she mentions with approval the prevailing "theory that all that Southern Negroes needed was to learn how to make good servants and lay brick" (279).

The pragmatism of both Washingtons, Du Bois admits through his plot structure, holds genuine appeal. He allows his characters to inhabit the world of compromise for over a hundred pages, an almost freestanding "realist" section that has a precise analogue in *Dark Princess.* After falling in love with Zora, Bles repeats the mistake made by Will in *Contending Forces* when he too abandons his chosen mate upon learning of her secret past as a coerced prostitute. He goes, of course, to Washington, where he finds a new and diametrically opposed muse and mentor in Caroline Wynn who, seeing limitless upwardly mobile potential, attempts to make him over into a phony, constituency-free "Negro leader" (269). Meanwhile, heartbroken Zora has found work as a lady's maid for Mrs. Vanderpool, of all people. The year and a half of corrupt, worldly wanderings ends only when Zora revives her utopian dream by determining to buy the swamp where she grew up. Her return to Toomsville is marked by a perfectly Du Boisian ambiguity as to whether she is heading to success or doom. She gets off the train in "ghostly morning light" (333), while the good teacher Miss Smith sits "in fatal resignation, awaiting the coming day" (334). As in *Souls,* a glimmer of light may indicate the beginning or the end of hope. Even with no guarantee of success, Du Bois's heroines choose faith.

Opposing the prevailing and alluring current of cynicism and compromise is a stubborn idealism that often appears quixotic or even insane. An early debate between ethereal Zora and skeptical Bles sets up the novel's central opposition. To Bles's fear that "dreams ain't—nothing," Zora swiftly responds "Oh yes, they is! . . . There ain't nothing but dreams" (19). Zora's guiding philosophy is a radical anti-materialism. White people "don't really rule; they just thinks they rule. They just got things,—heavy, dead things. We black folks is got the spirit," she explains to Bles (46). Tutored by Zora, Bles begins to value "spirit" over "things." He acquires the ability to see the world not as it is but as it should be: in short, as a utopian. As Caroline tells him: "You are so delightfully primitive; you will not use the world as it is but insist on acting as if it were something else" (279). According to this sequence, to be "primitive" is to reject the conditions imposed by modernity, a rejection that Du Bois represents as both wise and also productive. Bles and Zora's refusal to "use the world as it is" ultimately produces a paradigm of collectivist self-determination.

Zora's dream is a bold and ambitious if geographically limited one. She chooses to locate her utopia in the very heart of the neo-plantation system: a swamp of "crawling slime" where her grandmother runs a whorehouse catering to white aristocrats, thus perpetuating slavery relations in the sexual as well as economic arena (203). It was there that Zora herself had been raped as a young girl. Yet it is she who recognizes the blighted old swamp as "the place of dreams," in the words of Du Bois's chapter title, or in her own formulation "where the Dreams lives" (78). Especially in contrast with the neutral tones of the Washington chapters, Du Bois's language here is outrageously romantic. To clear the swamp, which Zora and Bles do together, is to brave "the yawning gates of hell" (93). When Zora sees the first harvest of cotton, "These new-born green things hidden far down in the swamp, begotten in want and mystery, were to her a living wonderful fairy tale come true. . . . They were her dream-children . . . they were her Hope" (125). It is in response to the infant seedlings that she articulates her own Morrisian philosophy of culture and production—"Everything ought to have the chance to become beautiful and useful"—in direct opposition to the earlier judgment of "culture and work" as "quite incompatible" (127).

In contrast with Bellamy's developmentalism, there is a heavy spiritual component here. The novel's corrupt, worldly middle section ends as soon as Zora sets foot in a church (293), and it is in a different church that she first spreads the idea of collectively buying the swamp (369). After these turning points, her vision steadily gains in clarity and structure. To the initial plan for a farm that would support Miss Smith's school, Zora adds a settlement house for orphan girls. The close of the novel sees the utopia still growing, with Bles projecting

> one central plantation of one hundred acres from school. Here
> Miss Zora will carry on her work and the school will run a model
> farm with your help. We want to centre here agencies to make
> life better. We want all sorts of industries; we want a little hospital
> with a resident physician and two or three nurses; we want a
> cooperative store for buying supplies; we want a cotton-gin
> and saw-mill, and in the future other things." (403–4)

In proper utopian fashion, the blueprint includes the near-comprehensive areas of education, health, commerce, agriculture, and industry: in other words, everything except art, which the aesthetically minded Zora will presumably place in the ample category of "other things." Even at this late point, Du Bois shows the two still pushing the limits of the possible with "a proposal a little too daring for them, a bit too far beyond their experience" (405). Unlike those of Bellamy, Morris, Howells, and Gilman, this very provisional utopia is far from facing the threat of stasis, which would indeed be a luxury in comparison with the hard work of establishing the community. Zora recognizes even five pages from the end that "the battle's . . . just begun" (430). Such an admission would never be made in a classical utopian novel, but would later dominate the outlook of the "critical utopias" of the 1960s and 1970s.[16]

Du Bois prevents his readers from knowing the outcome of Zora and Bles's daring cooperative venture. Even if completely successful, it will never be more than a cooperative settlement on a miniscule scale—which is why Du Bois must follow Hopkins in moving abroad for his next venture into quasi-utopian fiction. In fact, though limited to the American South, *Quest* already anticipates *Dark Princess*'s transnational romance in some ways.

The need for solidarity among people of color emerges as part of Du Bois's persistent critique of Washington. At a posh New York dinner party, Northern and Southern white elites unite in rejecting academic education for Negroes. On the point that the colored races should be educated only as far as their limited capacity would allow, "the Englishman, instancing India, became quite eloquent" (149). Here Du Bois introduces a topic—the analogy between various experiences of colonial and quasi-colonial oppression—that he wisely does not develop within this novel, but will revisit in *Dark Princess*. In the same way, one description of Zora shows her to be a precursor to Kautilya. Standing amid her flourishing field of cotton, the lovely Alabaman looks "ethereal, splendid, like some tall, dark, and gorgeous flower of the storied East" (157). If American blacks and Raj-ruled Indians suffer parallel problems, their solutions are also parallel: both groups can fight racist pragmatism with exotic, mythic beauty.[17] Further, in both cases Du Bois implicitly incorporates aesthetic reform into his utopian project, using a preexisting discourse of Oriental romance to assert a nonwhite physical ideal.

The two novels are structurally quite similar in that each has a corrupt, worldly middle section bookended by genuine attempts at different (local or global) forms of utopianism. The Homeric underworld in both cases is the arena of electoral politics, whether in Washington (*Quest*) or Chicago (*Dark Princess*). In each novel's roughest plot, boy meets, loses, and finds again an ideal girl, who ultimately helps him define and carry out what Du Bois in *Dark Princess* would call "world work."[18] Despite that second novel's title, the eponymous princess is only a revolutionary muse for the American protagonist, Matthew Towns. Its opening sees him at a loss for where to put his world-changing energies: the gifted medical student has been barred from a mandatory obstetric rotation by a vindictive Southern dean, a strategic refusal that effectively ended Matthew's career. We already know that he, like Reuel, will not develop into one of Frances Harpers's upstanding medical professionals. On self-imposed exile in Berlin, Matthew meets the beautiful and politically committed Princess Kautilya of Bwodpur, India, and through her a nascent coalition of the world's colored elite. An instant convert, he goes to work for a New York–based Kautilya contact but ends up in Illinois' Joliet State Prison, blamed for an aborted train sabotage that he had in fact averted. That literal captivity gives way to the metaphoric imprisonment that is Matthew's life in the arid and amoral city of Chicago. Just as Caroline Wynn becomes Bles's Washington mentor, the calculating and materialistic Sara Andrews recognizes Matthew's natural charisma, arranges for his release from prison, and grooms him to become another disconnected, manufactured politician. Matthew aimlessly accommodates Sara's plan, which includes a loveless marriage as part of the complete bourgeois-fantasy package, until Kautilya reappears to rescue him from a life bereft of romance and belief. He walks away from both the marriage and the promising political career, cleansing his soul through manual labor and another temporary absence from the Princess. Finally summoned back to his own hometown in Virginia, he learns that Kautilya has given birth to their son, who in a mystical multicultural ceremony becomes "Maharajah of Bwodpur" and "Messiah to all the Darker Worlds" (311). Like Zora and Bles at the end of *Quest,* the two lovers reunite to continue their ongoing struggle for justice, but now with a new generation in tow.

Because Du Bois's fiction has conventionally been read only as an extension of his political thought, it is easy to overlook the formal similarities of his first two novels. Both plot structures reinforce the need to imagine and work toward the impossible. As Nellie McKay points out, the central female characters of *Quest* and *Dark Princess* correspond neatly in that Zora and Kautilya both fill the role of "ideal heroine," opposing Caroline Wynn and Sara Andrews's ambitious, self-centered schemers.[19] We can take McKay's observation further by connecting individual characters to novelistic form. Caroline and Sara represent a politics of limitation, while Zora and Kautilya open intimidating realms of possibility. In both novels, as in *Of One Blood* before them, the better way does not materialize until the very end, but then overwhelms the reader's memory. Once we see utopia, the focus of the whole novel retroactively shifts to lead up to its construction.

However, what Princess Kautilya produces is quite different from the two hundred acres that Zora cultivates in *Quest.* While Du Bois's first novel places its faith in agrarian collectivism, the author of *Dark Princess* takes a cue from Hopkins to locate hope in a "world movement" of "the darker peoples" (16–17). In its lofty and supranational goals, so different from those of Bellamy, Howells, and Morris, the novel also continues to exhibit the negative influence of Booker T. Washington even thirteen years after his death. "I was young when I . . . was sent to Hampton," Matthew remembers. "There I was unhappy. They insisted on making me a farmer" (11). This blunt characterization of the Hampton Institute, Washington's first inspiration for Tuskegee, could not be farther from Washington's own in *Up from Slavery.*

To Washington, Hampton "seemed to me to be the largest and most beautiful building I had ever seen. . . . I was one of the happiest souls on earth."[20] For Matthew and for Du Bois, a vocational institute will not be sufficient as locus of utopian possibility. What this novel envisions instead is even farther from Washington's achievements than anything that Zora dared to imagine in *Quest:* a mystical and expanded global South. It is Kautilya who makes the crucial conceptual leap of combining Africa, Asia, Latin America, and the American South into what she, echoing Du Bois himself, calls "a world of colored folk" (278). "Take your geography and trace it," she writes to Matthew in what is to my mind the novel's most important passage. "From Hampton Roads to Guiana is a world of colored folk, physically beautiful beyond conception; socially enslaved, industrially ruined, spiritually dead, but ready for the breath of Life and Resurrection. South is Latin America, east is Africa, and east of east lies my own Asia" (278). Du Bois's unprecedented technique here lies somewhere between Bellamy's use of real Boston topography in *Looking Backward* and More's wholesale invention of a new island: it consolidates existing but far-flung continents into a metaphoric totality.[21] The result is what Kautilya calls "the black belt of the Congo, the Nile, and the Ganges" (286).

With its portrayal of a consolidated global South, *Dark Princess* offers a prehistory of the region that would come to be known as the Third World. Extrapolating wildly from his experience with the Universal Races Congress of 1911, Du Bois invents a "Great Central Committee of Yellow, Brown and Black" scheming to liberate that aggregated terrain (296). His later work never abandons the solidarity formulation that he allows Kautilya to develop here. It was he who had insisted that the National Association for the Advancement of Colored People be given a name that would afford symbolic inclusion to non-whites globally. As late as 1957 he still wrote of "a world of coloured folk" of whom he had only gradually become aware.[22] Du Bois's fictional use of that "world of colored folk" in his 1928 novel reveals both the immense force and also some of the problems with his global map of solidarity.

For Du Bois, as for Hopkins, the answer to political oppression is a total abandonment of realism. Du Bois uses the genre of romance to argue against a politics of compromise, and he uses an abstracted version of India to anchor that romance. Like Hopkins, he unwrites previous novels at the same time that he writes his own. While Hopkins responds to Frances Harper's call for race uplift through professionalism, Du Bois answers not only Harper (and Washington) but also a whole school of white American realists. Though he shared the political outlook of realist writers Upton Sinclair and Abraham Cahan, his literary affinity belonged far more with H. G. Wells.[23] Both privileged the power of the imagination through speculative fiction (in the widest sense of that term), with the crucial difference that Du Bois's imagination always remained optimistic, while Wells invented profoundly bleak scenarios. As Maurice Lee shows convincingly, Du Bois in *Quest* exhibits a generic double consciousness by combining realism and romance. Pure realism was in that period too pessimistic, Lee argues, and pure romance too invested in national reconciliation at the cost of black humanity; therefore Du Bois merges them into "wonderful fact," a new hybrid genre that incorporates "a realist's eye for social critique" and "a romancer's faith in possibility."[24] But *Dark Princess*, with its subtitle "A Romance," is a very different case. Rather than simply incorporating realism, Du Bois parodies its conventions only to subvert them from within through the tool of utopian romance.[25]

As in *Quest*, Du Bois uses divergent literary styles in each section, presenting Chicago in a hard-realist mode reminiscent of Theodore Dreiser and Upton Sinclair, rendering India in the decadent, otherworldly Orientalism of Baudelaire and other Oriental Renaissance figures, and dreaming of the American South as a hazy agrarian motherland familiar from Harlem Renaissance works like Jean Toomer's *Cane*. The resulting novel tends to cause problems for genre-minded readers. Arnold Rampersad calls it a "queer combination of outright propaganda and Arabian tale, of social realism and quaint romance, " while for Eric Sundquist its divergent modes are "at best awkwardly unified."[26] Du Bois's contemporaries, too, had found the conjunction of plain and elevated language, of politics and romance, of local and international settings, to be unsettling or inappropriate. An alternate view finds such readings inadequate, based as they are on a constricting realist viewpoint. Claudia Tate, in her introduction to the novel's latest edition, holds that "if his critics had judged the novel according to the values of an eroticized revolutionary art instead of the conventions of social realism, they probably would have celebrated *Dark Princess* as a visionary work."[27] Both Tate and Paul Gilroy see the novel, and especially its closing scene of multicultural pageant, as a model for a new black political idealism.[28] Both are right that the novel's shifts in genre are so obvious and pronounced that they must be understood as deliberate, though I would explain those shifts differently. Rampersad attributes them to the tension between secular and sacred; Tate, in *Psychoanalysis and Black Novels,* sees them as demonstrating the incompatibility of social activism and eroticism.[29] But since the shifts in genre coincide with shifts in geography—the novel alternates not only between realist and romantic registers but more specifically between realism in Chicago and romantic millenarianism in the expanded Black Belt—we can read them as showing the difficulties and disjunctures inherent in a global politics of solidarity. Concurrent movements for self-determination, *Dark Princess* shows, mythologize and exploit each other as often as they genuinely empower.

Before we travel to the incipient utopia, it will be helpful to see how meticulously Du Bois crafts the hyper-realist landscape it opposes. Therefore I will begin not with the global South but with its amoral urban foe. Because Du Bois follows the time-honored tradition of equating women with places, we can see the contrast between his realist and romantic sections by looking at two passages on Sara's and Kautilya's clothes. Each example finds the representative female away from home—Kautilya in Berlin and Sara in Washington—but each woman still carries with her the prime characteristics of the territory she embodies. As Sara waits in a Ku Klux Klan office to lobby for Matthew's release, "She had on a new midnight-blue tailor-made frock with close-fitting felt hat to match, gay-cuffed [sic] black kid gloves, gun-metal stockings, and smart black patent leather pumps" (119). This description, crammed with harsh plosives and made up of sharply hyphenated adjectives, few verbs, and not one adverb, gives a prosaic account of the commonplace items that make up Sara's outfit. The sentence's only instance of figurative language—"gun-metal" for gray—is one that connotes violence and inorganicity. Contrasting sharply is our first view of Princess Kautilya, a passage rife with dynamism and mystery even as it conveys the same category of information:

> He could see the faultlessness of her dress. There was a hint of
> something foreign and exotic in her simply draped gown of rich,
> creamlike silken stuff and in the graceful coil of her hand-
> fashioned turban. Her gloves were hung carelessly over her
> arm, and he caught a glimpse of slender-heeled slippers and sheer
> clinging hosiery. There was a flash of jewels on her hands and a
> murmur of beads in half-hidden necklaces. (8)

This is no static portrait but a spectator event, filtered through Matthew's reactions and set out parcel by parcel over time. Soft, drawn-out sibilants dominate its tone. Embedded verb forms like "draped," "hung," "caught a glimpse," and "clinging" bring a sense of motion. Far from identifiable and ordinary materials like felt and kid, Kautilya's clothes are of indeterminate composition: "creamlike silken stuff" that both piques curiosity by denying specification, and also offers a metaphor of nourishment in lieu of Sara's "gun-metal." Other figurative language abounds, in turban's "coil," "flash of jewels," and "murmur of beads." Necklaces are "half-hidden"; mystery remains. As we will see, Du Bois infuses all the passages treating both India and the conceptualized global South with that same ambience of elusiveness and possibility.

With the two sartorial descriptions above as guideposts, we may enter Sara's Midwestern milieu. The novel consists of four sections, each named after Matthew's current profession (or, in the case of "The Maharajah of Bwodpur," that of his son) and each associated through an original epigraph with a season. Even though Part III, "The Chicago Politician," spans more than two years, Du Bois firmly ties those years to "*Winter. Winter, jail and death. . . . Dirt and frost, slush and diamonds, amid the roar of winter in Chicago*" (109). The 100-page section occurs almost exclusively in that city; taken by itself, it reads on the multiple levels of topic, plot structure, references, and language as a prototypical turn-of-the-century realist novel. The main topic of this section is a perennial realist one: an individual's inauguration into the politics of compromise. Du Bois organizes his version of that story into a recognizable Chicago-realist form: as in Dreiser's *Sister Carrie*, one character's economic and social rise both causes and intersects with another character's fall, each mapped in a neat trajectory. Upton Sinclair receives tribute as well: when blacklisted from all contracting jobs, a desperate Matthew looks for work in the stinking stockyards made familiar in *The Jungle* (281). Finally, the writing itself, as we have seen from the stark but detailed description of Sara's outfit, embraces the mundane minutiae of urban existence: street numbers, ward numbers, bus routes, and weekly salaries.

Indeed, Du Bois's research trail shows verisimilitude to have been a priority in this Chicago section, especially in contrast with his passages on India. Striving for utmost accuracy in matters like local politics, neighborhood demographics, and even Matthew's prison number, Du Bois sent out no fewer than fifteen letters to contacts in Chicago. Even after sending

Dark Princess to his publisher, Du Bois wrote four more letters pertaining to the Chicago section. Three inquired into "the Negroes in Chicago politics" and the superpower project that Sara forces Matthew to support. The fourth aims to pin down Sara's purchasing habits by asking

> If a colored person of wealth was going to buy some new furniture
> and have the interior of their new apartment decorated, what
> chance in Chicago would they have to do the work? This
> information is for my novel and I want it right away. I want the
> lady to say that she has consulted this firm about her furniture and
> that firm about interior decorations.[30]

Though no reply survives, one presumably arrived, for the corrected version of *Dark Princess* has Sara telling fiancé Matthew proudly that "I've been up to Tobey's to select the furniture, and Marshall Field is doing the decorating" (139). Such a comment follows the well-worn realist convention of rendering consumption, especially of the conspicuous variety, in painstaking if disapproving detail.

As a result of Du Bois's careful research, the Chicago of *Dark Princess*, like that of *Sister Carrie* and *The Jungle* earlier and *Native Son* a decade later, is a recognizable, navigable, precisely mapped urban grid. Despite Du Bois's self-deprecatory claim that "the only thing that connects the novel with Chicago is my general knowledge of the colored group there," he had in fact bolstered that "general knowledge" with copious investigation into prison numbers, department stores, and electoral results.[31] The author's object in this section, as he explained to one Chicago source, was to "work in enough realism to make my message clear."[32] That "realism" partakes in the project that Kaplan identifies in her *Social Construction:* it is formidable, stultifying, and generative only of status quo. Indeed, the only transformative fantasy available in this Chicago comes when Sammy Scott "envisaged a political machine to run all black Chicago" (111).

Barrenness is the prime characteristic of this dystopian locale. In this instance, again, Sara Andrews exemplifies Chicago's qualities. Before marrying Matthew, Sara is described as "prim" (158), "thin, small" (109), "immaculate" (111), "physically 'pure' almost to prudery" (113), "calculating" (132), and evocative of "cleanliness, order, cold, clean hardness, and unusual efficiency" (109). "Be careful of the veil," she warns her new husband just after their wedding. For Du Bois this is a doubly significant detail: according to a conventional reading of "the veil," it shows Sara's protectiveness toward her virginity; to use the language of *Souls*, it also reveals her deference to the barriers of segregation. As far as we can tell, the marriage is never consummated: "there had been no honeymoon, no mysterious nesting" (145), for Sara "disliked being 'mauled' and disarranged" (153). Matthew's suggestion that they have a baby brings only "uncomprehending astonishment. 'Certainly not!' she had answered" (153). Sara's counterpart in New York, who appears only briefly, is a kind-eyed cabaret girl who dances sinuously and goes home with Matthew intermittently. The cities differ in that decadent New York can accept sexual pleasure while Chicago hides behind a mask of legitimacy; but neither can be a site of regeneration. In Du Bois's formulation, the move between Northern cities merely sustains the frustration of reproductive capacity initiated in Matthew's exclusion from obstetric rounds.

Strategic placement of mimetic details, an overall atmosphere of barrenness, clean arcs of character success and failure: such techniques, in their very abundance, ultimately convert realism into hyperrealism. Whereas the realist texts from Kaplan's *Social Construction* never break their frame, Du Bois inserts the realist "Chicago Politician" section amid a larger narrative that will unwrite its constructed realism. Even within the section, Du Bois makes it patently clear that Chicago's realist world is its own sort of fiction. Once allied with Sara and Sammy, and now inculcated in Chicago values and ambitions, Matthew acknowledges through the narrator that "all his enthusiasm, all his hope, all his sense of reality was gone" (126). Realism, then, necessitates the loss of not only hope and enthusiasm but even reality. Luckily, Du Bois can now wield the weapon of romance; and combating Chicago realism in the novel's remaining pages will mean combating all the ills of America and modernity, for "Chicago is the epitome of America. . . . Chicago is the American world and the modern world, and the worst of it" (284). With his wintry Chicago, Du Bois creates a geography in a synecdochial relationship to modern capitalist America. The rest of his novel dismantles that geography, as Chicago's winter thaws and melts into a Southern spring.

Within that barren, hopeless environment, the only refuge available to Matthew—and by extension to the reader—is Matthew's tiny bachelor apartment. During his early days with the political machine, Matthew fills the rooms with all that realism will not tolerate: an ugly Chinese god (representing both foreignness and faith), a fabulously rich and dynamic carpet, and later, Kautilya. As Matthew first encounters his prize possession, "This rug was marvelous. It burned him with its brilliance. It sang to his eyes and hands. It was yellow and green—it was thick and soft; but all this didn't tell the subtle charm of its weaving and shadows of coloring" (128). The magic carpet provides the only instance in a cold and static Chicago landscape of this sort of sensual language, with a profusion of gerunds evoking motion and vitality. Capable of burning Matthew, it generates warmth to melt the icy edifice of realism, while Du Bois's insistence that his own description "didn't tell" its full beauty participates in a romantic commonplace by signaling the unspeakable truths that evade characterization in language.

Dark Princess's last section occurs largely within this bubble of romance, before moving its finale to Virginia. It is in this exoticized refuge that Kautilya narrates her own history and that of her region. Because Hopkins's international solution in Of One Blood centers on Ethiopia, the novel participates in an Africanist rhetoric of ancientness and originality. Dark Princess places India at the core of a worldwide anti-colonial movement; accordingly the language of Orientalism, and its attendant imagery of wealth, luxury, and spice, oppose the impersonal machine that is Chicago. Kautilya's histories, like the room in which she recounts them, are characterized by all the required elements of nineteenth-century Orientalism. The India that she presents is dynastic, decadent, luxurious, unmappable, and ultimately unknowable. In a typical scene, "Before my face rose every morning the white glory of the high Himalayas, with the crowning mass of Gaurisankar, kissing heaven. Behind me lay the great and golden flood of Holy Ganga. On my left hand stood the Bo of Buddha and on my right the Sacred City of the Magmela" (228). Such a mythic and impossible geography contrasts utterly with the previous panoramas of Chicago and New York that feature cold, stark buildings within a rationalized, labeled, and accurate city grid.[33] As Kautilya continues her history, "All about me was royal splendor, wealth and jewels and beautiful halls, old and priceless carpets" (228). Here Du Bois reinforces another standard Orientalist image, one that he himself would debunk a few years later. As he wrote in a 1931 Amsterdam News column, "It is from [Akbar's] time that the legend of wealth and jewels and power comes down to us."[34] While his column acknowledges the language of "wealth and jewels" as a "legend," Du Bois's own novel reinforces that legend.

A further ingredient of the standard exoticized description—Asia as land of contrasts—still endures today in countless travel brochures. Du Bois reproduces that cliché as well, with Kautilya's description of her home as "loveliest and weirdest of lands; terrible with flame and ice, beautiful with palm and pine, home of pain and happiness and misery" (227). This hyperbole comes in answer to Matthew asking "from what fairyland you came?," thus depicting India not only as a place of extremes but as a place, like Hopkins's Telassar, that is not even human. Du Bois's dedication of the novel to Titania reinforces that depiction by equating Shakespeare's fairy queen with Kautilya and therefore India with fairyland.[35]

In *Dark Princess*'s Chicago section, India and Kautilya function not as a geographical reality and a human reality, respectively, but rather as conceptual categories powered by the vocabulary and imagery of Orientalism. The land and the woman oppose Chicago realism on the multiple levels of language, politics, and genre. Through the cracks of the urban firmament, Kautilya "filled all his imagination, all his high romance, all the wild joys and beauty of being" (145). The effect of the Chicago milieu, in turn, is to fragment the utopian internationalism that coheres around the imagined person of Kautilya. Before arriving there, Matthew had assured Kautilya that "Your dream of the emancipation of the darker races will come true in time" and will "light anew a great world-culture" (102). The Chicago analogue to that dream, as mentioned earlier, is Sammy Scott's less grandiose and more cynical vision of "a political machine to run all black Chicago" (111). Months of immersion in realpolitik rob Matthew of hope, prompting him to tell Kautilya's Japanese envoy that "The dream at Berlin was false and misleading. We have nothing in common with other peoples. We are fighting out our own battle here in America with more or less success. We are not looking for help beyond our borders" (150). Du Bois constructs the generic and geographical units of his novel in such a way that Chicago's boundaries trap Matthew, while a mythic India offers a way back out.

Ultimately, with Kautilya's help, Matthew resists the allure of compromise and returns to "the vision of world work" that he had tried to banish during those rationalized and provincial Chicago days (136). What is this work, and what world does it serve? As Ken W. Warren helps to clarify, *Dark Princess* explores two different types of global activism, one democratic and the other aristocratic or, in Warren's terms, oligarchical.[36] We see the latter version most clearly in the Council of the Darker World, which seeks the cultural and intellectual ascendancy of their own aristocracy. Here, Du Bois combines his own experiences at the Universal Races Congress of 1911 and at the helm of several Pan-African Congresses with the radical elitism of Okakura's Pan-Asian movement. However, this elitist globalism is not the "world work" that dominates *Dark Princess*. Only a few pages into the novel, Du Bois demonstrates the failure of the oligarchical approach by showing the contempt of the world's colored aristocracy toward "the rabble," whether brown or white.[37] Together, Matthew's mother and Kautilya develop an alternative kind of "world work" based on labor, love, and reproduction. While the failed model has its origins in actual events, this second category is deliberately mythical. The work of real or fictional conferences having proven too limited, imagination and procreation take over. The space that makes this new globalism possible is no European capital, but rather the expansive and fecund terrain of the American South, especially Prince James County, Virginia.

Far from Hopkins's prison of endogamy, this South is a hospitable and fertile Arcadia. Even Atlanta, in *Souls of Black Folk* characterized largely by "sordid money-getting," now functions as a site of hope and fertility in comparison with the fruitless Chicago and New York.[38] During his professional incarnation as "The Pullman Porter," Matthew visits the Southern capital with his friend and coporter Jimmie. The two stop in at "a pretty little cream and green cottage. . . . Before Matthew could ask what it all meant, out of the house came a girl and the tiniest of babies." As Jimmie explains, "'Been married a year,' he said. 'Married before I knew you, but the wife was working in Chicago and wouldn't come until I could set up a regular home. But the baby brought her, and I got the home'" (74). According to this sequence, Chicago and child-rearing are incompatible, South and domesticity synonymous. The baby itself, "amorphous and dark red-brown," is an avatar of the Black Belt.[39] On the train again, heading back to Chicago after the brief visit, Matthew muses on "That baby! That mother's face! There were, after all, some strangely beautiful things in life" (75). Strangeness and beauty, along with fertility, are qualities that remain in the South; nowhere in prosaic and rationalized Chicago, except in his Orientalist refuge, will Matthew use such words. In fact, the trip North will destroy Jimmie's domestic utopia; the very same chapter sees Jimmie lynched in Matthew's stead for a fabricated offense to a white woman.

Atlanta provides a temporary respite of tiny homes and tinier babies, while Prince James County expands that limited instance of self-determination and reproduction onto a global scale. Despite its apparent geographical spec ificity, Matthew's birthplace is in fact as imaginary as "Bwodpur": Virginia's counties honor Princes Edward, George, and William, but not James. Matthew's memories depict Virginia as a warm, comfortable region with only two identifying features, his mother and her farm. His early visit home conveys the area as a vague, subjective landscape characterized by "the soft glow of Autumn," "the dim, sweet morning," and a "magnificent—wonderful—beautiful—beautiful" vista (130–1). Months later, Kautilya's letters to Matthew—the same ones that transform the limited locale into a transnational Black Belt uniting Africa, Asia, and the American South—echo that romantic and insubstantial language.

Against Chicago's careful specificity, Virginia and India together open into a vague and constantly mutating soft, warm, brown Southern world. That world, with Kautilya as its foremost representative, first enters Matthew's mind as he sits in exile. In fact, within the logic of the text, it is Matthew's nostalgia for the colored South that conjures up the dark Princess. Homesick in Berlin, Matthew realizes that

> he never dreamed how much he loved that soft, brown world
> which he had so carelessly, so unregretfully cast away. What would
> he not give to clasp a dark hand now, to hear a soft Southern roll of
> speech, to kiss a brown cheek? To see warm, brown crinkly hair
> and laughing eyes. God—he was lonesome. So utterly, terribly
> lonesome. And then—he saw the Princess!" (7–8)

His memories of the South, rendered in sensual detail, in effect produce Princess Kautilya. What Matthew sees, following this conjuring, is not an individual but an essence of warmth and color. Matthew perceives her as "a glow of golden brown skin. It was darker than sunlight and gold; it was lighter and livelier than brown. It was a living, glowing crimson, veiled beneath brown flesh. It . . . glowed softly of its own inner radiance" (8). Kautilya, here, appears miraculously to replace a lost world that is both womblike and sexualized.

If Kautilya initially emerges to replace a lost maternal South, that South later provides a substitute for the missing Princess. When Matthew, recently released from Joliet State, visits Virginia at Christmas, "He knew now why he had come here. It was not simply to see that poor old mother. It was to walk in *her* footsteps" (131; italics in original). As in the earlier café scene, the South evokes Kautilya, now in the form of a palpable absence instead of a present essence; and once again, given Du Bois's use of pronoun instead of noun, Princess and "mother" are virtually interchangeable. Elsewhere, Matthew's unnamed and often voiceless mother is given life only through Kautilya. During that entire Christmas trip to Virginia, we never hear Matthew's mother speak. The last sentences of this first Virginia passage read: "She was sitting in the door, straight, tall, big, and brown. She was singing something low and strong. And her eyes were scanning the highway. Matthew leaped the fence and walked slowly toward her down the lane" (131). Like Kautilya in the "*her* footsteps" passage quoted above, Matthew's mother receives only a pronoun. In fact, no proper noun has intervened between "*her* footsteps" and "she was sitting," an omission that effectively consolidates the two strong, tall brown women. Silent during this entire sequence, Matthew's mother speaks for the first time only through Kautilya. As the Princess tells Matthew, "I went down again to Virginia and knelt beside your mother, and she only smiled. 'He ain't married,' she said. 'He only thinks he is . . . Wait, wait.' I waited" (224). If a Southern maternal nostalgia initially brought Kautilya into being, she in turn now reinvents the mother as a guru of vernacular wisdom.

Kautilya and Matthew's mother, then, repeatedly bring each other into being; at the same time, the text never deflects the possibility that Matthew has invented them both. Just as Reuel Briggs's flight from empiricism in *Of One Blood* brings the Ethiopian dream-city of Telassar into being, here the global South operates as a kind of wish-fulfillment for Matthew. Within the system that is Matthew's memory, South and Mother appear synonymous. His life story, as told to Kautilya, begins with his mother: "I was born in Virginia, Prince James County, where we black folk own most of the land. My mother, now many years a widow, farmed her little forty acres to educate me, her only child" (11). Elsewhere, in sequences that reinforce the invented quality of both South and Mother, the action that brings those figures into the narrative is not remembering but dreaming. Sailing back to New York as an ocean-liner scullion, Matthew drifts from demeaning, repetitive tasks into reverie: "The terrible, endless rhythm of the thing—paring, rising, falling, groaning, paring, swaying, with the slosh of the greasy dishwater, in the

hot close air, set Matthew to dreaming. He could see again that mother of
his that poor but mighty, purposeful mother—tall, big, and brown" (37).
As Kautilya provided panacea for exilic loneliness, the imagined visions of
his mother and her Southern agrarian world comfort Matthew amid inhos-
pitable surroundings.

Matthew reacts to circumstances of alienating, repetitive labor by dreaming of mother and home. Elsewhere, Du Bois presents Kautilya and the
global South as products of the same sort of wish-fulfillment. Still at sea,
after deflecting a set-up fight, "He slept and dreamed; he was fighting the
world" (41). On the next day, Matthew is back at the repetitive work of paring
potatoes:

> Matthew rose early and went to his task—paring, peeling, cutting,
> paring. Nothing happened. . . . So Matthew dropped back to his
> dreams. He was groping toward a career. He wanted to get his hand
> into the tangles of the world. . . . His sudden love for a woman
> above his station was more than romance—it was a longing for
> action, breadth, helpfulness, great constructive deeds. (42)

All his dreams—of the colored South, of his mother, of fighting the world, of
constructive work—cohere in the single person of the Princess. She appears
as if magically several times after the first materialization in Berlin: one
example out of many is her miraculous growth out of a pair of white satin
slippers, which themselves have suddenly emerged "on the outermost edge
of the forest of shoes" waiting to be shined by porter Matthew (89). It is this
magical, dreamlike figure, as mentioned earlier, who reconceptualizes Prince
James County, Virginia, into a great colored South, "a world of colored folk,
physically beautiful beyond conception . . . ready for the breath of Life and
Resurrection" (278). Compared especially with Bellamy's Boston, from
which Mesmerism and mystery have been banished, this is a utopia that
relies upon the power of the counterfactual.

The predicted resurrection arrives in the form of a ceremony anoint-
ing Kautilya and Matthew's baby boy, born without the knowledge of the
Chicago-mired father, as savior of the colored world. The novel's last scene
recalls Pauline Hopkins's political messianism from *Contending Forces* and
especially *Of One Blood*. Matthew is reborn into action even as control of the
novel and its soon-to-be-emancipated worlds passes to his son. *Dark Princess*'s
last section, "The Maharajah of Bwodpur," is the only one not named for

Matthew; cementing the motif of regeneration, this Spring section takes its title from the offspring instead of the unwitting father. To arrive at that communal scene of birth and rebirth, Matthew must first undergo a solitary voyage, a passage of sublime betweenness that marks the flight out of realism. To travel from Chicago to Virginia is to pass from the mechanical to the real. Even the telephone call summoning him home enacts that transition: "At first the voices came strained, far-off, unnatural, interrupted with hissings and brazen echoes. Then at last, real, clear, and close, a voice came pouring over the telephone in a tumult of tone" (301). Encapsulated here is the movement from "unnatural" to "real" and organically flowing. Following that call, Matthew endures a far more protracted and dangerous journey from unnaturalness to organicity. The plane ride lasts for seven hours and, for readers, three full pages. An excerpted version follows:

> The lights of Chicago hurried backward. . . . They left the great smudge of the crowded city and swept out over flat fields and sluggish rivers. Fires flew in the world beneath and dizzily marked Chicago. Fires flew in the world above and marked high heaven. Between, the gloom lay thick and heavy. It crushed in upon the plane. . . . His soul was afraid of this daring, heaven-challenging thing. He was but a tossing, disembodied spirit. There was nothing beneath him—nothing. There was nothing above him, nothing; and beside and everywhere to the earth's ends lay nothing. . . . In another hour Cincinnati—he groped at the map—yes, Cincinnati—lay in pools of light and shade, and the Ohio flowed like ink.
>
> Suddenly the whole thing became symbolic. He was riding Life above the world. He was triumphant over Pain and Death. He remembered death down there where once the head of Jimmie thumped, thumped, on the rails. He heard the wail of that black and beautiful widowed wife. . . . Some one touched his shoulder. He knew that touch. It was arrest, arrest and jail. But what did he care? He was flying above the world. He was flying to her.
>
> A soft pale light grew upon the world—a halo, a radiance as of some miraculous virgin birth. . . . Then over the whole east came a flush. . . . The clouds parted, melted, and ran before the gleaming glory of the coming sun. The earth lay spread like a sailing

picture—all pale blue, green, and brown; mauve, white, yellow and gold. (303–5)

Geographically and stylistically, the novel now rises out of the terrain of realism. After several repetitions of "above" and "beneath" or "below," Matthew and the narrative, caught between whatever dangers are above and below, find themselves free. Artificial light gives way to sunrise, and maps and borders to a dynamic, organic landscape. Matthew passes out of his own documented story, as it has so far been told, into an imagined future. The story he abandons is specifically one of violence and the foreclosure of paternity. The South, with "her" as its focal point, provides solace.

During this crucial transition, Matthew finally makes the leap from realism to utopian romance. To get to utopia, Matthew must rise off the map and enter an uncharted terrain. But this is far from the exploratory venture of Conrad's Kurtz or Gilman's three *Herland* voyagers, whose job is to render the "blank spaces" into a comprehensible topography. Herland, like Utopia before it, appears in precise and cartographically minded detail. Du Bois's narrator, on the other hand, shows Matthew leaving the domain of the legible, from named rivers that "flowed like ink," to a "symbolic" flight "above the world." If realism is not capable of writing what Du Bois wants, neither is conventional utopian fiction, for within this sequence India and the global South are not even allegedly documented places but thoroughly imaginative categories.

The novel closes with a ceremony that incorporates Matthew's wedding to Kautilya with the coronation of their infant son as not only Maharajah of Bwodpur but also "Messenger and Messiah to all the Darker Worlds" (311). Kautilya's heralded "east of east" miraculously arrives in Virginia in the form of the Hindu, Buddhist, and Muslim kings who join with the local Baptist clergy to pay tribute to that new savior. As in *Of One Blood*, a female interim ruler has held the throne for a more powerful king, with the difference that Kautilya gives birth to that heir, rather than awaiting his arrival from afar. Unlike the messianic utopianism of Hopkins, which relies on an unbroken ancient lineage, Du Bois's version hails miscegenation as liberation. To eugenicist claims that the darker races are inferior and that they will soon disappear, Du Bois responds on the eugenicists' own terms, using as ammunition the beautiful and costly "bubble of gold" that is Matthew and Kautilya's child.[40] If Hopkins, despite her rhetoric of purity, develops a new culturally hybrid Telassar at the end of *Of One Blood*, Du Bois here biologizes that hybrid utopia.

The novel's last scene lifts Matthew out of the barren landscape of Chicago realism, deposits him amid a mythical multicultural ceremony, and bestows upon him the reproductive power he has been denied ever since the opening of the novel. Within Du Bois's oeuvre, this scene finally realizes the utopian urge the author has been exploring since *The Souls of Black Folk*. With this last scene of syncretic coronation, Du Bois privileges the liberatory possibility of the imagination against a constructed modern world. India and the South, even if imaginary, allow him to write himself out of a dry, pessimistic white realism and into a strange new order that respects manual labor, accepts the political power of passion, and reconciles monarchy with racial hybridity. Where *Young India* combats stasis through its collective structure, enacting diversity even at the cost of a smooth surface to its utopia by including a range of writers with divergent and sometimes incompatible points of view, the notoriously solitary Du Bois here endorses an even more radical collectivism in the gathering of Kautilya with

> my Buddhist priest, a Mohammedan Mullah, and a Hindu leader
> of Swaraj . . . Japan was represented by an artisan and the blood of
> the Shoguns; young China was there and a Lama of Tibet; Persia,
> Arabia, and Afghanistan; black men from the Sudan, East, West,
> and South Africa; Indians from Central and South America, brown
> men from the West Indies, and—yes, Matthew, Black America was
> there too." (297)

Though the novel ends here, one is to presume that this collective will incubate into a fully realized utopia. Paul Gilroy, for one, views *Dark Princess*'s last chapter as a still-relevant paragon of amalgamation and solidarity, "an image of hybridity and intermixture that is especially valuable because it gives no ground to the suggestion that cultural fusion involves betrayal, loss, corruption, or dilution."[41] But what the potential utopia makes up for in population, it lacks in the kind of institutions that make even an imaginary social structure sustainable. The novel closes with the enthusiastic audience's apostrophe to "Messenger and Messiah to all the Darker Worlds," leaving no sense of where little Madhu and his newlywed parents will carry on their "world work." Now that Kautilya's womb has taken over as the repository of newness and hope, geography becomes secondary. With only that individual mechanism of ideological reproduction, the utopia promises to be even less enduring than the imperiled Telassar.

Further, Du Bois assembles his ephemeral utopia with unstable materials. In addition to framing both Kautilya and the global South as products of reactive fantasy on Matthew's part, *Dark Princess* presents an entirely fictitious India. Especially in comparison with the intensely mimetic Chicago, the India of the novel is no material realm but merely a field of associations and symbolisms bearing little resemblance to India's real history. Most implausible is the history that Du Bois has assigned to "Bwodpur," the birthplace of colored liberation. While Chicago's geography, politics, and commerce are rendered with a verisimilitude faithful to procured native-informant accounts, Kautilya's home state of "Bwodpur" in its very name is an imaginary and primarily symbolic entity. The name suggests Bahawalpur, a Punjabi princely state later incorporated into Pakistan. Aptheker, however, makes the undocumented claim (presumably on the basis of Kautilya's references to the Himalayas and to the Buddha) that Du Bois intended the fictional principality as Nepal.[42] In terms of historical accuracy, the choice hardly matters, for both Bahawalpur and Nepal remained staunchly and notoriously collaborationist from the mid-nineteenth century through the time at which Du Bois wrote and indeed up until Independence; thus both were highly unlikely to produce a credible nationalist leader from the ranks of their royal families. As opposed to the near-perfect correspondence between Sammy Scott and Edward H. Wright, Kautilya has no model; nor could she possibly have one. The idea that the female scion of an independent principality would become "the foremost living symbol of home rule in all India" negates the historical record, given that India's nationalist leadership arose out of not its aristocracy but its professional classes.[43]

India occupies an enormous symbolic space within Du Bois's global schema, yet he knew little of the region's history. In Du Bois's political columns, just as in *Dark Princess*, India represents the world's foremost possibility for anti-colonial liberation and one of the most useful models for African-Americans. Du Bois wrote several columns in *The Crisis* during the 1910s and 1920s extolling "Indian victories," "the Indian uprising," and "the struggle for independence in India."[44] In 1930 alone, six different columns mention India, hailing that year's Civil Disobedience campaign, encouraging readers to regard the Indian struggle with "reverence, hope, and applause," and proclaiming that "India will yet be free."[45] By 1943, Du Bois would conceptualize black America as an internal colony by way of an analogy with India: "Remember that we American Negroes are the bound colony of the United States just as India is of England."[46] In the following year, he would declare that "the greatest color problem in the world is that of India."[47]

Yet even as that "color problem" itself evolved, Du Bois's presentation of it remained fixed. In addition to the other brief mentions, Du Bois devoted two full columns, one before the height of Civil Disobedience and one after Independence, to setting out India's history. The 1931 article, also quoted twice above, reads

> What is India? It is an area of nearly 2,000,000 square miles, with
> a population of some 320,000,000. . . . It is inhabited by different
> races and tribes, speaking some two hundred different languages.
> These people are of all sorts and kinds. Some are Negroes; some
> are black folk, with straight hair; some are of the Chinese type, and
> some more nearly the European type;[48]

and the 1947 version

> What is India? It is 1,500 thousand square miles of territory, with
> four hundred millions of people. They are mixed descendents of
> Negroes and Negroids; Mongolians, Western Asiatics, and Eastern
> Europeans.[49]

Despite Du Bois's famously evolving mind, India remains the same: two columns, separated by sixteen years and one successful independence movement, define India through almost identical sequences. The earlier history goes on to quote a monologue of Kautilya's in response to Du Bois's question "What is India?" The column closes:

> This is India, and of its meaning and impression I have written
> in 'Dark Princess':
> 'India! India! Out of black India the world was born. Into
> the black womb of India the world shall creep to die. All that
> the world has done, India did, and that more marvelously,
> more magnificently. The loftiest of mountains, the mightiest
> of rivers, the widest of plains, the broadest of oceans—these
> are India.

Man there is of every shape and kind and hue, and the animal
friends of man, of every sort conceivable. The drama of life knows
India as it knows no other land, from the tragedy of Almighty God
to the laugh of the Bandar-log; from divine Gotama to the sons of
Mahmoud and the stepsons of the Christ.

For leaf and sun, for whiff and whirlwind; for laughter, and
for tears; for sacrifice and vision; for stark poverty and jeweled
wealth; for toil and song and silence—for all this, know India.
Loveliest and weirdest of lands; terrible with flame and ice,
beautiful with palm and pine, home of pain and happiness and
misery—oh, Matthew, can you not understand? This is India—can
you not understand?'[50]

Du Bois's novel, a product of his own imagination, now serves as an authentic representation of the region. That representation, in turn, offers an image
of India as inscrutable, hyperspiritual, and bizarre.

It is especially in comparison with Chicago's carefully researched verisimilitude that one can understand what an imaginary and ahistorical location
is the India of *Dark Princess*. As compared with the fourteen requests for
information on Chicago shopping, politics, and prisons, discussed above,
Du Bois sent only one letter on India. In November of 1927, *Dark Princess*
had already been sent to Harcourt, and only minor changes remained to be
made. One month earlier Du Bois had received a letter from Lala Lajpat Rai,
whom he had come to know during Rai's exile years in New York. In his
response to the letter, Du Bois closes by mentioning that "I am going to pub-
lish a novel in the spring. It touches India incidentally in the person of an
Indian princess. I am sending enclosed pages about her. I shall be glad to
have your criticism."[51] Du Bois sought no other such advice, despite having
been contacted by two other Indian nationalist organizers during that fall.
Even while approaching no less than eight individuals for their views on
Chicago electoral politics, Du Bois takes the corrections of one Indian as
definitive.

Du Bois's friendship with Lajpat Rai, his sole India consultant for *Dark
Princess*, comprises part of a larger history of internationalism in the period
around World War I. The Punjabi leader's five years living in Harlem and
working as "Indian Nationalist ambassador to America" brought him in
frequent contact with Du Bois. He formed close friendships with NAACP

co-founder Mary White Ovington, *Nation* editor and NAACP board member Oswald Garrison Villard, and birth control advocate Margaret Sanger, who also collaborated with Du Bois.[52] In 1916 Du Bois and Rai, along with Villard, Ovington, John Reed, Ida Tarbell, Walter Lippmann, James Weldon Johnson, and several other luminaries of New York's radical intelligentsia, became charter members of the Civic Club, a new organization for activism and reform.[53] Finally, there was the 1917 joint address for the Intercollegiate Socialist Society, an ambitious attempt at a holistic analysis of race, class, and colonialism. Following the lecture, a staff member of the U.S. War Department wrote to Du Bois that "Mr. Lajpat Rai seems anxious for trouble," asking whether the Indian "was inclined to make trouble here as well as in the world generally." No reply to the request survives; if there was one at all, it must have been deliciously acerbic.

Du Bois and Lajpat Rai shared not only some of the same colleagues and venues, but also many organizational goals, methods, and assumptions. Both believed firmly in the use of historical research toward achieving future progress; though they edited periodicals concurrently with each other, both had also written full-length histories and biographies. Both men believed as well in the utility of culture and art in political organizing, consistently including poems and sketches in their periodicals. The two shared an elitist, idealistic vision of group liberation. That elitism may be held responsible for each man's inattention to the plight of Indian and other Asian migrant laborers within the United States, despite the threats of the Asian Exclusion Leagues active during this period and the Hindu Exclusion Act that became law in 1917.[54] Rai lobbied against one version of the bill, largely on behalf of Indian students, but took little interest in migrant workers until much later; Du Bois, meanwhile, made no public mention of the anti-immigrant legislation or its intended objects.

A further area of overlap was in their complex responses to World War I, which both viewed as an imperialist conflict. During the war, each took the reluctant but strategic course of pledging open support to the Allies, despite personal misgivings and the disapprobation of others.[55] Supporting England's war effort, for Lajpat Rai, meant advocating Home Rule over Independence; it also meant refusing to agitate in favor of the twenty-nine "Hindu Conspiracy Case" defendants. As discussed in chapter 2, the case implicated Indian nationalists living in the United States of violating American neutrality by their anti-English activities. Rai, put under surveillance by association as well as for his own anti-English writings, effectively abandoned the defendants, who he felt were sullying the image of Indian nationalism.[56] Neither did Du Bois ever editorialize on the trial. Their postwar reactions converged similarly. After the declaration of Armistice, both men had high hopes that President Wilson's rhetoric of "self-determination" would apply to their own constituencies as well as to the holdings of the shattered Austrian Empire. Du Bois organized the Pan-African Congress of 1919 as an adjunct and advisor to the Paris Peace Conference, which he had originally hoped to attend; meanwhile, Rai sent telegram after telegram to Wilson, urging "that this victory of democracy over autocracy will be followed by an immediate grant of autonomy to India and other countries under the rule of the Allies."[57] Needless to say, both were sorely disappointed. Their shared experience makes its way into *Dark Princess* as Kautilya recalls bitterly that "there was nothing in this century as beautiful as the exaltation of mankind in November, 1918" that had falsely promised "as reward, freedom for India" (235).

Given the congruencies between their approaches and experiences, it is not surprising that Lajpat Rai would become Du Bois's main source on India on matters other than his novel. Du Bois's columns, too, rely heavily on Rai's pronouncements. Almost twenty years after Rai's death in 1929, Du Bois still cites the nationalist martyr on India's economy. The 1947 editorial "The Freeing of India," quoted above, reads: "The Indians are wretchedly poor. Lajpat Rai says: 'The people of India are the poorest on earth.'"[58] On the occasion of his death, Du Bois wrote in *The Crisis* that "every member of the 800,000,000 darker peoples of the world should stand with bowed heads in memory of Lajpat Rai, the great leader of India."[59] Four months later, another obituary appeared, this time in Du Bois's book review column: "Lajpat Rai is dead, a martyr to British intolerance. . . . Lajpat Rai understood and wrote about the Negro problem in America."[60]

Meanwhile, some of what Lajpat Rai "understood and wrote" contains analogies incompatible with the one Du Bois would later use to demonstrate black America's status as internal colony. Early in 1915, before the venerable founder's death, Rai used letters of introduction from Du Bois and Ovington to meet Booker T. Washington and tour Tuskegee. Rai took that trip, writes one biographer, because "he was anxious to study the problems of the Negro. . . . He felt that they were comparable to those of the depressed classes or untouchables in India"—not to the plight of India as a whole, as Du Bois would have it.[61] Ten years later, lecturing in opposition to a legislative quota for Muslims, Rai informed his audience that even "the colored people of the U.S.A. who socially form an entirely separate community with whom the white [sic] have hardly any social relation at all" never demanded group representation.[62] As opposed to Du Bois's contention that "we American Negroes are the bound colony of the United States just as India is of England," Lajpat Rai sets black and white America as analogous not to India and England, but to Muslim and Hindu India. Against Du Bois's solidarity equation, Lajpat Rai imagines himself in the majority position, and uses "the colored people of the U.S.A." to stand in for the minority Muslim position. Princess Kautilya may recognize that "you American Negroes . . . are a nation!" (17), but Lajpat Rai portrays a separate-but-contented community.

Much of Lajpat Rai's writing on the United States similarly fails to call attention to the active oppression and violence suffered by colored Americans. Rai habitually refers to the United States as a "land of freedom," with no mention of the inconsistent application of that much-vaunted freedom. His 1915 report on "Education in the United States" is so enthusiastic that Rai finds it necessary to close with the following caveat:

> The preceding account of education in the United States
> might lead my readers to suppose that America must be a
> paradise on earth, entirely free from sin, poverty, squalor,
> immorality and physical degeneration. By no means so. So far
> as sin and immorality are concerned America has as much of it
> as any other community or nation on earth; poverty and squalor
> perhaps she has less; physical degeneration perhaps the least.
> The fact is that considering the elements which make up her
> population she might be very much worse but for the care she
> takes in looking after the education and moral and physical
> welfare of her children.[63]

Rather than segregation or lynching, only a natural amount measure of immorality mars the previously rosy picture of U.S. social life. "The children of a nation are her capital," Rai continues, without acknowledging how recently it was that slavery had made this metaphor literally true. Similarly, Rai's "Open Letter to David Lloyd George," also written during the exile period, characterizes the slums of New York as "verily a paradise as compared with" those of urban India.[64] A year later, Rai again compared the United States favorably with Britain by measuring the nine newly commissioned Indians

in the British Army against the far larger number of African-American offi-
cers.[65] In this instance Rai does place black America in an analogous position to colonized India—but only in order to criticize British governance.

By the time Rai left the United States, he had acknowledged his host
nation's "Negro Problem," but still couched internal race relations as marginal to a larger understanding of national life. "When I came here for the
first time in 1905 I was a bit shocked by your treatment of the Negroes," he
said at his 1919 farewell address, "but otherwise I went back confirmed in my
admiration for America and her institutions."[66] Rai's most forceful indictment of racism in the United States came well after his departure, and then
only in defense of India. As previously discussed, Rai wrote to Du Bois in
October of 1927; Du Bois responded a month later with the "enclosed pages"
on India from *Dark Princess*. Rai's intent in that October letter was to seek
material to rebut Katherine Mayo's *Mother India*, a muckraking account of
child marriage and widow-burning that had enraged nationalist leaders.
After years of praising American freedom and social welfare, Rai now asked
Du Bois for instances of "the cruelties inflicted on your people by the whites
of America." Rather than the global solidarity work envisioned in Du Bois's
columns, this is investigation in aid of counterpropaganda.[67] Thus while Du
Bois treats India as a guiding force for the anti-colonial struggle, and cites
Lajpat Rai as a voice of India, that voice in turn speaks of white treatment of
black America only when it proves strategically useful. Lajpat Rai, Du Bois's
primary link to India, was not the internationalist that Du Bois wanted him
to be.

In fact, the two nationalists to whom Du Bois did *not* respond in 1927,
mentioned above, offered more of the rhetoric of egalitarian solidarity, if not
the substance. Using language closer to Du Bois's own than any used by
Lajpat Rai, journalist Shripad R. Tikekar wrote to Du Bois that

> The race-problem, I mean the fight between the black races on the
> one hand and the white people on the other is keen in India & as
> such all Indians have a feeling of sympathy towards the 'dark'
> Americans in their fight against the dominating white people. Can
> we take any lessons from your experience? Or would you like to
> listen to the sufferings of Indians engaged in the same fight?
> Whatever be our respective lots, I think it certain that we—in the
> same boat—can learn much by mutual exchange of thoughts.[68]

Despite the promising mentions of "sympathy" and "mutual exchange," no reply survives. Earlier that year, Abdur Raoof Malik, of the newly founded Bureau of Information in Gujranwala, wrote that "We ourselves being sufferers from the oppression alien rulers [sic] naturally view the struggle of Negroes with great sympathy." It is certain that Du Bois never replied to this request for information, since Nazir Ahmed Khan, the Bureau's secretary, sent a follow-up request in September.[69]

If India provides the seed for global colored liberation in *Dark Princess*, it is significant that Du Bois's main conduit to that key proto-nation envisioned their positions so differently. The romance of India, its ahistoricity, and the inconsistent analogy between colonized India and black America all demand that we approach the idea of a global South with caution. Throughout fictional and historical accounts of this seminal period in anticolonial organizing, the possibility of cross-group solidarity is both powerful and daunting. As quoted in the previous chapter, it was Lajpat Rai's double who enlightened Agnes Smedley's naïve protagonist in *Daughter of Earth* to the fact that Indian nationalism "was not only an historic movement in itself, but it was part of an international struggle for emancipation—that it was one of the chief pillars in this struggle."[70] However, as Rai's own pronouncements reveal, those pillars were uneven. The problem with analogy—as we saw in *Young India*'s 1920 volume—is that it reduces complex relationships to dichotomies, smoothes over intracolonized inequalities (e.g., between religions and castes within India), and erases the difference between the real experiences of colonialism and slavery, of wealth extracted from homelands and bodies transported as goods.

Of course, *Dark Princess* itself amply demonstrates the difficulties of solidarity politics. Within the novel, the trouble with coalitions comes across most clearly in the chapter that Du Bois later identified as his strongest.[71] When he meets with Kautilya's Council of the Darker World in Berlin, Matthew quickly detects "plain and clear the shadow of a color line within a color line, a prejudice within prejudice" in the racist and classist assumptions of the Japanese, Egyptian, and Arab delegates (22). Later Matthew and Kautilya, even while united in their chamber of romantic love, recognize the inherent difficulty of alliances. As Matthew tells his Princess, "'Here in America black folk must help overthrow the rule of the rich by distributing wealth more evenly . . . During the process they must keep step and hold tight hands with the other struggling dark peoples.' 'Difficult—difficult,' mused Kautilya, 'for the others have so different a path'" (256). Utopia's basis, then, is different paths, wobbly pillars, unstable analogies, and uneasy alliances.

I cannot complete my discussion of *Dark Princess* without noting the remarkable recent spate of critical interest in the novel.[72] In our own moment, one can conclude, this is what we want to believe in: the possibility for social change executed on the basis of intergroup solidarity. However, we also need to pay close attention to the problems the novel signals. Because it is a romanticized India that provides the basis for the emancipated world of color, and because the politics of the real India are often incompatible with those of Du Bois, *Dark Princess*'s transnational utopia is ultimately uninhabitable. The global Black Belt has a commensurate evanescence to Hopkins's Telassar as it lies in dread of "mighty nations penetrating" Africa—now not because of colonialism itself but because of the variety and divergence of ways to oppose it. Cross-continental utopias may offer valuable critiques of nationalism, but asserting a viable utopianism without making a specific territorial claim proves impossible.

Much as the anti-utopias of Forster, Huxley, and Zamyatin undermine the very premise of the developmentalist utopia, George Schuyler's serial novel *Black Empire* undermines the premise of Du Bois's utopian vision in *Dark Princess*. First published as a single volume in 1991, *Black Empire* appeared in two separate sections, "The Black Internationale: Story of Black Genius Against the World," and "Black Empire: An Imaginative Story of a Great New Civilization in Modern Africa," in the *Pittsburgh Courier* between 1936 and 1938. Despite their publication as a single novel, the two serial sequences serve quite different purposes. The first is a Du Boisian experiment in affirmative Orientalism, and the second a utopian parody that combines the least successful elements of *Looking Backward* and *Dark Princess*. "Black Empire" in particular penetratingly locates the problems set out between *Dark Princess*'s largely hopeful pages. The acerbic and unpredictable Schuyler, a gifted journalist and editor, invariably positioned himself outside the mainstream of American political thought. A Socialist Party member during the 1920s, Schuyler went on to write *The Communist Conspiracy against the Negroes* and the autobiography *Black and Conservative*. Whereas *Brave New World* effectively pillories the totalitarian aspects of classical utopias, "Black Empire" attacks their incomplete and open-ended antidotes.

A few years after reading *Dark Princess*, Schuyler proffered his own tale of global colored liberation under the pseudonym Samuel I. Brooks. In its entirety, *Black Empire* tells of the mysterious and virtually omnipotent Dr. Belsidus's successful battle for African liberation. Along with his inner circle (which includes the story's narrator, reporter Carl Slater), the prestigious Harlem doctor pursues a mutating goal that ranges from "Negro liberation" and "Negro control of the world" to, later in the book, simply a free Africa.[73] With Liberia as its first beachhead, the international elite fights through to the Congo and finally establishes a continent-wide "empire of black men and women working towards a cooperative civilization unexcelled in this world" (142). Even after Belsidus limits his objectives to a single continent, the novel's language remains transnational. Belsidus's collaborators initially travel "from wherever black men live" to meet in Harlem (25), and later assistance comes from "outlying districts of the Black Empire" in Malaysia, India, and America (256).

Though Schuyler characterized *Black Empire* as "hokum and hack work of the purest vein," its first installment, "The Black Internationale," in fact reflects an uncharacteristically optimistic segment of Schulyer's complex intellectual palette.[74] Even as "Black Empire" later ran in the *Courier,* Schuyler sent *The Crisis* an essay under his own name on anti-colonial internationalism, in which he traces the connections among the forces that enslaved and exploited colored people worldwide over the last centuries, and also among the resistance movements that arose in response. With the new Wilsonian rhetoric of self-determination, with the success of Gandhi's Non-Cooperation campaign, with Du Bois's several Pan-African Congresses, writes Schuyler, "the balance of power is shifting in the world."[75] "The Black Internationale" evinces that belief. Schuyler liberally sprinkles the adventure with utopian language; after the conspirators' first incursion into Africa, for example, "a new world has started" (115). These chapters also exhibit the influence of Du Bois specifically. Schuyler, whose enthusiasm for *Dark Princess* was unparalleled both in his own curmudgeonly reading experience and in that of the widely unloved novel, imitates among other aspects its Oriental motif.[76] Among other references, he describes Belsidus in story notes as a "combination of Garvey-Christ-Gandhi,"[77] includes one conspirator of "Hindu or Indian ancestry" (17), and draws Slater into the movement through use of "Teyoth, a Hindu drug that induces temporary insanity" (11). Like Matthew Towns, and indeed like Du Bois himself, Belsidus distrusts the nation-state.

He shows that distrust through his financial planning, hoarding "dozens of solid gold dishes" familiar from Norris's *McTeague* "so that I may, in the oriental manner, always have a supply of wealth that the white man's government will not molest" (12). As it does in *Dark Princess*, Asia here provides a road out of a despotic United States.

We can understand "The Black Internationale," then, as Schuyler's provisional tribute to Du Bois. Its utopia is imminent, open-ended, powered by the force of counterfactuality and affirmative Orientalism. In Schuyler's next serial sequence, "Black Empire: An Imaginative Story of a Great New Civilization in Modern Africa," we reach utopia proper—and here the troubles begin. "Black Empire" identifies all the problems implicit in Du Bois's "world of colored folk," also adding in many more of its own. As opposed to the suspenseful first story, this one begins in a far more conventionally utopian vein, enumerating the new state's innovations in the areas of medicine, nutrition, and communication. Rather than Du Bois, Schuyler appears to be channeling Bellamy, and inheriting his problem of excessive exposition. Here we have quintessentially utopian chapter titles like "Model Diet Kitchen Explained; Dr. Mason Tells of Advantages." Like so many classical utopias, these chapters contain genuine innovations as well as quasi-fascistic solutions. Schuyler invents a high-grade solar-powered radio, applies the raw-food diet that his Texas millionaire wife actually used on their child-prodigy daughter, but also imposes mandatory mass euthanasia. Moving quickly from melodrama to parody, Schuyler follows Forster and Huxley to hint that utopia will materialize as authoritarian paternalism.

In addition to calling into question the achievements and even the impulses of the Du Boisian "Black Internationale," "Black Empire" also anticipates the problems that would soon come with realizing postcolonial utopia. We will not be given the chance to see how the "Great New Civilization" will develop; the brief respite for imaginative construction rapidly gives way to invasion. Faced with losing their continental playground, former European enemies unite to reclaim it by force. Thus the deliberately provocational opening chapters give a mere glimpse at the unpalatable, totalitarian radicalism of the new society, before Schuyler abandons—or Europe prevents—its full realization. Now the overly expository Bellamyite chapter titles give way to more action-packed ones like "Martha and Her Group Shoot Their Way Out of Police Trap and Arrive at Rendezvous; London Bombed as Return Air Trip Begins." Schuyler appears to tire early on of the relatively plotless process of "building . . . a rational society," and reverts to the intrigue and armed combat that made up the first section (155). "Black Empire" closes just after the final battle, leaving the job of utopian reconstruction to the reader's imagination. Taken as a whole, Schuyler's serial utopia illustrates both the problems that *Of One Blood* and *Dark Princess* had solved (potential plotlessness, stasis, totalitarian bent) and also the new problems introduced by those dynamic, open-ended transnational utopias (internal discord, vulnerability to attack). As a self-professedly parodic text, it significantly undermines the goals and achievements of the anti-colonial utopia. "After a century of listening to black hustlers with Valhallas for sale," Schuyler would write a year later, "the Negro has become wary of schemes for instant salvation"—and even a dynamic, transnational utopia figures among them.[78]

As Alexander Bain explains, the transition from the provisional, hopeful quality of "The Black Internationale" to the sinister rationalization of "Black Empire" exemplifies Schulyer's discomfort with black internationalism as a political formation. Bain writes, "the problem for Schuyler was that the more 'clarity' black internationalism attained, the likelier it was to turn into something repugnant—more 'ancestral' than 'revolutionary.'"[79] This problem haunts utopian fiction at large: when Schuyler eschews "clarity," his judgment is of a piece with Huxley's anti-utopian critique in *Brave New World*. Utopia—particularly utopia without a concrete geographical foundation—teeters between poles of indistinctness and totalitarianism. Both *Dark Princess* and *Black Empire* confirm what we have already witnessed in J. T. Sunderland's transnational India: that a utopia based on solidarity is almost impossible to construct, even through fiction. In the case of *Dark Princess*, the anti-colonial imaginings of Du Bois's chief source on India do not accord with those of Du Bois himself. In *Black Empire*, Schuyler magnifies problems endemic to transnational utopia and to utopia more generally. In so doing he anticipates Richard Wright's pessimistic picture of anti-colonial solidarity in *The Color Curtain*.

III. Rationalism: Richard Wright

Near the end of *Dark Princess*, Kautilya proclaims boldly that "in 1952, the Dark World goes free" (297). As Arnold Rampersad points out, the most concrete realization of Kautilya's prediction is the pathbreaking 1955

Asian-African Conference in Bandung, Indonesia.[80] The twenty-nine formerly colonized nations that convened there might not yet have comprised Du Bois's complete "world of colored folk," but the Bandung Conference was certainly the closest realization to date of Du Bois's and Lajpat Rai's imaginary map of solidarity. Therefore I will close this chapter on transnational colored utopias by closely reading the best-known narrative of that conference, supplemented (with the Derridean overtones intended) by other first-person accounts. Richard Wright's 1956 travelogue *The Color Curtain* depicts the moment of transition from anti-colonial dream to postcolonial reality as one already rife with failure. Wright characterizes Du Bois's "world of colored folk" as a world of irrationality, mysticism, lack of specificity, and internal incoherence. Wright undercuts the "counterfactual," so important to Tagore, Coomaraswamy, Hopkins, and Du Bois, as a possible basis, or even a beginning, for political organizing. *The Color Curtain* evinces a developmentalist outlook on the part of Wright, who declares that the newly independent nations must foreswear mysticism and become "secular and practical."[81] At the same time, a historically rich or contrapuntal reading allows us to observe a far more serious problem emerge outside the text itself: namely, Cold War hegemony.

Wright's often novelistic account documents the collective achievements and shortcomings of what was just then coming to be known as the "Third World."[82] The book that Wright had wished to title "The Human Race Speaking" gives us an opportunity to see what becomes of the loose new utopianism discussed previously.[83] But with that fictional prediction at least partially realized, could Du Bois's borderless solidarity model coexist with a state system? Indeed, the Bandung Conference embodied the "Dark World" in its most purely statist incarnation (even though they figured heavily in discussion and even in the resulting Final Communiqué, the yet-unsuccessful liberation movements of Algeria, Morocco, and Tunisia and the group rights initiatives in South Africa and Palestine were not official attendees[84]). Such a stark delineation between colored communities widely recognized as sovereign (including those fully drawn into the orbit of a superpower, a problem I will discuss later) and those still struggling for political independence already represents a vast change from Du Bois's vision.

In typical Wright fashion, *The Color Curtain* fits in with neither of the two main interpretive schools regarding Bandung. Most accounts evince either an obvious anti-Communist slant, or else a romantic perspective on its ideals of solidarity. We see the first in the memoirs of pro-U.S. attendees like Ceylonese prime minister Sir John Kotelawala and New York congressman Adam Clayton Powell, Jr.[85] Among the radical left, on the other hand, Bandung gradually began to accrue an unmerited image of perfect harmony. In his 1963 "Message to the Grassroots," for example, Malcolm X presents the conference as a place where

> all the nations came together, the dark nations from Africa and Asia. . . . Once they kept [the white man] out, everybody else fell right in and fell in line. This is the thing that you and I have to understand. And these people who came together didn't have nuclear weapons, they didn't have jet planes, they didn't have all of the heavy armaments that the white man has. But they had unity.

As we will see from Wright's and Nehru's account, such a picture was far from true; it owes more to Du Bois's spiritualized picture of anti-colonial solidarity than to the realities of the conference. Yet Malcolm's poignantly optimistic version has strong staying power. Vijay Prashad and Bill Mullen summarize Bandung's current reputation when they call the conference "an anti-racist and anti-imperialist experiment with solidarity" and "the high water mark of twentieth-century anticolonial struggle," respectively. The utopian view of Bandung appears to color even perceptions of contemporary history: Zhang Yan, a Chinese journalist who reported on the conference, proclaimed in 1995 with mind-boggling confidence that "ever since, the Bandung spirit of peaceful coexistence between nations has been prevailing all over the world."[86]

Wright's portrayal is far less hopeful. What it conveys, more than anything else, is a kind of limbo. It shows how the newly independent nations have lost the energy of resistance and gained an unwelcome accountability, without achieving anything resembling the motivating utopia. Wright begins to perceive this limbo state even before departing for Asia, noting that one politically active Indonesian whom he interviews "had escaped a world that he did not want, but he did not know what kind of a world he did want." Utopian thinking, according to this diagnosis, has both fallen short and also ceased. One week, thousands of miles, and over a hundred pages later, Wright concludes that none of Africa's and Asia's leaders are better off than the hapless Indonesian. Rendering his overall thesis in full capitals, Wright virtually shouts with frustration that "all the men there represented governments that had already seized power and they did not know what to do with it" (207). For Wright, in other words, the post-independence conundrum comes down to there not having been sufficient specific visioning before independence.

As I will discuss, such a pessimistic picture stems in part, but not completely, from Wright's own proclivities. His tastes, after all, always did run more to the dystopian than the idyllic; not many writers can make the rural South (in *Uncle Tom's Children*) and the urban North (in *Native Son*) appear equally suffocating, oppressive, and bleak. The rare but potent Edenic moments in *Uncle Tom's Children*, most memorably a lazy afternoon at the swimming hole in "Big Boy Leaves Home," function purely as foils for the horrific violence that inevitably follows them.[87] To Wright, dreams are things that mock and deceive, rather than productively channeling energy as they do for Du Bois. In characterizing the entire contemporary world and especially Asia as made up of "millions of folk-minded masses trapped in the nets of fear, hunger and impossible dreams," Wright makes an absolute break from the romantic anti-colonialists who preceded him (54).

The book wrestles with failure even before depositing Wright in Indonesia. Its protracted first section, "Bandung: Beyond Left and Right" consists largely of Wright's obsessive attempt "to know the Asian personality" (20). Toward that Du Bious end he commissioned an extensive questionnaire from the social psychologist Otto Klineberg, unleashing it upon five native informants (one of whom may have been an informant not only for Wright but shortly afterward for the FBI).[88] Klineberg's questionnaire is itself a utopian endeavor. Filled with questions like "Do you want to see your country industrialized?," "Should intermarriage between the races be regulated by law?" and "What . . . is the best way to end racism?," it dwells in the fanciful realm of the conditional. But if the questionnaire gestures toward an ideal world, the answers never fulfill that promise. The interview results feel scattered and unfocused as Wright conveys them through the book's shortest paragraphs and most abrupt shifts. Even before Wright reaches the point at which he can deliver his conclusions, we feel that one of them must be a jarring lack of unity.

More importantly, Wright undermines his own data through the way that he conveys it to his reader. He makes the fascinating move of presenting the interviews neither as they occur (which would give a sense of immediacy and process), nor as a body through an impersonal research voice (which would give a sense of distance and objectivity), but rather as he him-self peruses them on the night train from Andalusia to Madrid. Thus excerpts and summaries of the interviews alternate disconcertingly with observations like "I lifted my eyes; the pastel-colored apartment buildings of Madrid were flashing by. I sighed" (70). At uneven intervals during the fifty-five pages in which Wright recounts his interviews, "the express train bumped along over the Spanish mountains toward Madrid" (26); "to the rocking of the train, I reflected" (31); "the express pounded on into the night as I pored over my notes" (33); "the Madrid express was rocking me to sleep" (55); and "in the morning light I stared at the tilting olive groves on the Spanish moun-tainsides; the train jolted toward Madrid" (63). The effect is so unsettling that it has led one recent critic to conclude erroneously that Wright conducted the interviews while actually in transit.[89] The method recalls Booker T. Washington's ostentatiously humble claim that he composed most of *Up from Slavery* "on board trains, or at hotels or railroad stations while I have been waiting for trains."[90] Both are self-conscious markers of an apparently artless realism, with Wright's technique testifying as well to his supremely transient state as an American exile in France. But the moving backdrop also serves to remind the reader that even at the end of this first journey Wright has come no nearer to defining the "pure Asian personality." Though Wright never says so directly, his method of presentation implies that such catego-ries as "the Asian mind" are in flux, and that his initial endeavor is therefore a misguided one (74). This first chapter frames the ultimately futile political exercise of Bandung with the futile intellectual exercise of pining down "the Asian," thus implicitly setting the stage for a still larger failure.

Wright's approach to the conference itself indicates a similar ambiva-lence. Despite setting out to counter the fear with which the West had greeted the conference, he still perpetuates the idea that Bandung rests on "negative unity," to use his own phrase (175). He shows with amused disgust how often Western journalists claimed prior to the conference that the only factor unit-ing the participating nations is their mutual hatred of the West. In addition to reproducing some of the hostile newspaper editorials, he also mocks a naïve French friend for asking, "her eyes wide with images of global racial revenge, 'What on earth have African Negroes and Burmese Buddhists in common?'" (17). But we must count Wright among those detractors, for he too notes that the participants share "nothing, it seemed to me, but what their past relationship to the Western world had made them feel" (12). Wright

never makes what could have been an easy rejoinder: that as newly independent nations the participants share particular issues of governance. This
would be the more utopian outlook, the belief that the unifying factor is not
a shared history of oppression but a shared openness of possibility.

Wright does make several attempts to find commonalities and equiva-
lences, or at least points of mutual comprehension, that rest on anything
other than a legacy of suffering. Upon arriving in Indonesia, he finds literal
common ground in the terrain itself. "The Javanese countryside reminded
me of Africa," Wright tells us, on the basis of peasant behavior, heat, buildings, commerce, and even "that same red earth" (129–30). He calls one of his
informants "the H. L. Mencken of Indonesia," thus at once paying his high-
est compliment and also framing Asia as kind of parallel universe to the
United States (53). But throughout the book, all of the instances of comprehension are negative, as in Wright's description of another informant as
being "as highly color-conscious as an American Negro" (44). By its close,
the conference does not look very different from the "war council" that the
Western press had feared (89). Nothing is defamiliarized, and our ethnocen-
tric perspective never shifts; we finish the narrative with the same preconceptions basically intact.[91] Toward the end of the book, Wright fools us briefly
into thinking that Bandung may have converted him, as "negative unity,
bred by a feeling that they [the delegates] had to stand together against a
rapacious West, turned into something that hinted of the positive" (175). But
we learn quickly that Wright means "positive" merely in a mathematical
sense (i.e., representing substance rather than deficit), not a moral one. The
delegates finally experience something in place of nothing only when "they
began to sense their combined strength; they began to taste blood" (175).
Absent here are any of the clichés of cultural anti-colonialism and affirmative Orientalism: that Asia and Africa can meet the West's material strength
with their own spiritual strength, or that the new nations might build their
future from reclaimed positive elements of the past. Instead, Wright
reiterates several times that the delegates hold in common only a history of
oppression and destruction. Like the Western press account that he cites so
disparagingly early in the book, he too concludes that the only basis for the
conference is a negative one.

Neither "negative unity" nor the bloodthirsty desire for revenge can
bring the conference a tangible sense of purpose. Wright builds to his
embittered conclusion that "All the men there represented governments

that had already seized power and they did not know what to do with it," quoted above, by assembling anecdotes to show how solidarity has floundered. He introduces, for example, "an American Negro who heard the 'call of race' and came to Bandung" (176). Entranced by this idea of global fellowship, traveling on his family's life savings, the Los Angeles mechanic "came thousands of miles to feel a fleeting sense of identity, of solidarity, a religious oneness with the others who shared his outcast state" but once there "understood absolutely nothing of what was going on about him" (177). The story contains an oblique condemnation of Bandung's entire premise: If "brown Mr. Jones" cannot comprehend the meaning of the proceedings, what use are they? The scene that Wright presents is one irreconcilably far from Du Bois's romance of oneness. Wright's sobering view of Bandung comes almost as a direct rejoinder to the psychedelic hallucination of Dark Princess, which Wright had years earlier dismissed as "only a romantic picture."[92]

Unlike Du Bois and the Young India collective, Wright also shows himself in The Color Curtain to be thoroughly uncomfortable with both biological and cultural hybridity. Despite his own exile history, he regards people who cross cultures with a removed pity. At various points throughout the book, Wright calls biculturalism a "problem" (42) and an "uneasy shifting back and forth" (120) that leads to "being a stranger to both worlds" (79). Further, as opposed to the pure and redemptive quality of Matthew and Kautilya's baby, here childhood is not a time of possibility but a dangerously vulnerable stage marked by susceptibility to infection. As elsewhere in The Color Curtain, Wright places his own opinions in the mouths of his interview subjects. In this case the amenable mouthpiece is Wright's host "Mr. P," who calls Indonesia "a baby country with many little childhood diseases" (105). As not only babies but hybrid babies, the new nations of the Bandung Conference would appear in Wright's estimation to have the gloomiest of prospects. Had Wright ever set out to compose a sequel to Dark Princess (admittedly, as terrible an idea as it is an unlikely one), if young Madhu even managed to survive rubella, he would grow into a confused, identity-conflicted adolescent.

As well as exhibiting discomfort with hybridity, Wright also differs from the anti-colonial utopians in his view of women's role in the new order. As opposed to Du Bois's feminist (if essentialized) vision of empowerment through fertility, Wright describes the "world of colored folk" in thoroughly masculinist terms. One of The Color Curtain's rare images of pure triumph, for example, is a scene in which spectating masses see for the first time "men of their color, race, and nationality arrayed in such aspects of power" (134). Elsewhere, Wright's scrutinizing attention to the conference's luminaries Chinese premier Zhou Enlai and Indian prime minister Jawaharlal Nehru places him in the category of reporters who presented Bandung as primarily a meeting of "Great Men." There were in fact women delegates, including Nehru's daughter and future Indian prime minister Indira Gandhi. Their absence comes in contrast to the deliberate inclusion in *Young India*, *Of One Blood*, and *Dark Princess* of women as actors in national (or transnational) liberation. Their roles may be temporally limited or symbolically cumbersome—in the case of *Of One Blood* and *Dark Princess*, the key women are interim figureheads awaiting a male messiah, and in the case of *Young India* they may be nameless mothers—but nonetheless those roles are crucial in the unfinished transition to full-blown utopia.

If neither hybridity nor shared history will suffice as organizing principles for a solidarity-based meeting, what does Wright offer in their stead? He names his own solution even while bemoaning its absence from Bandung: "secular and practical goals" (218). Wright's only hope lies in the Third World developing into a place of rationalism, unlikely given the "mystic-minded throng" that makes up the African and Asian masses (209). As Nina Kressner Cobb points out, Wright's developmentalism in *The Color Curtain* is of a piece with his "hostility, sympathy, repugnance and condescension" toward Africa in *Black Power*.[93] That earlier travelogue registers a view of Africa in utter contrast to Hopkins's romantic portrayal of ancient wisdom. Repulsed by all he sees, Wright resembles the unenlightened pre-Telassar Reuel searching in vain for "the march of progress" in Africa. Wright closes *Black Power* by counseling Nkrumah to "atomize the fetish-ridden past, abolish the mystical and nonsensical family relations that freeze the African in his static degradation."[94] In Kressner Cobb's psychoanalytic reading, Wright approaches Africa and Asia as aspects of his perennial subject—namely, himself—and since he considers his own breach with tradition a beneficial one, he can only conclude that the youthful nations that are his avatars ought to make the same break from their disempowering, burdensome histories.[95] To the extent that colonialism has already had that effect on Asia, Wright views it as a beneficial force, agreeing with one of his interview subjects that "in the long run, the impact of the West upon the East would undoubtedly be entered upon the credit side of the historical ledger" despite the pain of losing "irrational customs and traditions" (53). Wright wishes for a Third World free of what he sees as onerous spiritual pulls, much like Bellamy's Boston purged of Mesmerism.

At Bandung, that same developmentalism takes the form of incessantly identifying "race and religion" as the conference's hidden themes. By failing to define those terms, though, he demolishes his own analysis. He reminds us innumerable times (including in a chapter title) of the importance of race and religion; by the close of the book, those terms have lost meaning through repetition. Particularly problematic is "religion"; though Wright never gives a precise definition of "race" either, he does convey through quotes and examples the notion that race is a Western construction that has outlasted colonialism. "Religion," on the other hand, simply persists throughout as a mysterious, omnipresent, and destructive quality. Unlike other Bandung observers, Wright smells religion everywhere.[96] He is still in transit when the Palestine question provides his first exposure to what he deems religious fanaticism, though as we will see, he makes that determination with no evidence. As they fly from Rome to Cairo with other Bandung-bound reporters, an unnamed "dark-faced man" hands Wright a stack of photos:

> "What are these?" I asked.
> "Photos of Arab refugees driven by Jews out of their homes!"
> he said. "There are nine hundred thousand of them, homeless,
> starving . . ." [. . .]
> I leafed through the bundle of photos; they were authentic,
> grim, showing long lines of men, women, and children marching
> barefooted and half-naked over desert sands, depicting babies
> sleeping without shelter, revealing human beings living like
> animals. I peered up into the face of the journalist; his eyes were
> unblinking, hot, fanatic. This man was religious. It was strange
> how, the moment I left the dry, impersonal, abstract world of the
> West, I encountered at once: *religion*." (76–7; Wright's italics)

Amid the careful physical detail of the sequence, the lack of proof for the man's alleged faith is comparatively stunning. We are given no explanation for why he should appear "religious" and not, for example, humane—especially considering the "authentic" horror of the photos. If anything, their subject matter transcended religion, since Israel's 1955 Gaza offensive uprooted Christian as well as Muslim Arabs. (In fact, contrary to Wright's depiction of religion as a non-Western trait, the most salient quasi-religious force at play—Zionism—arose in Europe.) In equating outrage at Palestinian dispossession with religion, Wright indirectly redefines the latter term as any strongly held belief, though he holds back from including the West's alleged rationality among such beliefs. Unlike Du Bois's framing of realism as a construction, there is no intimation here that such "dry, impersonal" abstraction may be its own form of false idol. Just as he had been while recounting his native-informant interviews, Wright is still conspicuously in transit, suggesting that the diagnosis of "religion" ought to be a provisional one; yet it recurs innumerable times from that moment on.

In *The Color Curtain*'s most memorable anecdote, Wright manipulates an actual event in order to extend his verdict of superstition. This is the famous "Sterno episode," not coincidentally also the most novelistic moment of Wright's travelogue. The story runs thus: a nervous white American woman approaches Wright to get his insight on her own "Negro problem," namely the strange behavior of the black American journalist who shares her hotel room. Conventional and polite by day, the journalist has been creeping about the room late at night and crouching over an open flame. "Could she have been practicing voodoo, or something?" her fatuous room-mate asks Wright (184). With the helpful evidence of an empty can of Sterno, our narrator determines that the journalist has been straightening her hair with a hot comb under cover of night. Indeed, the shocked roommate confirms to Wright that the pitiable journalist, having run out of fuel, "begged and begged for a can of Sterno" (188). The incident provides Wright with a convenient opportunity to reflect on the depth of internalized racism: even in Indonesia, "where everybody was dark, that poor American Negro woman was worried about the hair she was born with" (186). Outside of *The Color Curtain*, though, the testimony of "that poor American Negro woman" tells an amusingly different tale. Ethel Payne, now widely recognized as a pioneer in black journalism, reported on the conference for the *Chicago Defender*. In a 1987 interview she tells of her hair troubles in Indonesia with a glee that utterly contradicts Wright's chapter title "Racial Shame at Bandung." She did indeed straighten her hair, ran out of Sterno in Bandung's extreme humidity, and told her friend Wright of her trouble. "If there's any Sterno in Bandung, I'll find it for you," Payne recounts Wright gallantly pledging.[97] There was not, but Wright found grain alcohol instead, showed Payne how to heat her comb with it, and even helped her comb her hair: "He'd pull sometimes, and then I'd pull the next. Together, we were frying my hair. It was the wildest thing you ever heard of!"[98] Even with Wright's assistance, Payne eventually decided that straight hair was not worth the trouble. "It was just getting to be ludicrous," Payne explains. Far from cringing in shame, for the remainder of the conference, "I would just put my little bonnet on, my little turban on, and let it go at that. But that was a hilarious moment, because he was trying so hard to help me."[99] And far from objectively and soberly judging, as he does in *The Color Curtain*, Wright here conspires in what he himself identified in print as the mythologization of white beauty.

Margaret Walker reads the critical alteration as a sign of Wright's "aversion to all black women."[100] While that may overstate matters, the story as it appears in *The Color Curtain* does show Wright saddling black women with pathologically insecure behavior. The fictional white roommate, mouthing liberal platitudes worthy of *Native Son*'s blind Mrs. Dalton, hardly fares better. But there is more at play here than Wright's misogyny. The author could have shown his own disgust with "racial shame" without inventing a middle-woman. What that implausible character provides is the association of self-hate with superstition, an association that in turn allows Wright to imply that rationalism can defeat both. As a fictional device, the white roommate serves to demonstrate how a hot comb may appear to an ignorant outsider as "voodoo"; thus the story fits better into the imposed frame of "race and religion." Even while mocking as cultural supremacy the belief that others are superstitious, he holds to what would become the Naipaulian idea of mystic-minded masses. Despite telling his straw woman to "get all that rot about voodoo out of your mind," he continues to view whole continents as riddled with superstition (188).

What will salvage Africa and Asia? How will these languishing regions begin to develop "secular and practical goals"? What the newly independent nations need, Wright implies, is more hardware and fewer abstractions. In the following exchange with the renowned journalist Mochtar Lubis, the topic at hand is once again Indonesia, but the point extends far beyond the archipelago.

> "How is the housing situation?" I asked Lubis.
>   "Desperate," he said. . . .
>   "What's holding up the building of houses? . . ."

"It takes about fifty dollars worth of Western materials to build
a house. . . . We don't even have nails; we can't make them."

" . . . can't a way be found to bypass this kind of dependence
upon the outside world? Can't Indonesia make nails, pipes, etc.?"

"No. Not yet. . . . We are still fighting a revolution,
nationalizing; there are strikes and much government control."

"Why are the people doing that instead of rebuilding?"

"Sentiment, politics. . . . They are trying to sweep out the last
of Western influence. They have their own ideas about what they
want." (97–8)

Wright uses the conversation to set up two parallel oppositions, delineating
types of activities ("fighting a revolution" versus "rebuilding") and types of
objects used in the activities (houses, nails, and pipes versus sentiment, politics, and ideas). One category is concrete, material, quantifiable, and the
other abstract. The contrast works beautifully on a rhetorical level, firmly
suggesting that all the intangible qualities so important to Du Bois not only
fail to help but in fact actively hinder the construction of a new order. As in
the Sterno episode discussed above, the dialogue here—especially the glar-
ingly non-oral "nails, pipes, etc."—seems apocryphal. Lubis, like Payne,
revealed Wright to have fabricated other quotes that appear in *The Color
Curtain*, though to my knowledge he did not comment on this particular
conversation.[101] Whether or not it occurred, Wright uses it cannily to undermine the romantic model of solidarity set out by Du Bois.

In *The Color Curtain* as elsewhere, one could go so far as to say that
Wright romanticizes rationalism. In fact, looking over alternative accounts
of the Bandung Conference, we find that it would take more than "secular
and practical goals" to salvage Du Bois's dream of a free darker world. As
pessimistic as Wright's narrative appears, many of Bandung's other commentators portray the conference with a still more skeptical bent. Our own
generation may wish to view the conference as an almost prelapsarian
moment free of Cold War pressures, but to some degree in Wright's account,
and even more so in others, the weeklong gathering proved already suscepti-
ble to the polarizing pull of the superpower era. To take two quite disparate
examples, Indian prime minister Jawaharlal Nehru and American reporter
Carl Rowan both convey a reality even less glorious than Wright's own
landscape of disappointment, confusion, and fanaticism. If all we can see

though Wright's narrowed eyes is irrationality and self-interested machina-
tions, Nehru's and Rowan's accounts unequivocally support at least the latter.
Their accounts of American spies and terrorist threats force us to reevaluate
Wright's perennial cynic as in fact mistakenly sanguine.

According to the accounts of Jawaharlal Nehru and others, the United
States sent several "Intelligence men" to infiltrate the sessions; but in fact,
implies Nehru, the United States had organized such solid support from
genuine delegates that its own spies proved superfluous. Turkey, Pakistan,
Iraq, Lebanon, and Iran "represented fully and sometimes rather aggressively, the pure American doctrine," Nehru told his government.[102] Again
surpassing Wright in pessimism, Nehru discerningly reads the conference
proceedings as predicting the coming catastrophe in Vietnam. "Turkey and
Pakistan generally supported the South Vietnamese representatives . . . This
means that America supports them. The future of Vietnam, therefore, is not
a hopeful one," Nehru concludes dryly.[103] If Bandung represents the realization of Dark Princess's fantasy, the conference is inaccessibly far from Du
Bois's ideal. What Wright renders with "controlled pessimism" appears elsewhere as simply an exercise in Bismarckian diplomacy.[104]

A careful look at other accounts of Bandung also alerts us to what
may be the most profound irony of the anti-colonial conference: Indonesia's
own imperial relationship to some of its neighboring islands. Both Rowan
and Nehru make offhand note of the terrorist warnings that redirect some
of the conference proceedings.[105] The references are to the militant group
Darul Islam, founded in 1942 to oppose first Dutch and then Indonesian
control of West Java. What we have, then, is an inkling of Indonesia's expansionist aspirations. That nascent expansionism would later become full-
blown with Indonesia's annexation of East Timor in 1975 under the approval
of Gerald Ford and Henry Kissinger—an act whose bloody repercussions
continue to emerge. As in Dark Princess's "color line within a color line,"
Indonesia's history proves that the experience of colonialism is no guarantee
against a government imposing it against a weaker population. Primarily
concerned with a single color line, Wright misses that subtext of Indonesian
imperialism.

The conference's failure fully to address the needs and concerns of
its African participants is yet another instance of the abstract notion of solidarity proving insufficient, one that appears across various accounts of
Bandung. This is an outcome that we could have predicted even from the

utopian writing of the pre-independence period. *Young India,* after all, proudly cites Indian assistance in the British colonization of East Africa, while *Dark Princess* bitterly dramatizes the "color line within a color line" that divides Kautilya's revolutionary Council of the Darker World. In this case, despite the inclusive label "Afro-Asian," "Negro Africa was the weakest part of the conference," as Wright states flatly (128). Other, less analytical reports implicitly confirm Wright by casting the African attendees as colorful curiosities. With the charismatic Nkrumah back at home, the four sub-Saharan delegations lose out completely in Bandung's pageant of personalities; Asian and Western accounts alike invariably diminish them to variants on "jet-black men . . . in flowing robes," as Carl Rowan puts it in this case. The conference's official *Pictorial Record* labels each of the many photographs of Sukarno, Nehru, and other luminaries but fails to name all but one African delegate (Liberia's Momulu Dukuly), not even doing some the courtesy of mentioning their countries ("Indira Gandhi with Delegates from Africa"; "Chief Delegate in traditional dress").[106] Amid this gathering of "the underdogs of the human race," there are apparently strata of influence and even humanness (12).

Africa's most memorable appearance in the final session at Bandung comes in Nehru's closing address. In a condescendingly well-meaning gesture, he ends by invoking his own region's responsibility toward Africa. Nehru concludes his speech with this rambling apology:

> I think that there is nothing more terrible, nothing more horrible
> than the infinite tragedy of Africa in the past few hundred years.
> When I think of it everything else becomes insignificant before
> that infinite tragedy of Africa ever since the days when millions of
> them were carried away into America or elsewhere: the way they
> were taken away, fifty per cent dying in the process, we have to
> bear that burden, all of us, I think the world has to bear it . . . And
> it is up to Asia to help Africa to the best of her ability, because we
> are sister continents.[107]

As he shifts from "Africa" to the unspecified and homogenous "millions of them," Nehru renders the continent and its people as grammatically interchangeable. With the needs of its few besieged islands of independence kept marginal to the conference's agenda, Africa once again plays the role of the silent partner.[108] This sense of "brown man's burden" is far from the closing panorama of equality that Gilroy observes in Du Bois. U.S. congressman Adam Clayton Powell, Jr., offers a different and still more sinister interpretation, reporting that Gold Coast delegate Kojo Botsio told him confidentially that "The British Foreign Office has agents on the scene here in Bandung and these agents have bluntly told me and other chiefs of the Sudan and the Gold Coast that if we opened our mouths and said anything more than the perfunctory word of greeting, the British government would not allow the Sudan nor the Gold Coast to achieve the Commonwealth status which they had been promised." In this case, the delicate position of the Gold Coast and Sudanese delegates points to the conference organizers' error in not inviting other national liberation movements—of Kenya, the Congo, and North Africa, among others—to participate officially. We see a significant imbalance here between sovereign states and independence movements, one that points to the flaws in a romantic notion of solidarity.

Beyond the problems of equality or equivalency, Wright and the other pragmatic commentators dwell on other omitted realities that further disrupt Du Bois's picture of a "world of colored folk." From solidarity to sanitation, the distance between their accounts and the hopeful prophesies of *Dark Princess* demonstrate what the great utopian failed or refused to consider. At various points in his travel account, Wright exhibits a quite justifiable concern with bodily functions and hygiene. With these topics we know we have left the Du Boisian universe in which bodies may bear babies and may suffer lynching, but labor pain and charred limbs never enter the picture. In Wright's Indonesia, normal human interaction, left unregulated, can prove disgusting and unsanitary: "I saw a young man squatting upon the bank of a canal, defecating in broad daylight into the canal's muddy, swirling water . . . A tiny boy was washing his teeth, dipping his toothbrush into the canal . . ." (94). If running water, in romantic discourse, unites far-flung regions and refreshes the spirit, here is the unpalatable realist antidote to that worn-out trope. Determined that his research and reporting will be absolutely thorough, Wright remarks that "Indonesian bathrooms are strange contraptions indeed; I tried futilely to determine how they originated" (117). Nehru's still more pragmatic Bandung writings corroborate this quintessentially anti-romantic preoccupation. As he reminded India's ambassador to Indonesia a few months before the conference, the viability of the transnational ideal that Bandung represents depends not on such abstractions as solidarity or understanding but on "an adequate provision of bath rooms and lavatories, etc. People can do without drawing rooms, but they cannot do without bath rooms and lavatories."[109] Attending to the most basic matters of sanitation, Nehru exhibits an even more prosaic outlook than Wright. Both explore a topic that would have interested Bellamy and even More, but certainly not romantic utopians like Hopkins or Du Bois, whose visions differ fundamentally from the reality of an undertaking like Bandung.

We find in Wright's view of Africa and Asia an eerie resemblance to that of the official organs of development. Here is the diagnosis of the United Nations "Measures for the Economic Development of Underdeveloped Countries," an influential 1951 policy document: "rapid economic progress is impossible without painful adjustments. Ancient philosophies have to be scrapped; old social institutions have to disintegrate; bonds of caste, creed, and race have to burst; and large numbers of persons who cannot keep up with progress have to have their expectations of a comfortable life frustrated."[110] Clearly, the culturally rich, often nostalgic utopias of Hopkins, Coomaraswamy, Tagore, and Du Bois would not be the defining visions for the postcolonial period. All the attributes that their affirmative Orientalism identifies as assets—mysticism, irrationality, spiritualism—are liabilities to Wright. As Bill Mullen concludes, Wright can only imagine a developmentalist cure for the ills of the Third World: "Wright's means of giving shape to this mass through a continued course of Western rationalization constituted an attempt to bleach it of its red, yellow, or even black excesses."[111] Reading alternate accounts of the Bandung Conference alerts us to Wright's critical misdiagnosis of the ailments of postcoloniality. His analysis is not too pessimistic, but alights on the wrong explanation: what is really controlling the shape of Bandung is the various forms of neo-colonialism, whether American, English, or Indonesian. Overly attuned to the foibles of religion, Wright misses the full story, which is just as disheartening if not more so. Bandung's lesson is far more ominous. During the Cold War period, as in our own era of "with us or against us," to be nonaligned—to be truly independent— would prove an impossible feat.[112]

Epilogue:
Multicultural Utopia?

"'It's all wrong,' Mr. P. said wearily. 'We made a revolution
and the common people fought and died to drive out the
Dutch. . . . We drove out the Dutch to build a good
society, now we have a class of Indonesians
who are acting more or less
like the Dutch.'"
—Richard Wright, *The Color Curtain*

What happened to the anti-colonial dream? The heady process of decolonization has brought about not utopia but corporate globalization, neo-colonial
economic and cultural relations, and widespread acceptance of developmentalist values. The arts-focused nation of *Young India* has given way to the
back office of the world; Pauline Hopkins's glorious Africa to a continent
decimated by structural adjustments and civil war; and J. T. Sunderland's
intrinsically anti-colonial United States to a full-scale imperial power. The
myth of developmentalism has achieved an absolute cognitive victory, to
the point that we have only recently begun to think outside of it.[1] Witness the
semantic evolution of Du Bois's "world of colored folk": from "Third World,"
with its derogatory implication of Cold War remnants; to "underdeveloped"
and then quickly to "developing," an adjective remarkable for its ability to be
at once euphemistic and prescriptive; and now, concurrently, to perhaps the
most sinister formulation yet, "emerging markets," another term that allows

any nonindustrialized country only one option for participating in a global community. The latter terms encapsulate the triumph of the teleological view seen in Bellamy's *Looking Backward,* in which "the more backward races are gradually being educated up to civilized institutions." Whether the action at hand is "being educated," "developing," or "emerging," the imperializing gerund remains consistent from 1888 to the present.

The literature of the postcolonial period abounds with examples of failed utopias. If the early-twentieth-century texts we have encountered thus far convey glorious vistas of possibility, post-independence writings explore the poetics of disillusionment. The passage from anti-colonial utopia to post-colonial reality occupies many writers from Africa and South Asia. One of the most poignant images of failed utopia comes early in Salman Rushdie's *The Moor's Last Sigh.* The idealistic Indian National Congress activist Camoens da Gama whispers to his dying wife of

> the dawning of a new world, Belle, a free country, Belle, above
> religion because secular, above class because socialist, above caste
> because enlightened, above hatred because loving, above
> vengeance because forgiving, above tribe because unifying, above
> language because many tongued, above colour because multi-
> coloured, above poverty because victorious over it, above ignorance
> because literate, above stupidity because brilliant.[2]

Camoens beautifully renders his pluralist dream, which later provides only the most heartbreaking contrast to the horrific violence that follows Indian independence. Even the most cursory encounter with the recent literature of Africa and South Asia as well as the Pacific and Caribbean regions will yield myriad further examples of postcolonial disappointment.[3]

The writers who appear in *Landscapes of Hope* offer clear answers as to why the promises of independence failed to materialize. Rabindranath Tagore and A. K. Coomaraswamy would find India's official priorities too derivative of Western values, particularly modernization and industrialization. Du Bois, throughout *Dark Princess,* anticipates and dramatizes structural problems with solidarity politics. George Schuyler predicts colonial revenge, albeit of a cruder and more obvious variety. Jawaharlal Nehru and others identify the Cold War pressures that would prevent new nations from growing in a natural and organic form. We can also turn to other trenchant analysts of postcolonial failure. In "The Pitfalls of National Consciousness,"

Frantz Fanon warns that national bourgeoisies will attempt to "advanta-geously replace the middle class of the mother country," a problem already described by Richard Wright's Mr. P. in the epigraph above.[4] Kwame Nkrumah offers the coinage "neo-colonialism," a pithy label that proves increasingly apt. For Immanuel Wallerstein, no independent state can suc-ceed when immersed in a capitalist world system.[5] In Marxian terms, it is incomplete revolution, whether inside or outside the nation, that doomed the anti-colonial utopia.

At the same time, we are constantly told that racism and colonialism are things of the past. Multicultural imagery and references to the end of history attempt to convince us that the anti-colonial utopia has been real-ized. None other than W. E. B. Du Bois presciently depicted this state of affairs several decades ago in his *Black Flame* trilogy, published between 1957 and 1961. The 1,000-page trilogy introduces several coalitions and col-laborations reminiscent of *Dark Princess*'s utopia. Just before closing, how-ever, it takes a drastically different turn. The trilogy's hero, the Du Boisian educator Manuel Mansart, is invited to a secret meeting in New York's posh Rainbow Room of "African rulers, West Indian officials and leaders of the Negroes of the United States."[6] Despite that promising premise, the group turns out to be bankrolled and controlled by America's most powerful busi-nessmen. Spearheaded by a Russian princess—in a Du Bois novel, already the sign of a dangerously retrograde movement—the self-interested alli-ance schemes to control Africa permanently. As the decadent and conserva-tive Princess Zegue announces to the gathered elite of the African diaspora, behind her are "some of the sixty men who own America and are the real rulers of one world" (337–8). They are manufacturers with an interest in South Africa, Rhodesia, the Congo, and North Africa; though originating from the United States, their interventions are never less than global. The "Big Sixty" present a Manichean scenario: "Will you join with the white race to help crush and beat back the crazy Chinese and Russian Communists, help bring that world back to its normal procedures; or will you join this rebellion against established authority—this revolt against civilization?" (339). The former course—the defense of civilization—consists of a false utopia that mimes equality in order to deflect Communism and thus keep Africa safe for Western industry. Here are Fanon's national bourgeoisies, not only replacing but openly colluding with an international capitalist class.

In *Worlds of Color,* Du Bois shows how positive internationalism (what would later be called "globalization from below") always breeds a coordinated repressive response, a reactionary counter-internationalism. In this case, it is all the more effective because it co-opts the language and imagery of liberation. What looks like anti-colonial solidarity actually serves to secure apparently limitless power for the globalizing forces of multinational industry. Here neo-colonialism proceeds with absolute and official complicity on the part of each national elite. As a result, as Princess Zegue portentously declares, "For five hundred years the British, French and German empires, and lately the United States, have ruled Europe, Asia, Africa, the Seas and all America. That rule has been temporarily disturbed in some areas. It will be restored and perpetuated—of that there is no shadow of doubt" (338).

Appropriately, the gathering comes in a chapter called "Death." On the most literal level, the title describes the worldly end of Du Bois's protagonist Mansart; but it also refers to the extinguishing of an ideal that Du Bois had held even before representing it in *Dark Princess,* at least since the first Pan-African Congress of 1900. The particular form of that internationalist ideal's demise is in fact worse than death: the old dream, rather than simply vanishing, succumbs to a new force that co-opts its rhetoric while robbing it of real transformative power. As Du Bois used his descriptions of Sara's and Kautilya's clothes to encapsulate the difference between a realist and a romantic politics, his rendering here of Princess Zegue's couture ensemble shows the malevolent Russian royal as an expensive counterfeit of all that Kautilya embodies:

> To her long, crimson-pointed hands, she was braceleted and
> ringed with a fortune in precious metals and blazing gems. Her
> bosom, with the contrivance of wire and elastic, was built out
> almost too full for her long, lithe limbs which undulated beneath
> billowing fabric whose embroidery must have kept a hundred
> skilled costumers working a hundred days until now their delicate
> folds concealed and at the same time revealed the perfection of her
> form. Her feet were shod in slippers of beaten gold and writhing
> silver. There was a studied harmony and simplicity in all her
> magnificence, and the total impression, when with a studied
> languor she extended her bejeweled hand to the guests, was beauty
> and opulence. (337)

This passage incorporates some of the extravagance and dynamism that characterized Telassar as well as both Kautilya and her utopia. As in Matthew's first sight of Kautilya, gerunds abound in the "blazing," "billowing," and "writhing" costume. But Du Bois makes clear through "contrivance" and the repetition of "studied" that this is a derivative, imitative version. Also new here is his close attention to the exploitative labor involved in assembling the outfit. Where Kautilya's clothes appear organic, these are falsely manufactured at great cost to their makers, even the "beaten gold and writhing silver" of this Princess's shoes having suffered for her deceptive beauty. Du Bois carefully assembles a figure and a group that superficially resemble Kautilya and her network of resistance, but at their core reek of artifice and abuse.

Forty years after Du Bois wrote *Worlds of Color,* proof of his fear comes in the form of the superficial multiculturalism increasingly espoused by American and multinational corporations. As Du Bois predicted in his final work of fiction, global capitalism in its most "progressive" mode now mitigates opposition by professing inclusivity. Karl Mannheim's definitions, introduced earlier, will help to clarify matters. Mannheim cautions us against understanding every "situationally transcendent idea" as utopian. In fact, some states of mind "incongruous with reality," to use his terms, actually serve to perpetuate existing power relations: his example is "the idea of Christian brotherly love . . . in a society founded on serfdom."[7] Centuries later, but through a similar method, multiculturalism provides a cover for the self-interested forces of corporate capital. In the "Benetton ad" version of anti-colonial utopia, a superficial concession to racial diversity erases deep inequalities of class and race. Several incisive commentators have recently expounded on this disturbing phenomenon. In his study of Afro-Asian solidarity, *Everybody Was Kung-Fu Fighting,* Vijay Prashad observes that "multicultural imperialism offers an allowance for so-called local cultures to remain intact as long as the cultural forms are those that facilitate consumerism." Prashad goes on to quote Angela Davis, who observes how multiculturalism ensures that "differences and diversities are retained superficially while becoming homogenized and harmonized politically."[8] Most recently, Jodi Melamed argues convincingly that "U.S. multiculturalism . . . legitimates as it obfuscates."[9]

Such a dynamic is hardly limited to the United States. Zadie Smith brilliantly dramatizes in *White Teeth* the way in which well-meaning multicultural pedagogy propagates an obligatory tolerance that ghettoizes culture and enforces essentialized identities.[10] On a larger scale, mainstream discussion of contemporary economic and cultural globalization portrays corporate capitalism as a force for healthy diffusion of cultures and ideas. Kwame Anthony Appiah's much-lauded *Cosmopolitanism: Ethics in a World of Strangers* is a case in point. While useful in places for its considered critique of identity politics and its explosion of false notions of authenticity, the book elsewhere presents a defense of global corporate pillage. Propounding the notion that all consumers will put a personal stamp on imported products, Appiah asks rhetorically, "What can you tell about someone's soul from the fact that she drinks Coca-Cola?"[11] While Appiah is right to contest crude unidirectional models of cultural influence, the fact remains that economic relations dictate basic human living conditions—and that today those conditions are far from fair or equitable. Throughout *Cosmopolitanism* Appiah sets up the most absurd brands of cultural nativism as scapegoats to vindicate economic globalization. From this point of view, the market is the ultimate anti-fundamentalist force. Indeed, Appiah writes that "if your concern is global homogeneity, this utopia [of radical Islam], not the world that capitalism is producing, is the one that you should worry about."[12] Rather, I would hold it incumbent upon us to worry about both. We can only construct better worlds, as the subjects of this study attempted to do, by eschewing fundamentalisms of all kinds, whether religious or economic. Compared with Leela Gandhi's fin-de-siècle affective communities or J. T. Sunderland's international relationships of sympathy, this new "market cosmopolitanism" is entirely bereft of their defining quality of resistance to an unjust order. As Bruce Robbins writes, contemporary "celebrations of cosmopolitan diversity have largely been uninterrupted by the issues of economic equality or geopolitical justice."[13] Those are precisely the issues that must occupy the inheritors of Lajpat Rai's and W. E. B. Du Bois's utopian aspirations.

This study had many beginnings: Thomas More's generic inauguration in 1516; Edward Bellamy's imaginative coup of 1888; 1903, when Pauline Hopkins took her fiction abroad and Du Bois struck out against the Washingtonian compromise; and Lajpat Rai's 1915 exile. More arranged the fortuitous marriage of fiction and political idealism. Bellamy revitalized utopia by moving it forward in time, also introducing the imperializing elements of linear history and racial purity. Lajpat Rai, Hopkins, and Du Bois further altered the utopian form by incorporating a punctuated time frame, embracing racial hybridity, and constructing borderless communities.

Contesting the teleological outlook of developmentalism, they transformed Bellamy's and Gilman's utopianism into something more useful for anti-colonial emancipation. But in so doing they also reinscribed preset categories of race and spirituality. Their anti-colonial utopianism faced new threats in the period of purported independence, the most pernicious of which may be appropriation. However, even those who view the path of history with regret recognize how important it is not to allow the constraints of the actual to set the limits of the possible. The impoverished options offered by Appiah—corporate globalization or nativist cultural nationalism—need not define the horizons of possibility. With careful attention to their central flaws of romanticization, expediency, and amorphousness, it is worth resurrecting the world-altering visions of the writers presented here—or, better still, creating our own utopian landscapes.

Notes

INTRODUCTION

1. Lala Lajpat Rai lecture quoted in "Explosion of Asia as Menace to Peace," *New York Evening Post* (September 22, 1917): 14.

2. W. E. B. Du Bois, *Dark Princess* (1928; reprint, Jackson, Miss.: Banner Books, 1995), 278. Subsequent references will be noted parenthetically in the text.

3. Fredric Jameson, *Archaeologies of the Future: The Desire Called Utopia and Other Science Fictions* (London: Verso, 2005), 3.

4. Charlotte Perkins Gilman, *Herland* (1915; reprint, New York: Pantheon Books, 1979), 54.

5. For the most succinct description of Western Orientalism, see Edward Said, *Orientalism* (New York: Vintage Books, 1979), 1–4. For Fox's extended discussion of "affirmative Orientalism," see Richard Fox, *Gandhian Utopia Experiments with Culture* (Boston: Beacon Press, 1989), 95–109. Also useful is the thoughtful essay "East of Said," in which Fox reflects on his adaptation of Said's model. Richard G. Fox, "East of Said," in *Edward Said: A Critical Reader*, ed. Michael Sprinker (London: Blackwell Publishing, 1992), 144–56.

6. Charles Chesnutt parodies that generalizing mind frame in his short story "Po' Sandy" when he has his white narrator refer to "the Oriental cast of the Negro's imagination." Chesnutt, *The Conjure Woman and Other Conjure Tales* (Durham, N.C.: Duke University Press, 1993), 46. Important critical studies of European and American Africanism include Christopher Miller, *Blank Darkness: Africanist Discourse in French* (Chicago: University of Chicago Press, 1986), V. Y. Mudimbe, *The Invention of Africa: Gnosis, Philosophy and the Order of Knowledge* (Bloomington: Indiana University Press, 1988), and Toni Morrison, *Playing in the Dark: Whiteness and the Literary Imagination* (New York: Vintage, 1993). Arturo Escobar succinctly

addresses the parallels and overlaps between Africanism and Orientalism, especially in relation to the discourse of development, in *Encountering Development: The Making and Unmaking of the Third World* (Princeton: Princeton University Press, 1993), 5–10.

7. T. Jackson Lears, *No Place of Grace: Antimodernism and the Transformation of American Culture, 1880–1920* (Chicago: University of Chicago Press, 1981).

8. Leela Gandhi, *Affective Communities: Anticolonial Thought, Fin-de-Siècle Radicalism, and the Politics of Friendship* (Durham, N.C.: Duke University Press, 2006), 11.

9. In some of the more material convergences between the Indian and Irish Home Rule movements, Irish-American activist Myron Phelps founded New York's Society for the Advancement of India in 1907; Dudley Field Malone helped establish the Friends of Freedom for India (with DuBois on its advisory board) in 1919; and Agnes Smedley and other Indian nationalists marched in the 1920 St. Patrick's Day parade. For details see Sobhag Mathur, *Echoes of the Indian National Movement in America* (Jodhpur: Kusumanjali Prakashan, 1996), especially chapter 1, "Indian Revolutionaries in America (1900–1920)." Such connections have been enormously fruitful for recent research in cultural history. For the influence of Irish nationalism on Garvey and other Caribbean writers see Michael Malouf, *Other Emerald Isles: Caribbean Revisions of Irish Cultural Nationalism* (Ph.D. diss., Columbia University, 2004). For Garvey's brand of Pan-Africanism as a utopian movement that relies on a rhetoric of motherland, see Robin D. G. Kelley, *Freedom Dreams: The Black Radical Imagination* (Boston: Beacon Press, 2002), 23–9.

10. For the broadest summary of his argument, see Benedict Anderson, *Imagined Communities: Reflections on the Origin and Spread of Nationalism* (London: Verso, 1983), 47–9.

11. F. Nnabuenyi Ugonna, "Introduction to Casely Hayford," in J. E. Casely Hayford, *Ethiopia Unbound: Studies in Race Emancipation* (London: Frank Cass and Company, 1969), viii.

12. Ian Christopher Fletcher, "Double Meanings: Nation and Empire in the Edwardian Era," in Antoinette M. Burton, ed., *After the Imperial Turn: Thinking With and Through the Nation* (Durham, N.C.: Duke University Press, 2003), 246.

13. For some of the contours and landmarks of that emerging field, see Sean Latham and Robert Scholes, "The Rise of Periodical Studies," *PMLA* 121.2 (March 2005), 517–31.

14. Some prominent examples of the first category include Bill Ashcroft, Gareth Griffiths, and Helen Tiffin, *The Empire Writes Back: Theory and Practice in Post-Colonial Literature* (London: Routledge, 1989); Barbara Harlow, *Resistance Literature* (New York: Methuen, 1987); part III of Anne McClintock, *Imperial Leather: Race, Gender, and Sexuality in the Colonial Contest* (London: Routledge, 2005); and chapter 3 of Said's own *Culture and Imperialism* (New York: Knopf, 1993). In the second and rapidly growing category, valuable and influential contributions have come from Wai Chee Dimock, Brent Hayes Edwards, Robin Kelley, Lisa Lowe, Vijay Prashad, Nikhil Singh, and Penny

Von Eschen. See especially Edwards, *The Practice of Diaspora: Literature, Translation, and the Rise of Black Internationalism* (Cambridge: Harvard University Press, 2003); Kelley, *Freedom Dreams;* and Prashad, *Everybody Was Kung-Fu Fighting: Afro-Asian Connections and the Myth of Cultural Purity* (Boston: Beacon Press, 2001).

15. Jenny Sharpe refutes this notion in her essay "Is the United States Postcolonial?" *Diaspora* 4:2 (1995): 181–98.

16. Edwards, *Practice of Diaspora,* 7.

17. See Karl Mannheim, *Ideology and Utopia: An Introduction to the Sociology of Knowledge* (New York: Harcourt, Brace & World, 1968), especially 173–6.

18. This is Weber's term, borrowed from Schiller, for the historical trend of rationalization and bureaucratization. For a fuller explanation see Max Weber, "Science as a Vocation" (1919), in *From Max Weber: Essays in Sociology,* eds. H. H. Gerth and C. Wright Mills (New York: Oxford University Press, 1958), 155.

19. Thomas More, *Utopia* (1516), ed. and trans. Edward Surtz (New Haven: Yale University Press, 1964), 83.

20. For more on the distinction between anti-utopia and dystopia, see chapter 1, note 58.

21. Krishan Kumar, *Utopia and Anti-Utopia in Modern Times* (Oxford: Basil Blackwell, 1987), 224; Tom Moylan, *Demand the Impossible: Science Fiction and the Utopian Imagination* (New York: Methuen, 1986).

22. See Moylan, *Demand the Impossible;* John Rawls, *The Law of Peoples* (Cambridge: Harvard University Press, 1999); and Immanuel Wallerstein, *Utopistics* (New York: New Press, 1998). Other coinages are Robert Schehr's "dynamic utopia" in *Dynamic Utopia: Establishing Intentional Communities as a New Social Movement* (Westport, Conn.: Bergin and Garvey, 1997) and David Harvey's "utopianism of process" in *Spaces of Hope* (Berkeley: University of California Press, 2000). For a brief bibliography of attempts to bring utopianism back into favor, see Erin McKenna's introduction to her philosophical study *The Task of Utopia* (Lanham: Rowman and Littlefield, 2001), esp. 13.

23. Marge Piercy, *Woman on the Edge of Time* (New York: Fawcett Crest, 1976), 96.

24. Bill Ashcroft, Gareth Griffiths, and Helen Tiffin, *The Post-Colonial Studies Reader* (London: Routledge, 1995), 183.

25. Both Vijay Prashad and Robin Kelley use "polyculturalism" to refer to a doctrine that rejects the idea of singular cultures meeting within a predetermined capitalist structure. Against multiculturalism, "polyculturalism, on the other hand, offers a dynamic view of history, mainly because it argues for cultural complexity." Vijay Prashad, *Everybody Was Kung-Fu Fighting: Afro-Asian Connections and the Myth of Cultural Purity* (Boston: Beacon Press, 2001), 66.

26. As M. Giulia Fabi writes of an earlier black utopia, we experience not "a fixed state of perfection but rather the utopia of a collective desire and commitment to strive towards social justice." M. Giulia Fabi, *Passing and the Rise of the African American Novel* (Urbana: University of Illinois Press, 2001), 70.

27. See Prashad, *Kung-Fu Fighting.*

CHAPTER 1

1. Gilbert Rist, *The History of Development: From Western Origins to Global Faith*, trans. Patrick Camiller (London: Zed Books, 1997), 40–3.

2. Frank E. Manuel and Fritzie P. Manuel, *Utopian Thought in the Western World* (Cambridge: Harvard University Press, 1979), 759; Kumar, *Utopia and Anti-Utopia*, 136.

3. Krishan Kumar, *Utopia and Anti-Utopia in Modern Times* (Oxford: Basil Blackwell, 1987), 137–8.

4. See Rist, *History of Development*, especially chapter 2, "The Metamorphosis of a Myth."

5. Robert Burton, *The Anatomy of Melancholy* (1621; reprint, Philadelphia: J. W. Moore, 1850), 62–3.

6. Joseph Conrad, *Heart of Darkness* (1902; reprint, London: Penguin Books, 1989), 33.

7. Rist, *History of Development*, 21.

8. Ania Loomba, *Colonialism/Postcolonialism* (London: Routledge, 2005), 23.

9. Hawthorne lived at Brook Farm for seven months in 1841, and published his derisive fictional account of the community in 1852. Its embittered narrator Miles Coverdale, too, writes ten years following his abortive experience. Early in *The Blithedale Romance*, Coverdale describes a "cheery . . . blaze" at Blithedale, but moves immediately to extinguish any warmth that blaze might convey to the reader:

"Vividly does that fireside re-create itself, as I rake away the ashes from the embers in my memory, and blow them up with a sigh, for lack of more inspiring breath. Vividly for an instant, but anon, with the dimmest gleam, and with just as little fervency for my heart as for my finger-ends! The staunch oaken logs were long ago burnt out. Their genial glow must be represented, if at all, by the merest phosphoric glimmer, like that which exudes, rather than shines, from damp fragments of decayed trees, deluding the benighted wanderer through a forest. Around such chill mockery of a fire some few of us might sit on the withered leaves, spreading out each a palm towards the imaginary warmth, and talk over our exploded scheme for beginning the life of Paradise anew."

In a few sentences, Hawthorne places the fire, the story he will tell through Coverdale, and even the noble ideals of utopian reform in an inaccessible past. Nathaniel Hawthorne, *The Blithedale Romance* (1852; reprint, New York: W. W. Norton, 1958), 37.

10. Charlotte Perkins Gilman, *Herland* (1915; reprint, New York: Pantheon Books, 1979), cover quote.

11. Edward Bellamy, *Looking Backward* (1888; reprint, New York: Penguin Books, 1986), 47. Subsequent references will be noted parenthetically in the text.

12. Karl Marx and Friedrich Engels, "Manifesto of the Communist Party" (1848), in *The Marx-Engels Reader*, ed. Robert C. Tucker (New York: W. W. Norton, 1978), 496.

13. Edward Bellamy to William Dean Howells, 17 June 1888, quoted in Jean Pfaelzer, *The Utopian Novel in America, 1886–1896* (Pittsburgh: University of Pittsburgh Press, 1984), 43.

14. For an extended reading of this "representational strategy of *racelessness by omission*," see M. Giulia Fabi, "'Utopian Melting': Technology, Homogeneity, and the American Dream in *Looking Backward*," in *Technology and the American Imagination*, ed. Francesca Bisutti De Riz and Rosella Mamoli Zorzi (Venezia, Italy: Supernova, 1994), 346–54.

15. Edward Bellamy, untitled letter, *The New Nation*, 3 October 1891: 567.

16. Thomas Peyser, *Utopia and Cosmopolis: Globalization in the Era of American Literary Realism* (Durham, N.C.: Duke University Press, 1998), 29.

17. Though absent from his unfailingly America-centric biographies, the Fabians figured prominently in Bellamy's political philosophy; he even wrote the introduction to the American edition of the *Fabian Essays in Socialism*. See G. Bernard Shaw, ed., *Socialism: The Fabian Essays* (Boston: C. E. Brown, 1894).

18. Beatrice Potter, Interview in *British Weekly*, 29 June 1893: 146, quoted in Ian Britain, *Fabianism and Culture: A Study in British Socialism and the Arts c. 1884–1918* (Cambridge: Cambridge University Press, 1982), 223.

19. George Bernard Shaw, Lecture delivered on 23 February 1900, quoted in Bernard Porter, *Critics of Empire: British Radical Attitudes to Colonialism in Africa 1895–1914* (London: Macmillan, 1968), 111.

20. Annie Besant, "Why I Am a Socialist" (1886), in *The Politics of Hope: The Origins of Socialism in Britain, 1880–1914*, ed. Edmund and Ruth Frow (London: Pluto, 1989), 36; Sidney James Webb, "What Socialism Means: A Call to the Unconverted" (1886), in *Hope*, 50–1.

21. Edward Bellamy, "Literary Notices," *Springfield Union*, 21 April 1877: 6, quoted in Sylvia E. Bowman, *Edward Bellamy* (Boston: Twayne Publishers, 1986), 81.

22. Frank E. Manuel and and Fritzie P. Manuel, *Utopian Thought in the Western World* (Cambridge: Harvard University Press, 1979), 458.

23. Kenneth M. Roemer, *Utopian Audiences: How Readers Locate Nowhere* (Amherst: University of Massachusetts Press, 2003), 117.

24. Thomas More, *Utopia* (1516), ed. and trans. Edward Surtz (New Haven: Yale University Press, 1964), 79.

25. Francis Bacon, *The New Atlantis* (1627); reprint in *Ideal Commonwealths: Francis Bacon, Thomas More, Thomas Campanella, James Harrington* (New York: Collier & Son, 1901), 120–1. I owe this reading of the "tirsan" ceremony to Jean Howard.

26. Howard P. Segal, "Utopia Diversified: 1900–1949," in *America as Utopia*, ed. Kenneth M. Roemer (New York: Burt Franklin, 1981), 333.

27. William Morris, "Review of *Looking Backward* by Edward Bellamy (1889)"; in Morris, *News from Nowhere and Other Writings*, ed. Clive Wilmer (London: Penguin, 1993), 357.

28. Morris, "Review of *Looking Backward*," 353.

29. Morris, "Review of *Looking Backward*," 354, 356.

30. A. L. Morton, *The English Utopia* (London: Lawrence & Wishart, 1952), 152, 171.

31. Marx and Engels, "Manifesto," 491.

32. Jean Pfaelzer, "The Impact of Political Theory on Narrative Structures," in Roemer, *America as Utopia*, 127.

33. William Dean Howells, *A Traveler from Altruria* (1894; reprint, New York: Sagamore Press, 1957), 181. Subsequent references will be noted parenthetically in the text.

34. See Johannes Fabian, *Time and the Other: How Anthropology Makes Its Object* (New York: Columbia University Press, 1983), especially 11–21 and Rist, *History of Development*, especially chapter 2, "Metamorphosis of a Myth." Lewis H. Morgan, *Archaic Society* (London: Macmillan, 1877), vii, quoted in Rist, *History of Development*, 41.

35. Anne McClintock, *Imperial Leather: Race, Gender, and Sexuality in the Colonial Contest* (New York: Routledge, 1995), especially 30–44.

36. McClintock, *Imperial Leather*, 37 and 32.

37. For one emblematic instance of this model, see Maine's 1872 legal history *Village Communities in the East and West*. As a land still in a stage through which "more civilized communities" have already passed, India is a legal historian's paradise, a place where "these dry bones live." Henry Maine, *Village Communities in the East and West* (London: John Murray, 1872).

38. William Dean Howells, *Through the Eye of a Needle* (New York: Harper & Brothers, 1907), 165–66. Subsequent references will be noted parenthetically in the text.

39. H. G. Wells employs the same device in *The Time Machine* (1895; reprinted London: Penguin Classics, 2005).

40. See, for example, the entries for "Altruria," "*A Traveler from Altruria*," "*Through the Eye of the Needle*," and "William Dean Howells" in Mary Ellen Snodgrass's error-ridden *Encyclopedia of Utopian Literature* (Santa Barbara: ABC-CLIO, 1995). More credible sources concur with Snodgrass to characterize Altruria as merely idyllic, overlooking the totalitarian dimensions that typify many utopias. See the Howells references in the essays by Donald C. Burt, Jean Pfaelzer, Kenneth M. Roemer, and Darko Suvin in Roemer, *America as Utopia*.

41. Kenneth Roemer, "Utopia and Victorian Culture: 1888–99," in Roemer, *America as Utopia*, 319.

42. Kenneth E. Eble, *William Dean Howells* (Boston: Twayne Publishers, 1982), 120; Edwin Cady, *The Realist at War: The Mature Years 1885–1920 of William Dean Howells* (Syracuse University Press, 1958), 200.

43. See Geir Lundestad, *"Empire" By Integration: The United States and European Integration, 1945–1997*. Oxford: Oxford University Press 1998.

44. Gilman, *Herland*, 2. Subsequent references will be noted parenthetically in the text.

45. Rokeya Sakhawat Hossain, "Sultana's Dream" (1905); reprint as *Sultana's Dream: A Feminist Utopia*, ed. Roushan Jahan (New York: Feminist Press at the City University of New York, 1988). For more on "Sultana's Dream," see chapter 2, note 2.

46. More, *Utopia*, 75–6.

47. Marouf A. Hasian, Jr., *The Rhetoric of Eugenics in Anglo-American Thought* (Athens: University of Georgia Press, 1996), 52. Hasian's is the only study to make the connection between slavery and eugenics.

48. Mark H. Haller, *Eugenics: Hereditarian Attitudes in American Thought* (New Brunswick: Rutgers University Press, 1984), 17.

49. Haller, *Eugenics*, 6.

50. The Cold Spring Harbor Laboratory (formerly the Eugenics Record Office) has an excellent online archive of historical materials from the American eugenics campaign. For an overview of the popular forms of eugenics see Steven Selden, "Eugenics Popularization," Cold Spring Harbor Laboratory Eugenics Archive, http://www.eugenicsarchive.org/eugenics/, accessed August 6, 2007.

51. The death of eugenics is a matter of heated debate among historians of the subject. Haller and several others assert that it faded from mainstream U.S. thought even before becoming tainted by association with Nazi genocide, while several more recent cultural historians trace the enduring influence of eugenic doctrine throughout the twentieth century, connecting it to the success of Richard Herrnstein and Charles Murray's 1994 bestseller *The Bell Curve* as well as the grand aspirations of the Human Genome Project. For examples of the latter, see Hasian, *Rhetoric*, and Wendy Kline, *Building a Better Race: Gender, Sexuality and Eugenics from the Turn of the Century to the Baby Boom* (Berkeley: University of California Press, 2001). In *The Nazi Connection: Eugenics, American Racism, and German National Socialism* (New York: Oxford University Press, 1994), Stephen Kuhl also departs from the earlier school by using archival materials to trace the active collaboration between American and German eugenicists.

52. Hardikar, *Lajpat Rai*, 39. N. S. Hardikar, *Lala Lajpat Rai in America* (New Delhi: Servants of the People Society, N.D.), 39.

53. Margaret Sanger, *An Autobiography* (1938; reprint, New York: Dover Publications, 1971), 369.

54. See, for example, Haller, *Eugenics*, 77–8 and Kline, *Building*, 16–31.

55. By the time that Gilman wrote *Herland*, laws allowing involuntary sterilization of prison and mental hospital inmates had been passed in Indiana (1907), California (1909), and Iowa (1911); fifteen states had sterilization laws by 1917. For a history of sterilization laws in the United States, see Kline, *Building*, 48–60.

56. Alys Weinbaum, *Wayward Reproductions: Genealogies of Race and Nation in Transatlantic Modern Thought* (Durham, N.C., and London: Duke University Press, 2004), 78.

57. To "mommick" is to rip into shreds.

58. For Moylan's definition of "critical utopia," see Tom Moylan, *Demand the Impossible: Science Fiction and the Utopian Imagination* (New York: Methuen, 1986), 10–2.

59. These are two distinct terms, often mistakenly used synonymously: dystopia, an older form present in Menippean satire and in Swift's *Gulliver's Travels,* which subsequently flourished in twentieth-century fiction and especially film; anti-utopia or negative utopia, an entirely new subgenre that first appeared around the turn of the century. I use "dystopia" to refer to a fictional representation of a place that, from the point of view of the narrator, is patently bad. Its inhabitants have never consented to any sort of social contract justifying its shortcomings, but rather find their behavior regulated by the threat of violence or expulsion. An anti-utopia or negative utopia, on the other hand, portrays a place that is not bad per se but functions exactly as it should, a place where most people are content with the utopian compromise to which they have implicitly consented. It is essentially a utopian society—but the author portrays it as a horror, and judges the compromise not to have been worthwhile. The contrast between the grim, bad-smelling aura of *1984* and the relentless cheer of *Brave New World* (two quite different texts, both formally and politically) exemplifies this distinction. As World Controller Mustapha Mond tells the Romantic rebels of *Brave New World,* "The world's stable now. People are happy; they get what they want, and they don't want what they can't get . . . they're blissfully ignorant of passion and old age; they're plagued with no mothers or fathers; they've got no wives, or children, or lovers to feel strongly about. . . . We've sacrificed the high art." Aldous Huxley, *Brave New World* (1932; reprint, New York: Perennial Library, 1969), 226. And in Zamyatin's version of the utopian trade-off, a newspaper declares "You are perfect; you are mechanized; the road to one-hundred-percent happiness is open!" Eugene Zamyatin, *We,* trans. Gregory Zilboorg (New York: E. P. Dutton, 1924), 167. The totalitarian society of *1984* offers no such benefits, merely omnipresent terror.

60. Edwin A. Abbott, *Flatland: A Romance of Many Dimensions* (1884; reprint, New York: Signet Classic, 1984), 43.

61. E. M. Forster, "The Machine Stops" (1909) in *The Collected Tales of E. M. Forster* (New York: Alfred A. Knopf, 1952). See 169 and 155 for positive eugenics; 166 for infant euthanasia.

62. Zamyatin, *We,* 14, 27, 116.

63. Zamyatin, *We,* 32.

64. Huxley, *Brave New World,* 1–6.

CHAPTER 2

1. I have discussed the few exceptions in the introduction. In the case of India, the only full-length source to make the connection between nationalism and utopianism is Richard Fox's *Gandhian Utopia: Experiments with Culture* (Boston: Beacon Press, 1989).

2. Rokeya Sakhawat Hossain, "Sultana's Dream" (1905); reprint as *Sultana's Dream: A Feminist Utopia*, ed. Roushan Jahan (New York: Feminist Press at the City University of New York, 1988), 17.

3. Fox, *Gandhian Utopia;* Anshuman Mondal, "Gandhi, Utopianism and the Construction of Colonial Difference," *Interventions* 3.3 (2001): 419–38.

4. Sandhya Shukla, *India Abroad: Diasporic Cultures of Postwar America and England* (Princeton: Princeton University Press, 2003), 175.

5. Manu Goswami, *Producing India: From Colonial Economy to National Space* (Chicago: University of Chicago Press, 2004).

6. The definitive source on the derivative nature of anti-colonial nationalism in India is Partha Chatterjee's *Nationalist Thought and the Colonial World: A Derivative Discourse?* (Minneapolis: University of Minnesota Press, 1993). More recently, Stephanie Newell offers an intriguing reading of "Great Man" biographies as a derivative discourse. See Newell, *Literary Culture in Colonial Ghana: How to Play the Game of Life* (Bloomington: Indiana University Press, 2002), 141–2.

7. Lala Lajpat Rai, "Mr. Lajpat Rai's Address," *Young India* III.2 (February 1920): 36.

8. Lala Lajpat Rai, "Suggestions to Hindu Students," *Young India* II.2 (February 1919): 40 [emphasis added].

9. Goswami, *Producing India,* 5.

10. Sarkar, *Modern India: 1885–1947* (Madras: Macmillan, 1983), 196–7.

11. *Young India* III.1 (January 1920): 1.

12. Benedict Anderson, *Imagined Communities: Reflections on the Origin and Spread of Nationalism* (London: Verso, 1983), especially 47–9.

13. Chatterjee, *Nationalist Thought,* 21.

14. Benedict Anderson, *The Spectre of Comparisons* (New York: Verso, 1998), 74.

15. *Young India* I.10 (October 1918): 1.

16. Christine Stansell, *American Moderns: Bohemian New York and the Creation of a New Century* (New York: Metropolitan Books, 2000), 176.

17. Lala Lajpat Rai, "Asia and the War," *The Masses* 9 (September 1916): 31.

18. Lala Lajpat Rai, "Young India," *Seven Arts* (October 1917): 743–58. See also Van Wyck Brooks, "Young America," *Seven Arts* (December 1916): 144–51; Seichi Naruse, "Young Japan," *Seven Arts* (April 1917): 616–26; and John R. Dos Passos, "Young Spain," *Seven Arts* (August 1917): 473–88.

19. Naeem Gul Rathore, *Indian Nationalist Agitation in the United States: A Study of Lala Lajpat Rai and the India Home Rule League of America, 1914–1920* (unpublished diss., Columbia University, 1965), 105.

20. Lala Lajpat Rai, "Mr. Lajpat Rai's Address," *Young India* III.2 (February 1920): 38.

21. For a quick summary of the role of defamiliarization in utopian fiction, see Kenneth M. Roemer, *Utopian Audiences: How Readers Locate Nowhere* (Amherst: University of Massachusetts Press, 2003), 26.

22. For a useful discussion and complication of this claim see Richard Halpern, *The Poetics of Primitive Accumulation: English Renaissance Culture and the Genealogy of Capital* (Ithaca, N.Y.: Cornell University Press, 1991), 145–6.

23. Alvin Johnson, "The Future of India," *Young India* III.4 (April 1920): 94.

24. Lala Lajpat Rai, "Ourselves," *Young India* I.1 (January 1918): 3.

25. Edward Bellamy, *Looking Backward* (1888; reprint, New York: Penguin Books, 1986), 198.

26. Anonymous, "The Black Hole Myth," *Young India* III.9 (September 1920): 199.

27. Anonymous, "Blacker than the 'Black Hole,'" *Young India* III.10 (October 1920): 234–5.

28. Benoy Kumar Sirkar [sic], "International India," *Young India* I.2 (February 1918): 12.

29. N. S. Hardiker, "United We Stand," *Young India* I.9 (September 1918): 15.

30. Anonymous, "The New Spirit in India," *Young India* III.8 (August 1920): 182; Hardiker, "Mohammedans of India," *Young India* III.4 (April 1920): 91.

31. Anonymous, "What Do Prominent Indians Say?," *Young India* I.1 (January 1918): 14.

32. N. S. Hardiker, "Selling their Birth Right for a Mess of Pottage," *Young India* II.1 (January 1919): 15. Led by anarchist and I.W.W. member Lala Har Dayal, the Ghadar Party advocated armed struggle in India and in the United States. For more on Har Dayal and Ghadar, see Harish K. Puri, *Ghadar Movement: Ideology, Organization and Strategy* (Amritsar: Garu Nanak Dev University, 1983).

33. *Young India* II.9 (September 1919): 214.

34. Ananda K. Coomaraswamy, "A Message," *Voice of India* I.1 (September 1944): 12.

35. Ananda K. Coomaraswamy, *Art and Swadeshi* (1911; reprint, New Delhi: Munshiram Manoharlal, 1994), 102.

36. Coomaraswamy, *Art and Swadeshi*, 3. Gandhi, who cites the Arts and Crafts movement's guiding spirit John Ruskin as one of his foremost influences, shared Coomaraswamy's and Tagore's hatred of industrialism and mechanization. Despite *Young India*'s many references to the ascendant nationalist leader, the periodical naturally fails to make any mention of his 1909 anti-industrial manifesto *Hind Swaraj*.

37. Ananda K. Coomaraswamy, *Medieval Sinhalese Art* (Broad Campden: Essex House Press, 1908), v.

38. John Ruskin, *The Two Paths* (1859), quoted in Partha Mitter, *Much Maligned Monsters: A History of European Reactions to Indian Art* (Chicago: University of Chicago Press, 1992), 245.

39. William Morris, "The Art of the People," in Morris, *Hopes and Fears for Art* (Boston: Roberts Brothers, 1882), 35.

40. Morris, "Art of the People," 36.

41. Morris, "Art of the People," 38.

42. Coomaraswamy, *Medieval Sinhalese Art*, ix.

43. Krishna Dutta and Andrew Robinson, *Rabindranath Tagore: The Myriad-Minded Man* (London: Bloomsbury, 1995), 160.

44. Roger Lipsey, *Coomaraswamy; Volume III, His Life and Work* (Princeton: Princeton University Press, 1977), 22.

45. Lipsey, *Coomaraswamy*, 22.

46. Coomaraswamy, *Art and Swadeshi*, 105.

47. Quoted in Jag Mohan, *Ananda K. Coomaraswamy* (New Delhi: Government of India, 1979), 24.

48. Mohan, *Coomaraswamy*, 61.

49. Quoted in Thomas Metcalf, *An Imperial Vision: Indian Architecture and Britain's Raj* (Berkeley: University of California Press, 1989), 143.

50. Ananda Coomaraswamy, "Our Art Section: Todi Ragini," *Young India* III.3 (March 1920): 50.

51. Ananda Coomaraswamy, "Art Section: Avolokitesvara Bodhisattva," *Young India* III.6 (June 1920): 122.

52. Ananda Coomaraswamy, "The Dying Man," *Young India* III.8 (August 1920): 170.

53. Ananda Coomaraswamy, "Sujata's Offering to Buddha," *Young India* III.12 (December 1920): 268.

54. Ananda Coomaraswamy, "Art Section: Infant Krishna with Yasoda," *Young India* III.9 (September 1920): 194.

55. Coomaraswamy, *Art and Swadeshi*, 70.

56. Ananda K. Coomaraswamy, *Introduction to Indian Art*, ed. Luisa Coomaraswamy (Delhi: Munshiram Manoharlal, 1966), 74.

57. Ananda Coomaraswamy, "Our Art Section: The Dance of Siva," *Young India* III.10 (October 1920): 218.

58. Ananda Coomaraswamy, "Art Section: Avolokitesvara Bodhisattva," *Young India* III.6 (June 1920): 122.

59. Ananda Coomaraswamy, "The Dying Man," *Young India* III.8 (August 1920): 170.

60. Ananda Coomaraswamy, "Note on the Study of Indian Art," *Young India* I.2 (February 1918): 7.

61. Ananda Coomaraswamy, "The Dying Man" *Young India* III.8 (August 1920): 170.

62. Mohammed Iqbal, "The New Temple," trans. Lajpat Rai and Coomaraswamy, *Young India* II.4 (April 1919): 74.

63. Ananda Coomaraswamy, "Our Art Section: Rama, Sita, and Lakshmana" *Young India* III.7 (July 1920): 146.

64. Ananda Coomaraswamy, "Notes on the Epics II: Mahabarata: Bhagavat Gita," *Young India* II.1 (January 1919): 12.

65. See Isaiah Berlin, "Rabindranath Tagore and the Consciousness of Nationality," in *The Sense of Reality: Studies in Ideas and Their History* (New York:

Farrar Strous and Giroux, 1997); Ashis Nandy, *The Illegitimacy of Nationalism: Rabindranath Tagore and the Politics of Self* (Delhi: Oxford University Press, 1994); Martha Nussbaum, "Patriotism and Cosmopolitanism," in *For Love of Country?: Debating the Limits of Patriotism*, ed. Joshua Cohen (Boston: Beacon Press, 1996); Amartya Sen, "Tagore and His India," in *India: A Mosaic*, ed. Robert B. Silvers and Barbara Epstein (New York: New York Review Books, 2000); and E. P. Thompson, introduction to *Nationalism*, by Rabindranath Tagore (London: Macmillan, 1991).

66. Rabindranath Tagore, *Nationalism* (New York: Macmillan, 1917), *passim*.

67. Tagore, *Nationalism*, 15.

68. Tagore, *Nationalism*, 119.

69. Tagore, *Nationalism*, 127.

70. Anonymous, "Book Reviews," *Young India* I.2 (February 1918): 23–4.

71. Anonymous, "Book Reviews," 24.

72. Anonymous, "Book Reviews," 25.

73. Anonymous, "At the Mother's Feet—(Communicated)," *Young India* I.1 (January 1918): 21.

74. Quoted in Sujit Mukherjee, *Passage to America: The Reception of Rabindranath Tagore in the United States, 1912–1941* (Calcutta: Bookland Private, 1964), 15.

75. Quoted in Mukherjee, *Passage to America*, 29.

76. E. P. Thompson, *Alien Homage: Edward Thompson and Rabindranath Tagore* (Delhi: Oxford University Press, 1993), 35.

77. Anonymous, "Bravo Tagore," *Young India* II.8 (August 1919): 171.

78. Anonymous, "Tagore's Secretary Free in England," *Young India* I.10 (October 1918): 8.

79. Nandy, *Illegitimacy*, 80.

80. Rabindranath Tagore, "India's Prayer," *Young India* I.5 (May 1918): 10, and "National Education," *Young India* I.9 (September 1918): 8.

81. Rabindranath Tagore, "The Day is Come," *Young India* I.1 (January 1918): 8.

82. Nemai Sadhan Bose, *Ramananda Chatterjee* (New Delhi: Ministry of Information and Broadcasting, 1974), 32.

83. Tagore, "The Captain Will Come to His Helm," *Modern Review* XXIII.4 (April 1918): 1.

84. Tagore, "Autumn," in *Young India* III.12 (December 1920): 281.

85. For a more detailed reading of the theme of iconography in *The Home and the World*, see my essay "The Home, the World, and the United States: *Young India*'s Tagore," *Journal of Commonwealth Literature* Volume 43, Number 1 (2008): 33–5.

86. Rabindranath Tagore, *The Home and the World*, trans. Surendranath Tagore (1919; reprint, London: Penguin Books, 1985), 36, 42. Subsequent references will be noted parenthetically in the text.

87. Quoted in Sen, "Tagore and His India," 60.

88. Georg Lukács, "Tagore's Gandhi Novel: Review of Rabindranath Tagore, *The Home and the World*," in *Reviews and Articles*, trans. Peter Palmer (London:

Merlin, 1983), 10. For a detailed rebuttal of Lukács' review, see Nandy, *Illegitimacy*, 15–9.

89. Mohandas Karamchand Gandhi, *Autobiography: The Story of My Experiments with Truth*, trans. Mahadev Desai (1948; reprint, New York: Dover, 1983), 419. That Gandhi never relies on *Bande Mataram* as a call to action should not be surprising, for despite his affinity for iconography, he consistently rejected those symbols and phrases that held any potential to divide. Early in his activist career he rejected the upper-caste sacred thread as a useful symbol of national purity, since untouchables could not wear it. Thus to Gandhi the sacred thread symbolized not purity or spiritual regeneration, but exclusion and hypocrisy. See *Autobiography*, 352. As a replacement, Gandhi identified the spinning wheel as the ideal golden-age icon. According to his vision, the *charkha* would provide production, employment, and propaganda at once; while the sacred thread "produced" exclusion, the *charkha* "produced" unity. Of course, Tagore disapproved even of this apparently benign icon as demeaning. For a summary of Tagore's criticism of Gandhi's *charkha* campaign, see Sen, "Tagore and His India," 73–4.

90. Dutta and Robinson, *Tagore*, 179.

91. Nandy, *Illegitimacy*, 19.

92. The negative valences of the term "communalism" often puzzle readers unfamiliar with the vocabulary of South Asian history. As opposed to the common European and American meaning of common possession or habitation, "communalism" in a South Asian context denotes violent religious separatism, or sectarianism.

93. Jennifer Burwell, *Notes from Nowhere: Feminism, Utopian Logic, and Social Transformation* (Minneapolis: University of Minneapolis Press, 1997), 64.

94. Partha Chatterjee in *The Nation and its Fragments* (Princeton: Princeton University Press, 1993) and Floya Anthias and Nira Yuval-Davis in their introduction to *Woman-Nation-State* (London: Macmillan, 1989) describe various stages of that process. See especially Chatterjee, Chapter Six, "The Nation and its Women," and Anthias and Yuval-Davis, 9–10.

95. Bruce Robbins, *Feeling Global: Internationalism in Distress* (New York: New York University Press, 1999), 161–2.

96. Anonymous, "Review of Tagore's *Sacrifice and Other Plays*," *Young India* I.2 (February 1918): 25.

97. Anonymous, "The Woman Movement in India," *Young India* II.11 (November 1919): 260; Anonymous, "Mrs. Sarojini Naidu," *Young India* II.10 (October 1919): 221.

98. Sarojini Naidu, "Awake," *Young India* I.7 (July 1918): 12.

99. Sarojini Naidu, "India to England," *Young India* II.10 (October 1919): 234.

100. Sarojini Naidu, "Panjab—1919," *Young India* II.8 (August 1919): 170.

101. Sarojini Naidu, "The Broken Wing," quoted in Anonymous, "Review of Sarojini Naidu's *The Broken Wing*," *Young India* I.10 (October 1918): 21.

102. Hughes's poem "Dreams" originally ran in *World Tomorrow*, a progressive Christian magazine founded and edited by one of *Young India*'s contributors, Norman Thomas.

103. Sarojini Naidu, "India," *Young India* II.7 (July 1919): 146.

104. James Cousins, *The Renaissance in India* (Madras: Ganesh and Company, 1918): 251. Quoted in Edward Marx, "Sarojini Naidu: The Nightingale as Nationalist," *Journal of Commonwealth Literature* 31.1 (1996): 55.

105. Anonymous, "Review of *Broken Wing*," 21.

106. Kumari Jayawardena, *The White Woman's Other Burden: Western Women and South Asia during Colonial Rule* (New York: Routledge, 1995).

107. Gertrude Boyle, "India Waking," *Young India* III.1 (January 1920): 19.

108. Amy Dudley, "Great India" *Young India* III.4 (April 1920): 89 [italics in original].

109. Amy Dudley, "Kali Mai" *Young India* II.9 (September 1919): 213.

110. Lala Lajpat Rai, "The Woman in India, No. I" *Young India* I.7 (July 1918): 17.

111. Anonymous, "Women in Indian Politics," *Young India* III.11 (November 1920): 244.

112. Sarojini Naidu, testimony to Joint Committee on Indian Reforms, quoted in Anonymous, "The Woman Movement in India": *Young India* II.11 (November 1919): 261.

113. Anonymous, "The 'Woman Movement' in India," *Young India* I.11 (November 1918): 7. this is a different article with the same title, from 1918.

114. Anonymous, "Woman Movement in India" (1919): 261.

115. Anonymous, "A Labor Revolt in the Fiji Islands," *Young India* III.5 (May 1920): 108.

116. Anonymous, "Indian Suffragists," *Young India* III.8 (August 1920): 172.

117. Anonymous, "A Labor Revolt in the Fiji Islands," *Young India* III.5 (May 1920): 108; "Indians in British East Africa," III.8 (August 1920): 185.

118. I.7 (July 1918): 3.

119. Quoted in Joan M. Jensen, *Passage from India: Asian Indian Immigrants in North America* (New Haven: Yale University Press, 1988), 213. Chapter 10, "'Hindu Conspiracy': Neutrality Laws," covers the case in detail.

120. Anonymous, "Book Reviews," *Young India* II.9 (September 1919): 215.

121. Anonymous, "A Labor Revolt in the Fiji Islands," *Young India* III.5 (May 1920): 108.

122. Anonymous, "Indians in British East Africa," *Young India* III.8 (August 1920): 185.

123. Francis Hackett, "The Opium Monopoly," *Young India* III.5 (May 1920): 111.

124. Anonymous, "Revolutions: By A Student of Revolutions," *Young India* I.12 (December 1918): 22.

125. Anonymous, "Farewell Dinners," *Young India* III.1 (January 1920): 11; "The Small and Subject Nations League and the *New York Times*," *Young India* II.1 (January 1919): 23.

126. *Young India* II.1 (January 1919): 2.

127. Anonymous, "Indians in British East Africa," *Young India* III.8 (August 1920): 185.

128. Anonymous, "India and the Philippines," *Young India* III.11 (November 1920): 244; and Anonymous, "The Philippines and India," *Young India* III.12 (December 1920): 269–70.

129. N. S. Hardiker, "Deporting Indian Laborers," *Young India* III.9 (September 1920): 214

130. Lala Lajpat Rai, "The New Internationalism," *Young India* I.4 (April 1918): 8.

131. Lajpat Rai, "New Internationalism," 9.

132. Lajpat Rai, "New Internationalism," 9.

133. Anonymous, "League Growing," *Young India* II.4 (April 1919): 1.

134. Anonymous, "Dr. Hardiker's Middle West Trip," *Young India* II.6 (June 1919): 138.

135. Rathore, *Indian Nationalist Agitation*, 134–5.

136. Lajpat Rai, "New Internationalism," 11.

137. Anonymous, "Dr. Hardiker's Middle West Trip," *Young India* II.6 (June 1919): 138.

138. Scott Nearing, "America to India," *Young India* III.5 (May 1920): 114.

139. Nearing, "America to India," 114.

140. Robert M. Buck, "Workers in India: Greetings from America," *Young India* III.5 (May 1920): 109.

141. Mayce Seymour, "To Lajpat Rai," *Young India* III.2 (February 1920): 26.

142. Anonymous, "Editorial Notes: What Does India Want?" *Young India* III.10 (October 1920): 220.

143. Anonymous, "Editorial Notes: Why America Should Sympathize," *Young India* III.12 (December 1920): 269.

144. Anonymous, "Editorial Notes: Daniel Webster on India"; "Editorial Notes: Andrew Carnegie and India"; "Editorial Notes: Mr. Asquith and India"; "Editorial Notes: Henry George on India," *Young India* III.10 (October 1920): 219–20.

145. Sunderland, "Mr. B. G. Tilak—An Appreciation," *Young India* III.9 (September 1920): 196.

146. Vijay Prashad, *Everybody Was Kung-Fu Fighting: Afro-Asian Connections and the Myth of Cultural Purity* (Boston: Beacon Press, 2001), 137 [italics in original].

147. Homi K. Bhabha, "The Black Savant and the Dark Princess," *ESQ: A Journal of the American Renaissance* 50.1–3 (2004): 140.

148. For more on the Nehruvian turn as a betrayal of anti-colonial ideals, see Fox, *Gandhian Utopia*, especially 169–83, and Chatterjee, *Nationalist Thought*, 131–66; for a novelist's view on dams and nuclear weapons, respectively, see Arundhati Roy's essays "The Greater Common Good" and "The End of Imagination," in Roy, *The Algebra of Infinite Justice* (London: Flamingo, 2002).

CHAPTER 3

1. The only work with the title "Black Utopia" examines antebellum communes: that is, William H. Pease and Jane H. Pease's study of uplift ideology, *Black Utopia: Negro Communal Experiments in America* (Madison: State Historical Society of Wisconsin, 1963). M. Giulia Fabi dedicates one chapter of her *Passing and the Rise of the African American Novel* (Urbana: University of Illinois Press, 2001) to examining utopian fiction within the larger rubric of racial passing. See pages 45–71.

2. W. E. B. Du Bois, *The Souls of Black Folk* (1903; reprint, New York: Dover, 1994), 162. Subsequent references will be noted parenthetically in the text.

3. See Edward Bellamy, *Looking Backward* (1888; reprint, New York: Penguin Books, 1986), 69–70, and Booker T. Washington, *Up from Slavery* (1901); reprinted in *Three Negro Classics* (New York: Avon Books, 1965), 108.

4. Amy Kaplan, *The Social Construction of American Realism* (Chicago: University of Chicago Press, 1988), 1.

5. Cedric Robinson, *Black Marxism: The Making of the Black Radical Tradition* (1983; reprinted Chapel Hill: University of North Carolina Press, 2000), 169.

6. For a discussion of Harper as mouthpiece of an evolutionary ideology of progress see Wilson Jeremiah Moses, *Afrotopia: The Roots of African American Popular History* (Cambridge: Cambridge University Press, 1998), 133.

7. Pauline E. Hopkins, *Contending Forces: A Romance Illustrative of Negro Life North and South* (1900; reprint, New York: Oxford University Press, 1988), 35–6. Subsequent references will be noted parenthetically in the text.

8. Pauline E. Hopkins, *Hagar's Daughter: A Story of Southern Caste Prejudice* (serialized 1901–2); reprint in *The Magazine Novels of Pauline Hopkins* (New York: Oxford University Press, 1988), 283. Subsequent references will be noted parenthetically in the text.

9. Pauline E. Hopkins, *Of One Blood; Or, The Hidden Self* (serialized 1902–3); reprint in *Magazine Novels*, 593. Subsequent references will be noted parenthetically in the text.

10. Thomas Hardy Leahey and Grace Evans Leahey, *Psychology's Occult Doubles: Psychology and the Problem of Pseudoscience* (Chicago: Nelson-Hill, 1983), 131–3; Maria Tatar, *Spellbound: Studies on Mesmerism and Literature* (Princeton: Princeton University Press, 1978), 20–1.

11. Nathaniel Hawthorne, *The Blithedale Romance* (1852; reprint, New York: W. W. Norton, 1958), 208.

12. Sutton E. Griggs, *Imperium in Imperio* (1899; reprint, Miami: Mnemosyne Publishing, 1969), 57, 190–6. Subsequent references will be noted parenthetically in the text.

13. Griggs remade Frazier Baker into Felix Cook, but the outline of the grisly story remains the same. The South Carolina state legislature recently voted to honor Baker with the state's first official acknowledgement of lynching. See Roddie Burris,

"Marker Will Honor S.C. Lynching Victims," *The State* (South Carolina) 21 May 2003, p. A1.

14. The vitriolic response of Mary Lefkowitz and others to Martin Bernal's *Black Athena: The Afro-Asiatic Roots of Classical Civilization* (New Brunswick, N.J.: Rutgers University Press, 1987) is the best-known recent example. As Wilson Moses reminds his readers, Bernal's general thesis had been presented as early as the eighteenth century with Constantin Volney's *The Ruins, or Meditation on the Revolutions of Empires* (1791). See Moses, *Afrotopia*, 6–7.

15. W. E. B. Du Bois, *The Quest of the Silver Fleece* (1911; reprint, Boston: Northeastern University Press, 1989), 362. Subsequent references will be noted parenthetically in the text.

16. For more on the "critical utopia," see chapter 1, page 62.

17. Later, as we will see, Du Bois complicates the notion of parallels among groups; here, however, he presents Zora and Kautilya as two versions of one romanticized essence.

18. Du Bois, *Dark Princess*, 136.

19. Nellie McKay, "W. E. B. Du Bois: The Black Women in His Writings," in *Critical Essays on W. E. B. Du Bois*, ed. William L. Andrews (Boston: Hall, 1985), 249–50.

20. Washington, *Up from Slavery*, 56–7.

21. As Bellamy tells it, it is only that real-world topography that convinces Julian West that he is in fact standing in the Boston of the future. Marveling at the grandeur of the urban panorama his host has shown him, West narrates, "Surely I had never seen this city nor one comparable to it before. Raising my eyes at last toward the horizon, I looked westward. That blue ribbon winding away to the sunset—was it not the sinuous Charles? I looked east—Boston harbor stretched before me within its headlands, not one of its green islets missing." Bellamy, *Looking Backward*, 55. We can see the same phenomenon as *News from Nowhere*'s Guest rows up a now-pristine Thames: using the permanence of geology to emphasize the marked change of all other aspects of life is one of the many techniques that Morris imitates from *Looking Backward*.

22. W. E. B. Du Bois, "Gandhi and the American Negroes," *Gandhi Marg* II.3 (1957): 174, 176.

23. Du Bois favorably reviewed many of Wells's works, titled his laudatory 1946 obituary of Wells "A World Great," and elsewhere called the writer "a great genius." See Herbert Aptheker, *Annotated Bibliography of the Published Writings of W. E. B. Du Bois* (New York: Kraus-Thomson, 1973), 79, 449. The consistent praise comes despite Wells's commendation of Washington and disparagement of Du Bois in his travelogue *The Future in America* (1906; reprint, New York: Arno Press, 1974). See discussion in David Levering Lewis, *W. E. B. Du Bois: Biography of a Race, 1868–1919* (New York: Henry Holt and Company, 1993), 362.

24. Maurice Lee, "Du Bois the Novelist: White Influence, Black Spirit, and *Quest of the Silver Fleece*," *African American Review* 33.3 (1999): 393.

25. This strategic use of realist conventions anticipates that of Marge Piercy in *Woman at the Edge of Time* (New York: Fawcett Crest, 1976), as identified by Tom Moylan. Moylan writes that Piercy "challenges realism, in all its associations with things as they are and 'must be,' from outside the limits of the genre by attacking with the fantasizing power of utopian science fiction." Tom Moylan, *Demand the Impossible: Science Fiction and the Utopian Imagination* (New York: Methuen, 1986), 150.

26. Arnold Rampersad, *The Art and Imagination of W. E. B. Du Bois* (Cambridge: Harvard University Press, 1976), 204; Eric Sundquist, *To Wake the Nations* (Cambridge: Harvard University Press, 1993), 620. See also Hanna Wallinger, "Secret Societies and Dark Empires: Sutton E. Griggs's *Imperium in Imperio* and W. E. B. Du Bois's *Dark Princess*," in *Empire: American Studies*, ed. John G. Blair and Reinhold Wagnleitner (Tubingen, Germany: Narr, 1997), 198, 203.

27. Claudia Tate, introduction to *Dark Princess*, by W. E. B. Du Bois (Jackson, Miss.: Banner Books, 1995), ix.

28. See Tate, introduction to *Dark Princess*, xxv, and Paul Gilroy, *The Black Atlantic: Modernity and Double Consciousness* (Cambridge: Harvard University Press, 1992), 144–5.

29. According to Rampersad, "The central problem involves the tension between the spiritual emphasis proper to this idea [that God is Love, etc] and the undeniably secular and political concerns that the author brought to his work. Here the story falters." Rampersad, *Art and Imagination*, 217. Tate writes that "the social (conscious) and erotic (partly unconscious) discourses do not cohere in *Dark Princess*." Claudia Tate, *Psychoanalysis and Black Novels: Desire and the Protocols of Race* (New York: Oxford University Press, 1998), 80.

30. W. E. B. Du Bois to Mildred Bryant Jones, November 22, 1927. Du Bois Papers. University of Massachusetts Amherst. Microfilm edition, 1980. On Jones and Du Bois's relationship see David Levering Lewis, *W. E. B. Du Bois: The Fight for Equality and the American Century, 1919–1963* (New York: Henry Holt and Company, 2000), 267–8 and *passim*.

31. W. E. B. Du Bois to Mrs. William C. Kenyon, May 3, 1934. Quoted in Herbert Aptheker, introduction to *Dark Princess*, by W. E. B. Du Bois (New York: Kraus-Thomson, 1974), 13.

32. W. E. B. Du Bois to Carl D. Thompson, November 17, 1927. Quoted in Aptheker, introduction to *Dark Princess*, 15.

33. To cite only one example: "Sammy's office was on State Street at the corner of Thirty-Second. Most of the buildings around there were old frame structures with living-quarters above and stores below. On each corner were brick buildings planned like the others, but now used wholly for stores and offices. The entrance to Sammy's building was on Thirty-Second Street" (111).

34. W. E. B. Du Bois, "The Wide, Wide World," *New York Amsterdam News* (October 7, 1931), 8.

35. For a helpful commentary on the Titania dedication see Brent Hayes Edwards, *The Practice of Diaspora: Literature, Translation, and the Rise of Black Internationalism* (Cambridge: Harvard University Press, 2003), 234–7.

36. Kenneth W. Warren, "An Inevitable Drift? Oligarchy, Du Bois, and the Politics of Race between the Wars," *boundary 2* 27.3 (2000): 153–169.

37. See all of *Dark Princess*, Chapter VI, especially 24.

38. Du Bois, *Souls*, 54.

39. Throughout *The Souls of Black Folk* Du Bois describes the soil of the Black Belt (especially Georgia) as red.

40. Several readers have noted the resemblance between little Madhu and the son whom Du Bois eulogized in his essay "Of the Passing of the First-Born," a resemblance that allows the baby of *Dark Princess* to compensate for the loss of Du Bois's own golden-haired child. See for example Alys Eve Weinbaum, *Wayward Reproductions* (Durham and London: Duke University Press, 2004), 35.

41. Gilroy, *Black Atlantic*, 144.

42. Herbert Aptheker, introduction to *Dark Princess*, by W. E. B. Du Bois (New York: Kraus-Thomson, 1974), 16.

43. Lewis mistakenly describes Lajpat Rai, son of a Bania (middle caste) village teacher, as "aristocratic" and a "fiery Brahmin." Lewis, *Fight for Equality*, 219.

44. References to India can be found throughout Du Bois's columns. See Aptheker, *Bibliography*, especially Part II, "Writings in Magazines Edited by Du Bois." For the columns from 1930, see Aptheker, 309–17.

45. Aptheker, *Bibliography*, 309–317.

46. W. E. B. Du Bois, "As the Crow Flies," *New York Amsterdam News* (April 10, 1943), 10.

47. W. E. B. Du Bois, "As the Crow Flies," *New York Amsterdam News* (February 26, 1944), 10.

48. Du Bois, "Wide, Wide World," 8.

49. W. E. B. Du Bois, "The Freeing of India," *Crisis* 54 (October 1947): 302.

50. Du Bois, "Wide, Wide World," 8.

51. Du Bois to Lajpat Rai, November 9, 1927. Du Bois Papers.

52. Hardikar, *Lala Lajpat Rai in America*, 39. For a surprisingly warm exchange between Du Bois and Sanger (who, in her irresponsibly undiscriminating zeal to spread the message of Malthusianism to all, lectured in front of such anti-black organizations as the Ku Klux Klan), see *The Correspondence of W. E. B. Du Bois*, ed. Herbert Aptheker (Amherst: University of Massachusetts Press, 1973), 301–2.

53. *The Civic Club of New York* (New York, September 1, 1916), 18–24, attached as Appendix to Naeem Gul Rathore, *Indian Nationalist Agitation in the United States: A Study of Lala Lajpat Rai and the India Home Rule League of America, 1914–1920* (unpublished diss., Columbia University, 1965), 302–6. Agnes Smedley, who volunteered as a secretary for Rai and the IHRL, signing many appeals for diplomatic recognition with her own pseudonym of "Pulin Behari Bose, special

representative of the Indian National Party in the United States," later contacted
Du Bois from Germany in search of "facts and figures on lynchings of the Negro
in America," and wrote a glowing portrait of Du Bois as "the most outstanding
figure among the Negroes" for the Calcutta monthly *Modern Review*. Janice R.
MacKinnon and Stephen R. MacKinnon, *Agnes Smedley: The Life and Times of an
American Radical* (Berkeley: University of California Press, 1988), 41; Aptheker,
Correspondence, 315; Agnes Smedley, "The Negro Renaissance," *Modern Review* 40.6
(December 1926): 657–61.

54. On the Exclusion Leagues and the legislation they advocated, see Joan M.
Jensen, *Passage from India: Asian Indian Immigrants in North America* (New Haven: Yale
University Press, 1988), especially chapter 7, "The Wrong Side of a Red Line: Legislative
Exclusion." Du Bois's silence on this matter is documented in Aptheker, *Bibliography*.

55. For Du Bois's strategic reaction to the war, see Manning Marable, *W. E. B.
Du Bois: Black Radical Democrat* (New York: Twayne Publishers, 1986), 94–6.
Du Bois later wrote with some chagrin that during the war years "I was swept into
the national maelstrom." From "Will the Great Gandhi Live Again," in *W. E. B.
Du Bois: A Reader*, ed. David Levering Lewis (New York: Henry Holt, 1995), 358.
Agnes Smedley dramatizes Lajpat Rai's cynicism about the war in *Daughter of Earth*.
Sardar Ranjit Singh, the Lajpat Rai character, tells the narrator: "Your War is for
democracy, you say. I doubt it—your principles do not extend to Asia, even though
Asia is three-fourths of the human race." Smedley, *Daughter of Earth* (New York:
Feminist Press, 1973), 264. Despite that cynicism, the IHRL passed a resolution in
June 1918 declaring "its hearty endorsement of the war aims of the United States
and the Allies, as expounded by President Wilson" and "its loyal support to the war
efforts of the United States and the Allies." *Young India* I.7 (July 1918): 4.

56. Rathore, *Indian Nationalist Agitation*, 91.

57. Rathore, *Indian Nationalist Agitation*, 112.

58. Du Bois, "The Freeing of India," 302.

59. W. E. B. Du Bois, "As the Crow Flies," *Crisis* 36.1 (January 1929): 1.

60. W. E. B. Du Bois, "The Browsing Reader," *Crisis* 36.5 (May 1929): 175.

61. Rathore, *Indian Nationalist Agitation*, 48.

62. Lala Lajpat Rai, "Presidential Address at the Bombay Hindu Conference,"
in *Lala Lajpat Rai: Writings and Speeches*, vol. II, ed. Vijaya Chandra Joshi (Delhi:
University Publishers, 1966), 247.

63. Lala Lajpat Rai, "Education in the United States," *Modern Review* 18.2
(1915): 131.

64. Lala Lajpat Rai, "Save India for the Empire: An Open Letter to David Lloyd
George," in *Lala Lajpat Rai: Writings and Speeches*, vol. I, ed. Vijaya Chandra Joshi
(Delhi: University Publishers, 1966), 266.

65. Summarized without attribution in Rathore, *Indian Nationalist Agitation*, 261.

66. Lala Lajpat Rai, "Farewell to America," in *Writings and Speeches*, vol. I, 390.

67. *Unhappy India*, the resulting anti-Mayo treatise, opens with Lajpat Rai's
apology that "It is with extreme reluctance amounting to pain that I have referred to

certain phases of American life. There is another side of American life—beautiful, noble, humane, full of the milk of human kindness for all races, all colours and all peoples of the world." This is a significantly different picture of American race relations from that conveyed in the pages of the *Crisis*. Lala Lajpat Rai, *Unhappy India* (Calcutta, Banna Publishing, 1928), x.

68. Shripad R. Tikekar to Du Bois, December 23, 1927. Du Bois Papers.

69. Nazir Ahmed Khan to Du Bois, September 29, 1927. Du Bois Papers.

70. Smedley, *Daughter of Earth*, 278–9.

71. Du Bois answered an anthologizer's request for "a few chapters which you think include your best writing in fiction" with this chapter from *Dark Princess* as well as the death of Zora's evil grandmother in *Quest*. Aptheker, *Correspondence*, 378.

72. Perhaps set off by Paul Gilroy's mention of *Dark Princess* in *Black Atlantic*, the novel has figured prominently in discussions of African diaspora literature, Afro-Orientalism, "racial globality," and revolutionary theory. See Homi K. Bhabha, "The Black Savant and the Dark Princess," *ESQ: A Journal of the American Renaissance* 50.1–3 (2004): 137-55; Edwards, *Practice of Diaspora*, 233–7; Robert Gregg and Madhavi Kale, "*The Negro* and the *Dark Princess*: Two Legacies of the Universal Races Congress," *Radical History Review* 92 (2005): 133-52; Bill V. Mullen, *Afro-Orientalism* (Minneapolis: University of Minnesota Press, 2004), 1–41; Claudia Tate, *Psychoanalysis and Black Novels: Desire and the Protocols of Race* (New York: Oxford University Press, 1998); Kenneth W. Warren, "An Inevitable Drift? Oligarchy, Du Bois, and the Politics of Race between the Wars," *boundary 2* 27.3 (2000): 153–69; and Alys Eve Weinbaum, *Wayward Reproductions* (Durham and London: Duke University Press, 2004), 200–14.

73. George S. Schuyler, *Black Empire*, ed. Robert A. Hill and R. Kent Rasmussen (1936–38; reprint, Boston: Northeastern University Press, 1991), 10, 12. Subsequent references will be noted parenthetically in the text.

74. Robert A. Hill and R. Kent Rasmussen, afterword to Schuyler, *Black Empire*, 310.

75. George S. Schuyler, "The Rise of the Black Internationale," *Crisis* (August 1938), in Schuyler, *Black Empire*, 336.

76. For the influence of *Dark Princess* on Schuyler, see Hill and Rasmussen, afterword to *Black Empire*, 289.

77. "Schuyler's story notes," Appendix A to Schuyler, *Black Empire*, 327.

78. George Schuyler, "Negroes Reject Communism," *American Mercury* 47 (1939): 176.

79. Alexander M. Bain, "*Shocks Americana!*: George Schuyler Serializes Black Internationalism," *American Literary History* 19.4 (2007), 946.

80. Arnold Rampersad, "Du Bois's Passage to India: *Dark Princess*" in *W. E. B. Du Bois: On Race and Culture*, ed. Bernard W. Bell, Emily R. Grosholz, and James B. Steward (New York: Routledge, 1996), 174.

81. Richard Wright, *The Color Curtain: A Report on the Bandung Conference* (1956; reprint, Jackson: Banner Books, 1994), 218. Subsequent references will be noted parenthetically in the text.

82. Margaret Walker claims that the conference itself "marked the first time the term was used in an international context." *Richard Wright: Daemonic Genius* (New York: Warner Books, 1988), 260. Carl Pletsch's seminal essay on modernization theory and the Cold War gives examples that predate the conference by several years. See Carl E. Pletch, "The Three Worlds, or the Division of Labor, circa 1950–1975," *Comparative Studies in Society and History* 23 (1981): 568–571.

83. Virginia Whately Smith, "Richard Wright's Passage to Indonesia," in *Richard Wright's Travel Writings: New Reflections*, ed. Virginia Whately Smith (Jackson: University of Mississippi Press, 2001), 90.

84. The conference's organizers invited delegates from the Gold Coast with the logic that independence was imminent, but Kenya, Guinea, Congo, Mali, and Nigeria, all of which would be independent within five years, were not included.

85. See Carlos P. Romulo, *The Meaning of Bandung* (Chapel Hill: University of North Carolina Press, 1956); John Kotelawala, *An Asian Prime Minister's Story* (London: George Harrap, 1956); and Adam Clayton Powell, Jr., *Adam by Adam: The Autobiography of Adam Clayton Powell, Jr.* (1971; reprint, New York: Citadel Press, 1994). For a wider discussion of how the black American anti-Communist press reported on Bandung, see Bill V. Mullen, *Afro-Orientalism* (Minneapolis: University of Minnesota Press, 2004), 66–7.

86. Malcolm X, "A Message to the Grassroots" (1963); reprinted in Malcolm X, *Malcolm X Speaks: Selected Speeches and Statements*, ed. George Breitman (New York: Pathfinder, 1990), 5–6; Vijay Prashad, "Badges of Color: An Afro-Dalit Story," *Z Magazine* (March 2000): 9; Mullen, *Afro-Orientalism*, 59; Zhang Yan, "I Wish I Had Met Richard Wright at Bandung in 1955 (Reflections on a Conference Attended by Both Wright and the Author," *Mississippi Quarterly: The Journal of Southern Cultures* 50.2 (1995): 277.

87. Just before the encounter with a white woman that leads to Big Boy's exile, his friend Bobo's lynching, and the shooting of two other boys, "a black winged butterfly hovered at the water's edge. A bee droned. From somewhere came the sweet scent of honeysuckles. Dimly they could hear sparrows twittering in the woods. They rolled from side to side, letting sunshine dry their skins and warm their blood. They plucked blades of grass and chewed them." Richard Wright, *Uncle Tom's Children* (1940; reprint, New York: HarperCollins, 1993), 229. That pleasant respite contrasts sharply with the gruesome outcome of "Big Boy" and many of the other stories in the collection.

88. Wright never acknowledges Klineberg's contribution within *The Color Curtain*, simply noting that "I had compiled a list of what I felt to be relevant questions" (20). But Amritjit Singh claims in his afterword that Wright designed the questionnaire "with the help of" Klineberg, whereas Wright biographer Michel Fabre attributes it to Klineberg alone. See Amritjit Singh, afterword to *The Color*

Curtain, by Richard Wright (Jackson: Banner Books, 1994), 230; Michel Fabre, *The Unfinished Quest of Richard Wright* (1973; reprint, Urbana: University of Illinois Press, 1993), 422. For the possibility that one of Wright's interview subjects may have been an FBI informant, see Addison Gayle, *Richard Wright: Ordeal of a Native Son* (Garden City: Anchor Press, 1980), 256, 316.

89. Yoshinobu Hakutani, "Richard Wright's Journey into Asia," in *Travel Writings*, 69.

90. Washington, preface to *Up From Slavery*, xxv.

91. Bill V. Mullen writes that "Wright primarily uses language of distance and Othering to describe the non-West." Mullen, *Afro-Orientalism*, 64.

92. Richard Wright, interview by Harry B. Weber, *New Jersey Herald-News*, 5 April 1941, reprinted in Michel Fabre, *Richard Wright: Books and Writers* (Jackson: University of Mississippi Press, 1990), 42.

93. Nina Kressner Cobb, "Richard Wright and the Third World," in *Critical Essays on Richard Wright*, ed. Yoshinobu Hakutani (Boston: G. K. Hall, 1982), 230.

94. Richard Wright, *Black Power: A Record of Reactions in a Land of Pathos* (New York: Harper and Brothers, 1954), 348.

95. Kressner Cobb, "Third World," 238.

96. This is a discrepancy that even sympathetic reviewers noted that at the time. *The Nation*'s reviewer, for example, writes that "Mr. Wright makes one peculiar judgment. He thinks that the air of Bandung was suffused by religious consciousness as well as by race. Other onlookers at the conference do not seem to have noticed the religion very much." Guy Wint, "The Impatience of the East," *The Nation* 172 (14 April 1956): 324, reprinted in *Richard Wright: The Critical Reception*, edited by John M. Reilly (New York: Burt Franklin, 1978), 276. For other first-person accounts of the Bandung conference see Carlos P. Romulo, *The Meaning of Bandung* (Chapel Hill. University of North Carolina Press, 1956), John Kotelawala, *An Asian Prime Minister's Story* (London: George Harrap, 1956), Carl T. Rowan, *The Pitiful and the Proud* (New York: Random House, 1956), and B. K. Nehru, *Nice Guys Finish Second* (New Delhi: Viking, 1997).

97. Ethel Payne, Interview by Kathleen Currie, Washington Press Club Foundation, 22 September 1987, 69.

98. Payne, Interview, 70.

99. Payne, Interview, 70.

100. Walker, *Daemonic Genius*, 267.

101. Responding to excerpts that ran in the transatlantic journal *Encounter* before *The Color Curtain*'s publication, Lubis wrote that Wright's Indonesian contacts "were amazed to read Mr. Wright's notebooks in which Mr. Wright quotes them saying things which they never said." Here Lubis refers not to his own conversations with Wright, but to that of an unnamed Indonesian novelist whom Wright portrays as anti-Japanese. Mochtar Lubis, "Through Colored Glasses?" *Encounter* (March 1956): 73.

102. Jawaharlal Nehru, "Note to Chief Ministers," in Jawaharlal Nehru, *Selected Works of Jawaharlal Nehru*, ed. Ravinder Kumar and H. Y. Sharada Prasad, Second Series, vol. 28 (New Delhi: Oxford University Press, 2001), 131–2.

103. Nehru, "Note to Chief Ministers," 134.

104. Singh, afterword to *Color Curtain*, 232.

105. Rowan, *Pitiful*, 385; Nehru, "Note to Chief Ministers," 130.

106. *Pictorial Record of the Asian-African Conference* (Jakarta: National Committee for the Commemoration of the Thirtieth Anniversary of the Asian-African Conference, 1985), 58.

107. Jawaharlal Nehru, "A Historic Milestone in Cooperation," in Nehru, *Selected Works*, 128.

108. Adam Clayton Powell, Jr., *Adam by Adam: The Autobiography of Adam Clayton Powell, Jr.* (1971; reprint, New York: Citadel Press, 1994), 112–3.

109. Jawaharlal Nehru, letter to B.F.H.B. Tyabji, 20 February 1955, in Nehru, *Selected Works*, 100.

110. United Nations Department of Social and Economic Affairs, "Measures for the Economic Development of Underdeveloped Countries" (New York: United Nations, 1951), quoted in Escobar, *Encountering Development*, 3 and 4. Arturo Escobar, *Encountering Development: The Making and Unmaking of the Third World* (Princeton, N.J.: Princeton University Press, 1994).

111. Mullen, *Afro-Orientalism*, 66.

112. George W. Bush, press conference, November 6, 2001. http://archives.cnn.com/2001/US/11/06/gen.attack.on.terror/ accessed July 15, 2007.

EPILOGUE

1. This is the situation that Sylvia Wynter sets out to remedy in her essay "Is 'Development' a Purely Empirical Concept, or also Teleological? A Perspective from 'We-the-Underdeveloped,'" in *Prospects for Recovery and Sustainable Development in Africa*, ed. A. F. Yansane (Westport, Conn.: Greenwood Press, 1996), 299–316. Similarly, Arturo Escobar writes that by the 1970s, "development had achieved the status of a certainty in the social imaginary" such that "it seemed impossible to conceptualize social reality in other terms." Escobar, *Encountering Development*, 5.

2. Salman Rushdie, *The Moor's Last Sigh* (New York: Pantheon, 1996), 51.

3. Ralph Pordzik discusses many such examples in *The Quest for Postcolonial Utopia: A Comparative Introduction to the Utopian Novel in the New English Literatures* (New York: Peter Lang, 2001), which despite its title is thoroughly immersed in dystopia. Some other novels centered on the disillusionments of postcoloniality include Bessie Head's *When Rain Clouds Gather* (1968; reprinted London: Heinemann, 1995); Ngũgĩ wa Thiong'o's *Devil on the Cross* (1983; reprinted London: Heinemann, 1985); Earl Lovelace's *The Wine of Astonishment* (London: Heinemann, 1986); Ken Saro-Wiwa's *Sozaboy: A Novel in Rotten English* (1986; reprinted London:

Longman, 1995); and M. G. Vassanji's *The In-Between World of Vikram Lall* (New York: Random House, 2005).

4. Frantz Fanon, *The Wretched of the Earth* (New York: Grove Press, 2005), 149.

5. Kwame Nkrumah, *Neo-Colonialism: The Last Stage of Imperialism* (London: Thomas Nelson and Sons, 1965); Immanuel Wallerstein, "Dependence in an Interdependent World: The Limited Possibilities of Transformation within the Capitalist World Economy," *African Studies Review* 17.1 (1974).

6. W. E. B. Du Bois, *Worlds of Color* (New York: Mainstream Publishers, 1961), 73.

7. Karl Mannheim, *Ideology and Utopia: An Introduction to the Sociology of Knowledge* (New York: Harcourt, Brace & World, 1968), 173, 175.

8. Vijay Prashad, *Everybody Was Kung-Fu Fighting: Afro-Asian Connections and the Myth of Cultural Purity* (Boston: Beacon Press, 2001), 61.

9. Jodi Melamed, "The Spirit of Neoliberalism: From Racial Liberalism to Neoliberal Multiculturalism," *Social Text* 29.4 (2006): 14.

10. See Zadie Smith, *White Teeth* (New York: Random House, 2000), 129–30.

11. Kwame Anthony Appiah, *Cosmopolitanism: Ethics in a World of Strangers* (New York: W. W. Norton, 2006), 102.

12. Appiah, *Cosmopolitanism*, 144.

13. Bruce Robbins, "Cosmopolitanism: New and Newer," Review of Kwame Anthony Appiah, *Cosmopolitanism: Ethics in a World of Strangers, boundary 2* 34.3 (2007): 51.

Bibliography

Abbott, Edwin A. *Flatland: A Romance of Many Dimensions.* 1884. Reprint, New York: Signet Classic, 1984.

Anderson, Benedict. *Imagined Communities: Reflections on the Origin and Spread of Nationalism.* London: Verso, 1983.

———. *The Spectre of Comparisons.* New York: Verso, 1998.

Anthias, Floya, and Nira Yuval-Davis, eds. *Woman-Nation-State.* London: Macmillan, 1989.

Appiah, Kwame Anthony. *Cosmopolitanism: Ethics in a World of Strangers.* New York: W.W. Norton, 2006.

Aptheker, Herbert, ed. *The Correspondence of W. E. B. Du Bois.* Amherst: University of Massachusetts Press, 1973.

———. *Annotated Bibliography of the Published Writings of W. E. B. Du Bois.* New York: Kraus-Thomson, 1973.

———. Introduction to *Dark Princess,* by W. E. B. Du Bois. New York: Kraus-Thomson, 1974.

Ashcroft, Bill, Gareth Griffiths, and Helen Tiffin. *The Empire Writes Back: Theory and Practice in Post-Colonial Literature.* London: Routledge, 1989.

———. *The Post-Colonial Studies Reader.* London: Routledge, 1995.

Bacon, Francis. *The New Atlantis.* 1627. Reprint in *Ideal Commonwealths: Francis Bacon, Thomas More, Thomas Campanella, James Harrington.* New York: Collier & Son, 1901.

Bain, Alexander M. "*Shocks Americana!*: George Schuyler Serializes Black Internationalism," *American Literary History* 19.4 (2007): 947–63.

Bellamy, Edward. *Looking Backward.* 1888. Reprint, New York: Penguin Books, 1986.

Berlin, Isaiah. *The Sense of Reality: Studies in Ideas and Their History*. New York: Farrar Strous and Giroux, 1997.

Bernal, Martin. *Black Athena: The Afro-Asiatic Roots of Classical Civilization*. New Brunswick, N.J.: Rutgers University Press, 1987.

Besant, Annie. "Why I Am a Socialist." 1886. In *The Politics of Hope: The Origins of Socialism in Britain, 1880–1914*, ed. Edmund and Ruth Frow, 32–40. London: Pluto, 1989.

Bhabha, Homi K. "The Black Savant and the Dark Princess," *ESQ: A Journal of the American Renaissance* 50.1–3 (2004): 137–55.

Booker, M. Keith. *The Post-Utopian Imagination*. Westport: Greenwood, 2002.

Bose, Nemai Sadhan. *Ramananda Chatterjee*. New Delhi: Ministry of Information and Broadcasting, 1974.

Bowman, Sylvia E. *Edward Bellamy*. Boston: Twayne Publishers, 1986.

Brecher, Jeremy, Tim Costello, and Brendan Smith. *Globalization from Below: The Power of Solidarity*. Cambridge: South End Press, 2000.

Britain, Ian. *Fabianism and Culture: A Study in British Socialism and the Arts c. 1884–1918*. Cambridge: Cambridge University Press, 1982.

Brooks, Van Wyck. "Young America." *Seven Arts* (December 1916): 144–51.

Burton, Robert. *The Anatomy of Melancholy*. 1621. Reprint, Philadelphia: J. W. Moore, 1850.

Burwell, Jennifer. *Notes from Nowhere: Feminism, Utopian Logic, and Social Transformation*. Minneapolis: University of Minneapolis Press, 1997.

Cady, Edwin. *The Realist at War: The Mature Years 1885–1920 of William Dean Howells*. Syracuse, N.Y.: Syracuse University Press, 1958.

Casely-Hayford, J. E. *Ethiopia Unbound*. London: C. M. Phillips, 1911.

Chatterjee, Partha. *Nationalist Thought and the Colonial World*. Minneapolis: University of Minnesota Press, 1998.

———. *The Nation and Its Fragments*. Princeton: Princeton University Press, 1993.

Chesnutt, Charles. *The Conjure Woman and Other Conjure Tales*. Durham, N.C.: Duke University Press, 1993.

Cobb, Nina Kressner. "Richard Wright and the Third World." In *Critical Essays on Richard Wright*, edited by Yoshinobu Hakutani, 228–39. Boston: G. K. Hall, 1982.

Conrad, Joseph. *Heart of Darkness*. 1902. Reprint, London: Penguin Books, 1989.

Coomaraswamy, Ananda K. "A Message." *Voice of India* I.1 (September 1944): 12.

———. *Art and Swadeshi*. 1911. Reprint, New Delhi: Munshiram Manoharlal, 1994.

———. *Medieval Sinhalese Art*. Broad Campden: Essex House Press, 1908.

Deegan, Mary Jo. Introduction to Charlotte Perkins Gilman, *With Her in Ourland: A Sequel to Herland*, edited by Deegan and Michael R. Hill. Westport, Conn.: Greenwood Press, 1997.

Delany, Martin. *Blake, or the Huts of Africa*. 1859. Reprinted Boston: Beacon Press, 1971.

Dos Passos, John R. "Young Spain." *Seven Arts* (August 1917): 473–88.

Douglas, Ann. "The Therapeutic Retreat." Review of *No Place of Grace: Antimodernism and the Transformation of American Culture, 1880–1920*, by T. J. Jackson Lears. *The Nation* (19 December 1981): 675–77.

Du Bois, W. E. B. "As the Crow Flies." *Crisis* 36.1 (January 1929): 1.

———. "As the Crow Flies." *New York Amsterdam News* (April 10, 1943), 10.

———. "As the Crow Flies." *New York Amsterdam News* (February 26, 1944), 10.

———. *Dark Princess*. 1928. Reprint, Jackson, Miss.: Banner Books, 1995.

———. "Gandhi and the American Negroes." *Gandhi Marg* II.3 (1957): 174, 176.

———. "Sensitive Liberia." *Crisis* 28.1 (May 1924), 10.

———. "The Browsing Reader." *Crisis* 36.5 (May 1929): 175.

———. "The Freeing of India." *Crisis* 54 (October 1947): 302.

———. "The Negro Mind Reaches Out." In *The New Negro, An Interpretation*, edited by Alain Locke, 385–414. New York: Atheneum, 1925.

———. *The Ordeal of Mansart*. 1957. Reprint, New York: Kraus-Thomson, 1976.

———. *The Quest of the Silver Fleece*. 1911. Reprint, Boston: Northeastern University Press, 1989.

———. *The Souls of Black Folk*. 1903. Reprint, New York: Dover, 1994.

———. "The Wide, Wide World." *New York Amsterdam News* (October 7, 1931), 8.

———. *W. E. B. Du Bois: A Reader*, edited by David Levering Lewis. New York: Henry Holt, 1995.

———. "Will the Great Gandhi Live Again." In *W. E. B. Du Bois: A Reader*, edited by David Levering Lewis, 358–60. New York: Henry Holt, 1995.

———. *Worlds of Color*. New York: Mainstream Publishers, 1961.

Dutta, Krishna, and Andrew Robinson. *Rabindranath Tagore: The Myriad-Minded Man*. London: Bloomsbury, 1995.

Eble, Kenneth E. *William Dean Howells*. Boston: Twayne Publishers, 1982.

Edwards, Brent Hayes. *The Practice of Diaspora*. Cambridge: Harvard University Press, 2003.

Escobar, Arturo. *Encountering Development: The Making and Unmaking of the Third World*. Princeton: Princeton University Press, 1995.

Fabi, M. Giulia. *Passing and the Rise of the African American Novel*. Urbana: University of Illinois Press, 2001.

———. "'Utopian Melting': Technology, Homogeneity, and the American Dream in *Looking Backward*." In *Technology and the American Imagination*, edited by Francesca Bisutti De Riz and Rosella Mamoli Zorzi. Venezia, Italy: Supernova, 1994. 346–54.

Fabian, Johannes. *Time and the Other: How Anthropology Makes Its Object*. New York: Columbia University Press, 1983.

Fabre, Michel. "Margaret Walker's Richard Wright: A Wrong Righted or a Wright Wronged?" *Mississippi Quarterly* 42.4 (Fall 1989): 429–50.

————. *Richard Wright: Books and Writers*. Jackson: University of Mississippi Press, 1990.

————. *The Unfinished Quest of Richard Wright*. 1973. Reprint, Urbana: University of Illinois Press, 1993.

Fanon, Frantz. *The Wretched of the Earth*. New York: Grove Press, 2005.

Fletcher, Ian Christopher. "Double Meanings: Nation and Empire in the Edwardian Era." In Antoinette M. Burton, ed., *After the Imperial Turn: Thinking With and Through the Nation*. Durham, N.C.: Duke University Press, 2003: 246–59.

Forster, E. M. *The Collected Tales of E. M. Forster*. New York: Alfred A. Knopf, 1952.

Fox, Richard. *Gandhian Utopia: Experiments with Culture*. Boston: Beacon Press, 1989.

Frow, Edmund, and Ruth Frow, eds. *The Politics of Hope: The Origins of Socialism in Britain, 1880–1914*. London: Pluto, 1989.

Gandhi, Leela. *Affective Communities: Anticolonial Thought, Fin-de-Siècle Radicalism, and the Politics of Friendship* (Durham, N.C.: Duke University Press, 2006.

Gandhi, Mohandas Karamchand. *Autobiography: The Story of My Experiments with Truth*. 1948. Translated by Mahadev Desai. Reprint, New York: Dover, 1983.

Gayle, Addison. *Richard Wright: Ordeal of a Native Son*. Garden City: Anchor Press, 1980.

Gilman, Charlotte Perkins. *Herland*. 1915. Reprint, New York: Pantheon Books, 1979.

————. *With Her in Ourland: A Sequel to Herland*. Edited by Mary Jo Deegan and Michael R. Hill (Westport, Conn.: Greenwood Press, 1997.

Gilroy, Paul. *The Black Atlantic: Modernity and Double Consciousness*. Cambridge: Harvard University Press, 1993.

————. *There Ain't No Black in the Union Jack*. Chicago: University of Chicago Press, 1991.

Goswami, Manu. *Producing India: From Colonial Economy to National Space*. Chicago: University of Chicago Press, 2004.

Gregg, Robert and Madhavi Kale. "*The Negro* and the *Dark Princess*: Two Legacies of the Universal Races Congress." *Radical History Review* 92 (2005): 133–52.

Griggs, Sutton E. *Imperium in Imperio*. 1899. Reprint, Miami: Mnemosyne Publishing, 1969.

Gubar, Susan. "*She* in *Herland*: Feminism as Fantasy." In *Coordinates: Placing Science Fiction and Fantasy*, edited by George E. Slusser, Eric S. Rabkin, and Robert Scholes, 139–49. Carbondale: Southern Illinois University Press, 1983.

Hakutani, Yoshinobu. *Critical Essays on Richard Wright*. Boston: G. K. Hall, 1982.

———. "Richard Wright's Journey into Asia." In *Richard Wright's Travel Writings: New Reflections*, edited by Virginia Whately Smith, 63–77. Jackson: University of Mississippi Press, 2001.

Haller, Mark II. *Eugenics: Hereditarian Attitudes in American Thought*. New Brunswick, N.J.: Rutgers University Press, 1984.

Halpern, Richard. *The Poetics of Primitive Accumulation: English Renaissance Culture and the Genealogy of Capital*. Ithaca, N.Y.: Cornell University Press, 1991.

Hardikar, N. S. *Lala Lajpat Rai in America*. New Delhi: Servants of the People Society, N.D.

Hardt, Michael and Antonio Negri. *Empire*. Cambridge: Harvard University Press, 2000.

Harlow, Barbara. *Resistance Literature*. New York: Methuen, 1987.

Harvey, David. *Spaces of Hope*. Berkeley: University of California Press, 2000.

Hasian, Marouf A., Jr. *The Rhetoric of Eugenics in Anglo-American Thought*. Athens: University of Georgia Press, 1996.

Hassan, Narin, and Ed Chan. "Review of *The Quest for Postcolonial Utopia: A Comparative Introduction to the Utopian Novel in the New English Literatures*, by Ralph Pordzik." *Utopian Studies* 12.2 (2001): 362–4.

Hawthorne, Nathaniel. *The Blithedale Romance*. 1852. Reprint, New York: W. W. Norton, 1958.

Hill, Robert A., and R. Kent Rasmussen. Afterword to *Black Empire*, by George S. Schuyler. Boston: Northeastern University Press, 1991.

Hopkins, Pauline E. *Contending Forces: A Romance Illustrative of Negro Life North and South*. 1900. Reprint, New York: Oxford University Press, 1988.

———. *Hagar's Daughter: A Story of Southern Caste Prejudice*. 1901–2. Reprint in *The Magazine Novels of Pauline Hopkins*. New York: Oxford University Press, 1988.

———. *Of One Blood; Or, The Hidden Self*. 1902–3. Reprint in *The Magazine Novels of Pauline Hopkins*. New York: Oxford University Press, 1988.

Hossain, Rokeya Sakhawat. "Sultana's Dream." 1905. Reprint in *Sultana's Dream: A Feminist Utopia*, edited by Roushan Jahan. New York: Feminist Press at the City University of New York, 1988.

Howells, William Dean. *A Traveler from Altruria*. 1894. Reprint, New York: Sagamore Press, 1957.

———. *Through the Eye of a Needle*. New York: Harper & Brothers, 1907.

Huxley, Aldous. *Brave New World*. 1932. Reprint, New York: Perennial Library, 1969.

Iyer, Vijay, and Michael Ladd. Program Notes to *In What Language? A Song Cycle of Lives in Transit*. Live performance at The Asia Society, New York, 2003.

James, Henry. *Daisy Miller.* 1878. Reprint, New York: Dover Publications, 1995.

Jameson, Fredric. *Archaeologies of the Future: The Desire Called Utopia and Other Science Fictions.* London: Verso, 2005.

————. "Of Islands and Trenches: Neutralization and the Production of Utopian Discourse." In Jameson, *The Ideologies of Theory: Essays 1971–1986.* Minneapolis: University of Minnesota Press, 1988.

Jayawardena, Kumari. *The White Woman's Other Burden: Western Women and South Asia during Colonial Rule.* New York: Routledge, 1995.

Jensen, Joan M. *Passage from India: Asian Indian Immigrants in North America.* New Haven: Yale University Press, 1988.

Jones, Andrew F., and Nikhil Pal Singh. "Guest Editors' Introduction." *positions: east asia cultures critique* 11.1 (2003): 1–9.

Kaplan, Amy. *The Social Construction of American Realism.* Chicago: University of Chicago Press, 1988.

Kaplan, Amy, and Donald Pease, eds. *Cultures of United States Imperialism.* Durham, N.C.: Duke University Press, 1993.

Kelley, Robin D. G. *Freedom Dreams: The Black Radical Imagination.* Boston: Beacon Press, 2002.

Kline, Wendy. *Building a Better Race: Gender, Sexuality, and Eugenics from the Turn of the Century to the Baby Boom.* Berkeley: University of California Press, 2001.

Kotelawala, John. *An Asian Prime Minister's Story.* London: George Harrap, 1956.

Kühl, Stephen. *The Nazi Connection: Eugenics, American Racism, and German National Socialism.* New York: Oxford University Press, 1994.

Kumar, Krishan. *Utopia and Anti-Utopia in Modern Times.* Oxford: Basil Blackwell, 1987.

Kumar, R. P. "Origin and Development of Periodicals in English before Independence—I. Survey of Periodicals." *International Library Review* 16 (1984): 183–202.

————. "Origin and Development of Periodicals in English before Independence—II. Cessation of Periodicals." *International Library Review* 16 (1984): 203–08.

Lajpat Rai, Lala. "Asia and the War." *The Masses* 9 (September 1916): 31.

————. "Farewell to America." In *Lala Lajpat Rai: Writings and Speeches,* vol. I, edited by Vijaya Chandra Joshi, 390–6. Delhi: University Publishers, 1966.

————. "Presidential Address at the Bombay Hindu Conference." In *Lala Lajpat Rai: Writings and Speeches,* vol. II, edited by Vijaya Chandra Joshi, 243–57. Delhi: University Publishers, 1966.

————. "Save India for the Empire: An Open Letter to David Lloyd George." In *Lala Lajpat Rai: Writings and Speeches,* vol. I, edited by Vijaya Chandra Joshi, 255–80. Delhi: University Publishers, 1966.

————. *Unhappy India*. Calcutta: Banna Publishing, 1928.

—— "Young India." *Seven Arts* (October 1917): 743–58.

Leahey, Thomas Hardy, and Grace Evans. *Psychology's Occult Doubles: Psychology and the Problem of Pseudoscience*. Chicago: Nelson-Hill, 1983.

Lears, T. Jackson *No Place of Grace: Antimodernism and the Transformation of American Culture, 1880–1920*. Chicago: University of Chicago Press, 1981.

Lee, Maurice. "Du Bois the Novelist: White Influence, Black Spirit, and *Quest of the Silver Fleece*." *African American Review* 33.3 (1999): 389–400.

Lewis, David Levering. *W. E. B. Du Bois: Biography of a Race, 1868–1919*. New York: Henry Holt and Company, 1993.

————. *W. E. B. Du Bois: The Fight for Equality and the American Century, 1919–1963*. New York: Henry Holt and Company, 2000.

Lipscy, Roger. *Coomaraswamy; Volume III, His Life and Work*. Princeton: Princeton University Press, 1977.

Lock, Graham. *Blutopia: Visions of the Future and Revisions of the Past in the Work of Sun Ra, Duke Ellington, and Anthony Braxton*. Durham, N.C.: Duke University Press, 1999.

Loomba, Ania. *Colonialism/Postcolonialism*. London: Routledge, 2005.

Lubis, Mochtar. "Through Colored Glasses?" *Encounter* (March 1956): 73.

Lukács, Georg. "Tagore's Gandhi Novel." Review of *The Home and the World*, by Rabindranath Tagore. In Lukacs, *Reviews and Articles*, translated by Peter Palmer. London: Merlin, 1983.

Lundestad, Gier. *The American "Empire" and Other Studies of US Foreign Policy in a Comparative Perspective*. London: Oxford University Press.

MacKinnon, Janice R., and Stephen R. MacKinnon. *Agnes Smedley: The Life and Times of an American Radical*. Berkeley: University of California Press, 1988.

Maine, Henry. *Village Communities in the East and West*. London: John Murray, 1872.

Mannheim, Karl. *Ideology and Utopia: An Introduction to the Sociology of Knowledge*. Translated by Louis Wirth and Edward A. Shils. New York: Harcourt, Brace & World, 1968.

Manuel, Frank E., and Fritzie P. Manuel. *Utopian Thought in the Western World*. Cambridge: Harvard University Press, 1979.

Marable, Manning. *How Capitalism Underdeveloped Black America*. Boston: South End Press, 1983.

————. *W. E. B. Du Bois: Black Radical Democrat*. New York: Twayne Publishers, 1986.

Marx, Edward. "Sarojini Naidu: The Nightingale as Nationalist." *Journal of Commonwealth Literature* 31.1 (1996): 47–62.

Marx, Karl. *The Marx-Engels Reader*. Edited by Robert C. Tucker. New York: W. W. Norton, 1978.

Marx, Karl, and Friedrich Engels. "Manifesto of the Communist Party." 1848. In *The Marx-Engels Reader,* edited by Robert C. Tucker, 469–500. New York: W. W. Norton, 1978.

Mathur, Sobhag. *Echoes of the Indian National Movement in America.* Jodhpur: Kusumanjali Prakashan, 1996.

McClintock, Anne. *Imperial Leather: Race, Gender, and Sexuality in the Colonial Contest.* New York: Routledge, 1995.

McKay, Nellie. "W. E. B. Du Bois: The Black Women in His Writings." In *Critical Essays on W. E. B. Du Bois,* edited by William L. Andrews, 230–52. Boston: Hall, 1985.

McKenna, Erin. *The Task of Utopia.* Lanham: Rowman and Littlefield, 2001.

Melamed, Jodi. "The Spirit of Neoliberalism: From Racial Liberalism to Neoliberal Multiculturalism," *Social Text* 29.4 (2006): 1–25.

Metcalf, Thomas. *An Imperial Vision: Indian Architecture and Britain's Raj.* Berkeley: University of California Press, 1989.

Miller, Christopher. *Blank Darkness: Africanist Discourse in French.* Chicago: University Of Chicago Press, 1986.

Mitter, Partha. *Art and Nationalism in Colonial India, 1850–1920: Occidental Orientations.* Cambridge: Cambridge University Press, 1994.

———. *Much Maligned Monsters: A History of European Reactions to Indian Art.* Chicago: University of Chicago Press, 1992.

Mohan, Jag. *Ananda K. Coomaraswamy.* New Delhi: Government of India, 1979.

Mondal, Anshuman. "Gandhi, Utopianism and the Construction of Colonial Difference." *Interventions* 3.3 (2001): 419–38.

More, Thomas. *Utopia.* 1516. Edited and translated by Edward Surtz. New Haven: Yale University Press, 1964.

Morris, William. *News from Nowhere.* 1890. Reprint, in *News from Nowhere and Other Writings,* edited by Clive Wilmer. London: Penguin, 1993.

———. "The Art of the People." In Morris, *Hopes and Fears for Art.* Boston: Roberts Brothers, 1882.

Morrison, Toni. *Playing in the Dark: Whiteness and the Literary Imagination.* New York: Vintage, 1993.

Morton, A. L. *The English Utopia.* London: Lawrence & Wishart, 1952.

Moses, Wilson Jeremiah. *Afrotopia: The Roots of African American Popular History.* Cambridge: Cambridge University Press, 1998.

Moylan, Tom. *Demand the Impossible: Science Fiction and the Utopian Imagination.* New York: Methuen, 1986.

———. *Scraps of the Untainted Sky: Science Fiction, Utopia, Dystopia.* Boulder: Westview Press, 2000.

Mudimbe, V. Y. *The Invention of Africa: Gnosis, Philosophy and the Order of Knowledge.* Bloomington: Indiana University Press, 1988.

Mukherjee, Sujit. *Passage to America: The Reception of Rabindranath Tagore in the United States, 1912–1941.* Calcutta: Bookland Private, 1964.

Mullen, Bill V. *Afro-Orientalism*. Minneapolis: University of Minnesota Press, 2004.

Nandy, Ashis. *The Illegitimacy of Nationalism. Rabindranath Tagore and the Politics of Self*. Delhi: Oxford University Press, 1994.

Naruse, Seichi. "Young Japan." *Seven Arts* (April 1917): 616–26.

Nehru, B. K. *Nice Guys Finish Second*. New Delhi: Viking, 1997.

Nehru, Jawaharlal. "A Historic Milestone in Cooperation. " In Nehru, *Selected Works of Jawaharlal Nehru*, edited by Ravinder Kumar and H. Y. Sharada Prasad, Second Series, Volume 28, 125 8. New Delhi: Oxford University Press, 2001.

———. "Note to Chief Ministers." In Nehru, *Selected Works of Jawaharlal Nehru*, edited by Ravinder Kumar and H. Y. Sharada Prasad, Second Series, Volume 28, 129–38. New Delhi: Oxford University Press, 2001.

———. *Selected Works of Jawaharlal Nehru*. Edited by Ravinder Kumar and H. Y. Sharada Prasad, Second Series, Volume 28. New Delhi: Oxford University Press, 2001.

Neville-Sington, Pamela, and David Sington. *Paradise Dreamed: How Utopian Thinkers Have Changed the Modern World*. London: Bloomsbury, 1993.

Newell, Stephanie. *Literary Culture in Colonial Ghana: How to Play the Game of Life*. Bloomington: Indiana University Press, 2002.

Nkrumah, Kwame. *Neo-Colonialism: The Last Stage of Imperialism*. London: Thomas Nelson and Sons, 1965.

Nussbaum, Martha. *For Love of Country?: Debating the Limits of Patriotism*. Edited by Joshua Cohen. Boston: Beacon Press, 1996.

Panahi, Jafar. "Open Letter to the National Board of Review of Motion Pictures." April 30, 2001.

Patai, Daphne, ed. *Looking Backward, 1988–1888: Essays on Edward Bellamy*. Amherst: University of Massachusetts Press, 1988.

Payne, Ethel. Interview by Kathleen Currie. Washington Press Club Foundation. 22 September 1987.

Pease, William H., and Jane H. *Black Utopia: Negro Communal Experiments in America*. Madison: State Historical Society of Wisconsin, 1963.

Peyser, Thomas. *Utopia and Cosmopolis: Globalization in the Era of American Literary Realism*. Durham, N.C.: Duke University Press, 1998.

Pfaelzer, Jean. "The Impact of Political Theory on Narrative Structures." In *America as Utopia*, edited by Kenneth M. Roemer, 117–32. New York: Burt Franklin, 1981.

———. *The Utopian Novel in America, 1886–1896*. Pittsburgh: University of Pittsburgh Press, 1984.

Pictorial Record of the Asian-African Conference. Jakarta: National Committee for the Commemoration of the Thirtieth Anniversary of the Asian-African Conference, 1985.

Piercy, Marge. *Woman on the Edge of Time*. New York: Fawcett Crest, 1976.

Pletch, Carl E. "The Three Worlds, or the Division of Labor, circa 1950–1975."
    Comparative Studies in Society and History 23 (1981): 568–71.

Pordzik, Ralph. *The Quest for Postcolonial Utopia: A Comparative Introduction to
    the Utopian Novel in the New English Literatures*. New York: Peter Lang, 2001.

Porter, Bernard. *Critics of Empire: British Radical Attitudes to Colonialism in
    Africa 1895–1914*. London: Macmillan, 1968.

Powell, Adam Clayton, Jr. *Adam by Adam: The Autobiography of Adam Clayton
    Powell, Jr.* 1971. Reprint, New York: Citadel Press, 1994.

Prashad, Vijay. "Badges of Color: An Afro-Dalit Story." *Z Magazine* (March
    2000): 8–10.

———. *Everybody Was Kung-Fu Fighting: Afro-Asian Connections and the Myth of
    Cultural Purity*. Boston: Beacon Press, 2001.

Rampersad, Arnold. "Du Bois's Passage to India: *Dark Princess*." In *W. E. B. Du
    Bois: On Race and Culture*, edited by Bernard W. Bell, Emily R. Grosholz,
    and James B. Steward. New York: Routledge, 1996.

———. Foreword to *The Quest of the Silver Fleece*, by W. E. B. Du Bois. Boston:
    Northeastern University Press, 1989.

———. *The Art and Imagination of W. E. B. Du Bois*. Cambridge: Harvard
    University Press, 1976.

Rathore, Naeem Gul. *Indian Nationalist Agitation in the United States: A Study of
    Lala Lajpat Rai and the India Home Rule League of America, 1914–1920*. PhD
    diss., Columbia University, 1965.

Rawls, John. *The Law of Peoples*. Cambridge: Harvard University Press, 1999.

Reilly, John M., ed. *Richard Wright: The Critical Reception*. New York: Burt
    Franklin, 1978.

Rist, Gilbert. *The History of Development: From Western Origins to Global Faith*.
    London: Zed Books, 2003.

Robbins, Bruce. "Cosmopolitanism: New and Newer." Review of Kwame
    Anthony Appiah, *Cosmopolitanism: Ethics in a World of Strangers*. *boundary
    2* 34.3 (2007): 47–60.

———. *Feeling Global: Internationalism in Distress*. New York: New York
    University Press, 1999.

Robinson, Cedric. *Black Marxism: The Making of the Black Radical Tradition*.
    1983. Reprint, Chapel Hill: University of North Carolina Press, 2000.

———. "Du Bois and Black Sovereignty: The Case of Liberia," *Race and Class*
    32.2 (1990): 39–50.

Roemer, Kenneth M., ed. *America as Utopia*. New York: Burt Franklin, 1981.

———. "Utopia and Victorian Culture: 1888–99." In *America as Utopia*, edited
    by Kenneth M. Roemer, 305–32. New York: Burt Franklin, 1981.

———. *Utopian Audiences: How Readers Locate Nowhere*. Amherst: University
    of Massachusetts Press, 2003.

Romulo, Carlos P. *The Meaning of Bandung*. Chapel Hill, N.C.: University of
    North Carolina Press, 1956.

Rowan, Carl T. *The Pitiful and the Proud*. New York: Random House, 1956.

Roy, Arundhati. *The Algebra of Infinite Justice*. London: Flamingo, 2002.

Roy, Supriya, ed. *Tagoreana in* The Modern Review. Calcutta: Viswa-Bharati, 1998.

Rushdie, Salman. *The Moor's Last Sigh*. New York: Pantheon, 1996.

Said, Edward. *Culture and Imperialism*. New York: Vintage Books, 1993.

———. *Orientalism*. New York: Vintage Books, 1979.

Sanger, Margaret. *An Autobiography*. 1938. Reprint, New York: Dover Publications, 1971.

Sarkar, Sumit. *Modern India: 1885–1947*. Madras: Macmillan, 1983.

Schaer, Roland, Gregory Claeys, and Lyman Tower Sargent, eds. *Utopia: The Search for the Ideal Society in the Western World*. New York: Oxford University Press, 2000.

Schehr, Robert. *Dynamic Utopia: Establishing Intentional Communities as a New Social Movement*. Westport: Bergin and Garvey, 1997.

Schuyler, George. *Black Empire*. Edited by Robert A. Hill and R. Kent Rasmussen. 1936–8. Reprint, Boston: Northeastern University Press, 1991.

———. "Negroes Reject Communism." *American Mercury* 47 (1939): 176–81.

Segal, Howard P. "Utopia Diversified: 1900–1949." In *America as Utopia*, edited by Kenneth M. Roemer, 333–46. New York: Burt Franklin, 1981.

Sen, Amartya. "Tagore and His India." In *India: A Mosaic*, edited by Robert B. Silvers and Barbara Epstein, 53–106. New York: New York Review Books, 2000.

Sharpe, Jenny. "Is the United States Postcolonial?" *Diaspora* 4:2 (1995): 181–98.

Shaw, G. Bernard, ed. *Socialism: The Fabian Essays*. Boston: C. E. Brown, 1894.

Shukla, Sandhya. *India Abroad: Diasporic Cultures of Postwar America and England*. Princeton: Princeton University Press, 2003.

Singh, Amritjit. Afterword to *The Color Curtain*, by Richard Wright. Jackson: Banner Books, 1994.

Slusser, George E., Eric S. Rabkin, and Robert Scholes, eds. *Coordinates: Placing Science Fiction and Fantasy*. Carbondale: Southern Illinois University Press, 1983.

Smedley, Agnes. "The Negro Renaissance." *Modern Review* 40.6 (December 1926): 657–61.

———. *Daughter of Earth*. New York: Feminist Press, 1973.

Smith, Virginia Whately. "Richard Wright's Passage to Indonesia." In *Richard Wright's Travel Writings: New Reflections*, edited by Virginia Whately Smith, 78–115. Jackson: University of Mississippi Press, 2001.

Smith, Zadie. *White Teeth*. New York: Random House, 2000.

Snodgrass, Mary Ellen. *Encyclopedia of Utopian Literature*. Santa Barbara: ABC-CLIO, 1995.

Sprinker, Michael, ed. *Edward Said: A Critical Reader*. London: Blackwell Publishing, 1992.

Stansell, Christine. *American Moderns: Bohemian New York and the Creation of a New Century.* New York: Metropolitan Books, 2000.

Sundquist, Eric. *To Wake the Nations.* Cambridge: Harvard University Press, 1993.

Tagore, Rabindranath. *Nationalism.* New York: Macmillan, 1917.

———. *The Home and the World.* 1919. Translated by Surendranath Tagore. Reprint, London: Penguin Books, 1985.

Tatar, Maria. *Spellbound: Studies on Mesmerism and Literature.* Princeton: Princeton University Press, 1978.

Tate, Claudia. Introduction to *Dark Princess,* by W. E. B. Du Bois. Jackson, Miss.: Banner Books, 1995.

———. *Psychoanalysis and Black Novels: Desire and the Protocols of Race.* New York: Oxford University Press, 1998.

Thompson, E. P. *Alien Homage: Edward Thompson and Rabindranath Tagore.* Delhi: Oxford University Press, 1993.

———. Introduction to *Nationalism,* by Rabindranath Tagore. London: Macmillan, 1991.

———. *William Morris: Romantic to Revolutionary.* New York: Pantheon Books, 1955.

W. E. B. Du Bois Papers. W. E. B. Du Bois Library. University of Massachusetts at Amherst.

Walker, Margaret. *Richard Wright: Daemonic Genius.* New York: Warner Books, 1988.

Wallerstein, Immanuel. "Dependence in an Interdependent World: The Limited Possibilities of Transformation within the Capitalist World Economy." *African Studies Review* 17.1 (1974).

———. *Utopistics.* New York: New Press, 1998.

Wallinger, Hanna. "Secret Societies and Dark Empires: Sutton E. Griggs's *Imperium in Imperio* and W. E. B. Du Bois's *Dark Princess.*" In *Empire: American Studies,* edited by John G. Blair and Reinhold Wagnleitner, 197–210. Tubingen, Germany: Narr, 1997.

Warren, Kenneth W. "An Inevitable Drift? Oligarchy, Du Bois, and the Politics of Race between the Wars." *boundary 2* 27, no. 3 (2000): 153–69.

Washington, Booker T. *Up from Slavery.* 1901. Reprint, in *Three Negro Classics,* 23–205. New York: Avon Books, 1965.

Webb, Sidney James. "What Socialism Means: A Call to the Unconverted." 1886. In *The Politics of Hope: The Origins of Socialism in Britain, 1880–1914,* edited by Edmund and Ruth Frow, 41–57. London: Pluto, 1989.

Weber, Max. *From Max Weber: Essays in Sociology,* edited by H. H. Gerth and C. Wright Mills. New York: Oxford University Press, 1958.

Weinbaum, Alys. "Reproducing Racial Globality: W. E. B. Du Bois and the Sexual Politics of Black Internationalism." *Social Text* 67 (2001): 15–41.

———. *Wayward Reproductions*. Durham, N.C., and London: Duke University Press, 2004.

Wells, H. G. *The Future in America*. 1906. Reprint, New York: Arno Press, 1974.

Wilde, Oscar. *The Soul of Man under Socialism and Selected Critical Prose*. London: Penguin, 2001.

Wint, Guy. "The Impatience of the East." Review of *The Color Curtain*, by Richard Wright. *The Nation* 172 (14 April 1956): 324.

Wright, Richard. *Black Power: A Record of Reactions in a Land of Pathos*. New York: Harper and Brothers, 1954.

———. *The Color Curtain: A Report on the Bandung Conference*. 1956. Reprint, Jackson: Banner Books, 1994.

———. *Uncle Tom's Children*. 1940. Reprint, New York: HarperCollins, 1993.

Wynter, Sylvia. "Is 'Development' a Purely Empirical Concept, or also Teleological? A Perspective from 'We-the-Underdeveloped.'" In *Prospects for Recovery and Sustainable Development in Africa*, ed. A. F. Yansane. Westport, Conn.: Greenwood Press, 1996, 299–316.

X, Malcolm. "Message to the Grassroots." In *Malcolm X Speaks: Selected Speeches and Statements*, edited by George Breitman, 3–17. New York: Pathfinder, 1990.

Young India. New York. 1918–1920.

Zamiatin, Eugene. *We*. Translated by Gregory Zilboorg. New York: E. P. Dutton, 1924.

Zhang Yan. "I Wish I Had Met Richard Wright at Bandung in 1955 (Reflections on a Conference Attended by Both Wright and the Author." *Mississippi Quarterly: The Journal of Southern Cultures* 50.2 (1995): 277–87.

Index